HEARING IN TIME

Psychological Aspects of Musical Meter

Justin London

OXFORD
UNIVERSITY PRESS

2004

OXFORD
UNIVERSITY PRESS

Oxford   New York
Auckland   Bangkok   Buenos Aires   Cape Town   Chennai
Dar es Salaam   Delhi   Hong Kong   Istanbul   Karachi   Kolkata
Kuala Lumpur   Madrid   Melbourne   Mexico City   Mumbai   Nairobi
São Paulo   Shanghai   Taipei   Tokyo   Toronto

Copyright © 2004 by Oxford University Press, Inc.

Published by Oxford University Press, Inc.
198 Madison Avenue, New York, New York 10016

www.oup.com

Oxford is a registered trademark of Oxford University Press

All rights reserved. No part of this publication may be reproduced,
stored in a retrieval system, or transmitted, in any form or by any means,
electronic, mechanical, photocopying, recording, or otherwise,
without the prior permission of Oxford University Press

Library of Congress Cataloging-in-Publication Data
London, Justin.
Hearing in time : psychological aspects of musical meter /
by Justin London.
p.   cm.
Includes bibliographical references and index.
ISBN 0-19-516081-9
1. Musical meter and rhythm.   2. Musical perception.
I. Title.
ML3832.L65 2004
781.2′26—dc22   2003014964

9 8 7 6 5 4 3 2 1

Printed in the United States of America
on acid-free paper

A Song, for My Father

Acknowledgments

As is so often the case with scholarly projects, the book you are holding is not the book I set out to write. My first intention was to explore the nature of metric complexity, but it became apparent that before I could do that, I needed to examine basic research into temporal perception and cognition and its relevance for musical meter. Hence this book. A fuller exploration of metric complexity will have to wait for another volume. I have at least partially stuck to my original intention, however, in that *Hearing in Time* brings together research from two different fields: music psychology (which includes studies of temporal perception, motor behavior, and music perception and cognition) and music theory (which includes theories of rhythm and meter, tonal theory, and rhythmic and metric analysis).

In tackling such an interdisciplinary task I have had the help of many colleagues. On the music theory side of the aisle I wish to thank Kofi Agawu, Graeme Boone, Jim Buhler, Norman Carey, Rick Cohn, Zohar Eitan, Bob Gjerdingen, Gretchen Horlacher, Brian Hyer, Harald Krebs, Fred Lerdahl, Robert Morris, Jay Rahn, Brian Robinson, John Roeder, Frank Samarotto, and Larry Zbikowski, for their many helpful explanations, criticisms and comments. Special thanks to Jonathan Kramer and the participants in his seminar on rhythm at Columbia University who provided helpful feedback on an earlier version of the manuscript.

An even greater share of thanks must go to my nonmusicologist colleagues, whose assistance and explanations were essential in my ongoing education in psychology and cognitive science: Ric Ashley (also a card-carrying music theorist), Eric Clarke, Geoff Collier, Carolyn Drake, Anders Friberg, Richard Parncutt, Dirk Povel, Neil Todd, and Luke Windsor. Ed Large has been both a patient tutor in many areas of research as well as a delightful co-author. I would especially acknowledge the late Jeff Pressing, who always gave patient and lucid responses to my many queries; I among many will miss him. Henkjan Honing and Peter Desain have been both long-standing correspondents as well as congenial hosts, and this book benefited greatly from my visit to the Music, Mind, Machine lab of the Nijmegen Institute for Cognition and Information (at the University of Nijmegen) in the summer of 2000. Likewise Caroline Palmer, Mari Riess Jones, and David Huron were similarly gracious in inviting me to their labs at Ohio State University in the spring of 2001, and Professors Jones and Palmer made many helpful suggestions and criticisms of an early version of the manuscript. Last, but most assuredly not least, much thanks and appreciation to Bruno Repp for his careful reading of the entire manuscript. His unstinting critical commentary and unflagging encouragement was a model of peer review.

It is both pro forma and also true to add at this point that while much of what is correct and insightful in the book is a result of the aid of the scholars mentioned, I alone am responsible for whatever errors and problems remain.

This book would not have been possible without special material as well as intellectual support. The Mellon Endowment Fellowship of Carleton College provided for an extended sabbatical leave for the 2000–2001 academic year, during which much of the book was written. Likewise, the preparation of the musical and graphic examples was underwritten by publication subventions from the *Society for Music Theory*, the Lloyd Hibberd Publication Endowment Fund of the *American Musicological Society*, and funds provided by Shelby Boardman, Dean of Carleton College. Thanks, too, to Corey Sevett at Artisan Computer Graphics, for his meticulous work on the examples. Catharine Carlin and John Rauschenberg at Oxford University Press gave enthusiastic support and editorial assistance, and Robert Milks expertly guided the book through its design and production.

One does not see a project like this through from start to finish without help from those at home. My colleagues in the Carleton College Music department, especially Ronald Rodman, Steve Kelly, and Larry Archbold, were all that one could ask for in this regard. My wife, Betsey Buckheit, assisted with her meticulous copyediting, correcting, and indexing skills, but more important gave unswerving love and moral support.

Finally, a note about the dedicatee and the reference to Horace Silver. My father, Dr. Sheldon London, is a retired biochemist currently enjoying a return to the life of an active jazz musician. He taught me, largely by example, that both art and science have their rightful places in the house of the intellect.

Permissions

Permission to reproduce example 1.2, rendered by George Houle in his book *Meter in Music: 1600–1800* (©1987 by George Houle), was kindly provided by the author. Permission to reproduce example 4.2, taken from *The Rhythmic Structure of Music* by Grosvenor Cooper and Leonard Meyer (© by the University of Chicago), was kindly provided by the University of Chicago Press. Portions of chapter 2 are taken from my article in *Music Perception* 19.4 (2002), pages 529–50 (© the Regents of the University of California).

Contents

Hearing in Time

Introduction

What Is Meter and What Is It For?

If you ask a musician "what is musical meter?" you are likely to get a demonstration of various ways of counting time such as "one-la-lee, two-la-lee" or "one and two and three and . . . " The musician is also apt to mention time signatures, the number of beats in a measure, which note carries the beat, and so forth. Some also might talk about how meter is part of the rhythmic "feel" or "groove" that underlies a particular melody or accompaniment.

This characterization of meter usually presumes, especially in styles in which one has written notation, that meter is part of the music itself. A contemporary composer might acknowledge this by saying that meter is a parameter subject to precompositional manipulation (e.g., meter can be serialized in a 12-tone composition as readily as pitch). Likewise, a music theorist might say that meter is a necessary part of the structural representation of a piece of music.

A slightly different but perhaps more useful question would be to ask a musician "what is meter *for*?" For this question you are likely to get an answer along the lines of "to help you play the rhythms properly." For, in counting correctly, a musician is able to play the rhythmic figures at the right tempo and with the correct durational proportion(s). To put it another way, the performer's sense of meter guides the motor behaviors used in the production of musical sounds. Although beginners typically need to count out the meter when they learn and practice a piece of music, more experienced musicians usually do not (although, when confronted with complicated patterns, they may also count them out). Even when not actually playing or singing (e.g., when a musician reads through a score and imagines the sounds in his or her head), metric counting helps the musician hear how the music is supposed to go.

So our hypothetical musicians would recognize that meter is both "for something" as well as part of the music's feel or groove. This is somewhat correct. In counting according to one meter and not another, a musician gives a series of tones a particular rhythmic shape and nuance; their sense of the meter leaves a kind of residue in performance, such that the "same" series of notes played under different counting frameworks will have distinctive differences in its expressive timing and dynamics.

From the outset, it is important to grasp the distinction between *rhythm* and *meter*. Rhythm involves patterns of duration that are phenomenally present in the music, and these patterns often are referred to as *rhythmic groups*. It is important to note that these "patterns of duration" are not based on the actual duration of each musical event—as a rhythmic pattern can be played legato or staccato, for example—but on the *interonset interval* ("IOI") between the attack-points of successive events. By contrast, meter involves our initial perception as well as subsequent anticipation of a series of beats that we abstract from the rhythmic surface of the music as it unfolds in time. In psychological terms, rhythm involves the structure of the temporal stimulus, while meter involves our perception and cognition of such stimuli. To paraphrase Gjerdingen (1989), if "meter [is] a mode of attending," then rhythm is that to which we attend.[1]

Meter is a perceptually emergent property of a musical sound, that is, an aspect of our engagement with the production and perception of tones in time. To be sure, there are important differences in the function of meter for listeners versus performers, but here I will focus on those aspects of meter that hold for both (and, of course, performers are also listeners). The guiding hypothesis of this book is that meter is a particular kind of a more general behavior. The same processes by which we attend to the ticking of a clock, the footfalls of a colleague passing in the hallway, the gallop of a horse, or the drip of a faucet also are used when we listen to a Bach adagio, tap our toes to a Mozart overture, or dance to Duke Ellington. As such, meter is not fundamentally musical in its origin. Rather, meter is a musically particular form of *entrainment* or *attunement*, a synchronization of some aspect of our biological activity with regularly recurring events in the environment. Meter is more, however, than just a bottom-up, stimulus driven form of attending. Metric behaviors are also learned—they are rehearsed and practiced. For musical rhythms are often stereotypical, stylistically regular, and hence familiar. So we fit, so to speak, patterns of events in the world to patterns of time we have in our minds (and, as we will see, our bodies).

At the beginning of his book on *Auditory Scene Analysis*, Albert Bregman poses the rhetorical question "what is perception for?" He answers by saying that "the job of perception . . . is to take [our] sensory input and to derive a useful representation of reality from it" (1990, p. 3). In following the implications of this seemingly obvious answer, Bregman is led to the question of how it is we are able to determine which sounds in our environment go together, that is, what sounds can be thought of as belonging to a common source. To answer this second question Bregman developed his concept of auditory streams and the auditory scene and thus launched a thriving line of research. Here I propose a slightly different answer for meter. For meter is not just a part of the "representation of reality," a means of temporally indexing musical events. Rather, meter is one of the ways in which our senses are guided in order to form representations of musical reality. Meter provides a way of capturing the changing aspects of our musical environment as patterns of *temporal invariance*. Bregman's characterization of what perception is for can thus be amended: perception is not only for deriving representations of reality; perception also serves to guide our behavior, and this includes perceptual behavior (tracking a moving stimulus, such as another person), motor behavior (running toward or away from them), social behavior (talking to them), and so forth.

So, to return to the question "what is meter for?" we can say that metric entrainment allows listeners to synchronize their perception and cognition with musical rhythms as they occur in time. When we are entrained our attention literally "moves with the music," and this engenders and encourages our bodily movements as well—from tapping toes and swinging arms to dancing and marching. When performers perform (and presumably when composers compose) they use the same perceptual and cognitive mechanisms in directing their attention and hence their musically specific motor behavior(s).[2] Jeffrey L. Pressing takes an evolutionary point of view for this process, and he proposes the following hypothesis of "rhythmogenesis": "*Musical rhythm arises from the evolved cognitive capacity to form and use predictive models of events* [ital. in original]— specifically, predictions of the timing of anticipated future events" (2002, p. 295). He goes on to note "the time-scale of the elements [of a meter—N.B., Pressing's term in this article is "feel" or "groove"] must be those relevant for human action and predictions. This is in accordance with experimental findings, which show a correspondingly limited time-scale range in which temporal patterns engage human rhythmic responses" (2002, p. 296).

It seems clear, then, that hearing the temporal regularities in a series of tones, and attributing to them a particular coherence as an object in the auditory scene (to use Bregman's terms), is a musically peculiar instance of a more general perceptual and cognitive ability. "Peculiar" is the right adjective for this instance, for it must be acknowledged that when listening to music (whether in a concert hall, our automobile, or our living room) we are *not* attending to such sounds in terms of their normal ecological significance. As Roger Scruton (1997) has pointed out, musical sounds are not part of our normal sound world, hence he makes a distinction between sound in the physical world and musical tones in "acousmatic space." Musical tones are produced for their own aesthetic contemplation as sounds—they are ends in themselves, and not further markers of location, action, size, and so on. When we attend to the sound of the oboe in an orchestral work we are not trying to discern the location of the oboist, nor do we understand a decrescendo in the oboe part as an indication that the oboist is moving away from us. Rhythm, too, is distilled from its everyday ecological significance in the concert hall. As I have noted, rhythm signifies movement, but musical tones do not move. Rather, we hear a kind of virtual motion in a virtual, asousmatic space (Langer 1953; Gjerdingen 1994). Nonetheless, it is precisely because our musical perception is parasitic on other modes of auditory perception that we hear movement in rhythmic pattern, or a sense of distance and remoteness when a melody gets softer and softer. Music derives much of its expressive power from the residues of the normal ecological significance of patterned sounds when we hear them in aestheticized contexts.

Some Other Premises of This Book

The major premise of *Hearing in Time* is that meter is a form of entrainment behavior. A number of other significant premises stem from it. The first is that these entrainment behaviors are highly practiced: from early childhood we are steeped in a musical environment, and have many opportunities to develop and hone our attentional habits relative to particular musical styles. Moreover, as metric entrainment is intimately related to motor behaviors, it is worth noting that those behaviors are also highly practiced. While there significant differences from person to person in their rhythmic sensitivities and abilities, most of us are very good at walking, running, and, of course, listening to and performing music—for almost everyone can sing a simple tune. Therefore, when we attend to a piece of music, we are rarely starting from metric first principles. Indeed, our highly practiced habits allow us to be sensitive to subtle nuances of a performer's interpretation (whether in the context of Rubinstein's Chopin or Tony Williams's be-bop drumming).

A second premise is that as a kind of attentional behavior, meter is subject to a number of fundamental perceptual and cognitive constraints, and these constraints need to be taken into account in discussions of meter, especially music-theoretic descriptions of possible (i.e., "well-formed") versus impossible meters. These constraints in turn have implications for how musical gestures can create particular expressive effects. By casting a pattern of alternating long and short notes in a particular meter and at a particular tempo, for example, a composer may exploit the perceptual differences between them, so that one may talk about a perceptual or cognitive basis for rhythmic affect.

Organizational Overview

Hearing in Time considers meter in both Western and non-Western musical traditions and examines our rhythmic perception and performance in both the laboratory and the concert hall. In so doing, we find a rich range of rhythmic practices and metric abilities. At the same time, I also argue that in these different cultures and contexts meters are nonetheless subject to the same basic formal and cognitive constraints. As our capacity for entrainment is universal, the same sorts of rhythmically regular patterns will tend to give rise to similar metrical structures and similar musical effects.

The first two chapters survey the theoretical background and empirical research in the psychology of perception and motor behavior relevant to musical meter. Chapters 3, 4, and 5 then relate this research to specifically musical contexts. Chapters 3 and 5 examine the ways that our metrical attention interacts with rhythmic surfaces, while chapter 4 presents *Hearing in Time*'s core conceptions of metric well-formedness, along with a new form of metric representation. The metric taxonomy becomes more fine-grained as the book progresses, as I note only differences among *metrical types* (different "flavors of $\frac{3}{4}$," for example, based on different varieties of subdivision) but also distinguish each type according to tempo, what I call *tempo-metrical types*. For our perceived sense of a given meter will change with tempo, even if its formal architecture remains constant.

Chapter 6 is an analytical interlude, a tour of the rhythmic landscape in the first movement of Beethoven's Fifth Symphony. This analysis shows how our metrical attending can change—often dramatically—over the course of a piece. It is an antidote, in some sense, to the other parts of the book, both because those other parts are more theoretical and because they tend to focus on steady states of metrical entrainment, rather than its flux.

Chapters 7 and 8 take us to other musical traditions and cultures, where we find meters with non-isochronous beat patterns. These meters are related to the principles of well-formedness laid out in the previous chapters. A single set of well-formedness constraints for both Western and non-Western musics is proposed. One of those constraints, *maximal evenness* (a concept taken from tonal theory, specifically, that of well-formed musical scales), is shown to be a global constraint on metric hierarchies, a constraint with perceptual as well as formal motivations.

Chapter 9 concludes the book by presenting the *many meters hypothesis*. This hypothesis moves beyond tempo-metrical types to highly context-specific patterns of temporal expectation that govern our attention to as well as performance of rhythmic sequences. The many meters hypothesis gives an ecologically valid approach to our metric perception and cognition by recognizing that we acquire our metrical listening habits by listening to real-world, human performances of music. And whereas these performances rarely (at least until recently) involve mechanically perfect timing patterns, their timing patterns are stable, involving expressive nuances that are typical of certain styles and genres. It is these nuanced timing patterns that we internalize and come to expect. These patterns may be highly individuated—not just among substyles of a music (e.g., different senses of swing in different styles of jazz) but also in the idiosyncratic rhythmic behaviors of particular musicians (e.g., Glenn Gould's Bach). Highly skilled listeners may have hundreds of specific timing patterns at their command and can reflexively invoke the appropriate meter as the music demands.

The many-meters hypothesis is in sharp contrast to the standard music-theoretic view of meter as comprising a few archetypal patterns. It also differs from Christopher Hasty's recent and more radical rejection of the categorical separation between rhythm and meter. Hasty focuses on the uniqueness of each rhythmic experience, which he refers to as its durational and metrical "particularity." Hasty notes that "it is customary to view rhythm as a rich and fully sensuous embodiment of music's temporal progress and meter as rhythm's shadowy, schematic counterpart—abstract, mechanical, and devoid of any intrinsic expression. . . . What is lost in this simplification is the specifically temporal character of repetition and therefore the claim of meter to be regarded as fully sensible and expressive" (1997, p. viii). I heartily agree with Hasty regarding the sensible, embodied aspects of our metric experience; I hope to show how meter itself can be expressive and how it can embody (both figuratively and literally) expressive movement. At the same time, in considering meter as, most essentially, a kind of behavior, I also claim that these behaviors are stable, replicable, and learnable. Listening metrically involves our musical habits, and not just a few generic habits but a rich repertoire of metric responses to rhythmic patterns and processes.

1

Meter as a Kind of Attentional Behavior

Attention, Anticipation, and Synchronization

As we move through the world, we seek information: What is out there? Where is it? Where am I? In this way we locate ourselves in our environment, find things we need (doorknobs and doorways, food, books, companions) and avoid other things (gaps in the pavement, wild animals, unpleasant acquaintances). But our world is not just composed of static objects: things move and stuff happens. Most movements and events give rise to sounds, for sounds are indicators of change in our environment. In attending to the sonic traces of events, we are able to learn not only what is going on but also *when* those events occur, as sounds mark the path of events in time as well as in space. And if the events are temporally regular—footfalls, ticks of a clock, or notes in a melody—we can anticipate when future events will occur.

James J. Gibson, the father of ecological approaches to perception, noted that looking at the world does not present us a static picture but a constantly shifting set of edges, contours, colors, and intensities. Gibson realized that in such a dynamic environment the perceptual task is not to find what changes but, rather, to be able to discern what aspects of the environment do *not* change: "The *adjusting* of perceptual organs, the overt acts of attention in looking, listening, smelling, tasting, and touching, can now be understood as an activity of extracting the invariants from potential stimulation, that is, the act of optimizing the pickup of external information." (1982, p. 168). The notion of a perceptual invariant is crucial, for the invariant features of a spatial array are the keys to our perception of it. As Gibson surmised:

The available stimulation surrounding an organism has structure, both simultaneous and successive, and this structure depends on sources in the outer

9

environment. . . . Instead of postulating that the brain constructs information form the input of a sensory nerve, we can suppose that the centers of the nervous system, including the brain, resonate to information. (1966, p. 267)

Gibson's choice of the term "resonate" is both apt and suggestive. Gibson's work did not consider temporal phenomena, such as sound patterns, and he did not usually discuss attention per se. Yet if we consider the perception of sound patterns, such as music, it seems that in an analogous fashion temporal invariants (as opposed to spatial invariants) guide the perceiver to direct his or her attention to a particular (future) location in time (see also Iyer 2002, p. 394).

Ulric Neisser, whose work was strongly influenced by Gibson, described how interaction with the environment drives this resonance. He noted that "the cognitive structures crucial for vision are the anticipatory schemata that prepare the perceiver to accept certain kinds of information rather than others and thus control the activity of looking" (1976, p. 20). Neisser adds, however:

Although hearing requires no exploratory movements like those of the eyes or hands, it is fundamentally the same sort of cyclic activity. . . . The listener continuously develops more or less specific readinesses (anticipations) for what will come next, based on information he has already picked up. These anticipations—which themselves must be formulated in terms of temporal patterns, not of isolated moments—govern what he will pick up next, and in turn are modified by it. Without them, he would hear only a blooming, buzzing confusion. (1976, p. 27)

Neisser's echoes of William James here are apropos, for James himself noted that the attentive process depends on "(1) the accommodation or adjustment of the sensory organs, and (2) the anticipatory preparation from within of the ideational centers concerned with the object to which the attention is paid" (1890, p. 434) and that such "anticipatory thinking" is 'universally present' in our acts of attention" (p. 439).

The ecological theories developed by Gibson and his adherents tend to approach perception and cognition from a practical, survival-in-the-environment perspective—I hear a sound, and I turn toward it to learn more about its source (the size, distance, and possible threat or benefit the source represents). But in a musical context, we are not involved with "exploration" of our environment(s) in the same way. Listening to music occurs in contexts (concert halls, living rooms, automobiles) in which we regard the musical sounds qua sounds, as objects to be considered in and of themselves, rather than as signs of motion, location, and so on. To be sure, in the concert hall, musical sounds *are* the result of the musicians' actions: their playing or singing creates the sounds we hear. Musical sounds do have ecological significance in the world of musical performance as the kinds of sounds performers make. Likewise, at times music may play more directly on the normative ecological significance of a sound, as when Rimskii-Korsakov has an orchestra imitate the sonic size and spatial motion, not to mention the buzzing wings, of a flying insect, or when a waltz limns the footfalls and twirls of dancers in some virtual ballroom. But my larger point remains, namely, that musical sounds do not connect with events in the world in the way that nonmusical ambient sounds do (we don't worry about being stung by Rimskii-Korsakov's bumblebee!). At the same time, however, some aspects of musical sounds still supervene on our nonmusical engagement with sounds, especially and particularly with respect to their rhythm, as rhythm is a powerful indicator of motion and movement (Gjerdingen 1994).

Ecological approaches to temporal perception have influenced a great deal of research in rhythmic perception and cognition, specifically that of Mari Riess Jones and her colleagues. She describes our basic faculties for temporal attention as follows:

> Attention is cast from some reference event at one point in time toward a target event scheduled for a later time. . . [thus] attention itself is a dynamic, many-leveled affair based upon nested internal rhythms. We continually cast ourselves forward by rhythmically anticipating future events that may occur within small and larger time intervals. These paths form the patterns of mental space and time and so can establish for us that sense of continuity and connection that accompanies comprehension. (1981, p. 571)

Jones has proceeded to develop her own theory of attending: "A rhythmical approach to attending is one which assumes that people and other animals target attending over predetermined time intervals toward events in space and time in a rhythmical fashion. Attending is a energistic activity guided in part by explicitly dynamic schemes that are themselves set in motion or indeed synchronously driven by the ongoing temporal character of an environment" (1986, p. 19). Jones's notion of energistic activity here draws on the work of Daniel Kahneman (1973), who introduced the concept of attentional energy as a resource, of limited capacity, that could be selectively marshaled: "According to the rhythmic attending theory, people rely upon invariances abstracted from the temporal rhythmicities of a particular context to prepare attentionally for 'when' forthcoming events will happen. Attentional energy is thus temporally targeted" (Jones 1986, p. 23).

Jones's research program has been to develop a model of temporal attending, of systematic modulations in our attention and expectation (Barnes & Jones 2000). Of cardinal importance is the need to match our temporal expectancies to when events are going to happen in our environment:

> The interaction of the perceiver with moving world patterns is described by the principle of synchronization. Successive event onsets in world patterns si-

multaneously define a series of nested time periods, and corresponding to each world time period there is a synchronized perceptual rhythm with a similar period. (Jones 1976, p. 328)

This process of synchronization is also referred to as *entrainment* or *attunement*. Entrainment, strictly speaking, means that "in response to a periodic input, a physiological rhythm may become entrained or phase-locked to the periodic stimuli. In this case, there is a periodic rhythm so that for each N cycles of one rhythm there are M cycles of the second rhythm" (Glass & Mackey 1988, p. 13). As we will see, entrainment is at times more and at times less than a phase-locking of the listener's attentional rhythms with temporal regularities in the musical surface; but the idea that meter is related to, and may be a complex form of, entrainment behavior is a central hypothesis of this book. Musical meter is the anticipatory schema that is the result of our inherent abilities to entrain to periodic stimuli in our environment. To paraphrase Ulric Neisser, if such a schema represents anything, it represents the temporal arrangement of a series of events (Neisser 1978, p. 103).

Studies of Rhythmic Behavior

In musical and nonmusical contexts there have been many studies of rhythmic synchronization, anticipation, and attention. The simplest studies of entrainment involve having subjects tap along with a metronome at varying tempos (i.e., tapping in 1:1 coordination with metronome clicks). Tapping studies involve not only attention but also action, a behavior (tapping in synchrony) that depends on rhythmic attending. Studies of tapping go back to the 19th and early 20th century (e.g., Dunlap 1910; Stevens 1886; Woodrow 1932). These studies have shown that our tapping can be extremely precise, as we can reproduce a temporal interval with a high degree of consistency. However, tapping studies also have shown that our synchronization systematically deviates from the stimulus onset, as people tend to tap 20–60 ms before the metronome click.[1] Tapping studies also have shown that increasing the complexity of the behavior and stimulus may actually reduce the variability in both phase and period. For example, Semjen, Schulze, et al. (1992) found that having subjects "doubletime" (i.e., tap both on the clicks and between them) or tap on offbeats reduced the phase and period variance at moderate tempos. Wohlschläger and Koch (2000) found that tapping to extended tones tended to be more accurate than tapping to bare metronome clicks.

In most experiments, participants are simply instructed to tap with the pacing stimulus as accurately as possible; often they are then asked to continue tapping at the same rate, producing what are sometimes termed "paced" versus "unpaced" responses. It is an open question in many studies, however, of the extent to which participants are counting "metrically" as they tap. How subjects form or employ mental images related to their performance (imagined melodies or speech rhythms, for example), whether or not they use such strategies, and so forth, is usually not addressed. But clearly such questions as "Are subjects counting in twos or threes?" or "Are they imagining a melody or rhythmic cadence while they tap?" may be relevant. Repp (in press) found that there is a "subdivision benefit"—a reduction in the variability of asynchronies (or relative phase)—for patterns of tapping within certain tempo ranges that are at a slower rate than a pacing stimulus, 1:2, 1:3, or 1:4, and so on.

In addition to using tapping tests, researchers have studied our ability to notice and judge temporal displacements within a series of regular durations. Halpern and Darwin (1982) asked subjects to judge whether the last interval in a short series of four clicks was the same or different as preceding intervals (that is, whether the last click came early or late relative to their expectations based on the previous clicks) and found that sensitivity was related to tempo (see also Schulze 1989b). Likewise Schulze (1978) found that tempo change is more salient than the perturbation of a single element in an otherwise isochronous series of elements. More broadly, one gains an advantage when presented with a series of intervals rather than a single interval compared to a standard (Drake & Botte 1993; Hirsh, Monohan, et al. 1990). While a series of intervals gives subjects a number of tries to judge a baseline duration and thus better encode a standard for comparison with a target interval, at the same time these periodic stimuli can (and probably do) trigger a metric response in the listener, setting up a dynamic framework against which subsequent durations or onsets may be heard and measured.

Temporal expectations also play a role in judgments of completeness and closure as well as rhythmic or melodic alteration. Jones, Boltz, and Kidd (1982) presented short, nine-tone sequences and found that the detection of pattern alteration or displacement in a target sequence was facilitated by metric attending (that is, in sequences whose organization was designed to induce a pattern of accents). Jones and Ralston (1991), using a same/different judgment task, found that when pitch alterations were in metrically prominent positions subjects were better at noticing them. Boltz (1989) manipulated the structure of folk and folk-like melodies by compressing or expanding rhythmic pattern, so that their endings came either "early" or "late." As she also manipulated their cadential structure, Boltz found that the sense of closure was affected both by temporal and tonal manipulations. Dowling, Lung, and Herrbold presented subjects with familiar tunes such as "Frère Jacques," "Mary Had a Little Lamb," and "Twinkle, Twinkle Little Star" that were interleaved with "distractor" notes. They found that:

> [A subject's] ability to perform this auditory "hidden figures" task depended upon the rhythmic control of attention on the basis of expectancies developed through perceptual learning with melodies in the listeners' culture. Listeners

appear to have aimed expectancies in pitch and time at regions where events critical to the identification of melodies are likely to occur—regions defining "expectancy windows" through which target notes are perceived. Events outside these expectancy windows were not perceived as accurately as events within the windows. Listeners discerned interleaved melodies whose notes fell *on* the consistent temporal beat of a pattern better than they did melodies whose notes fell *off* the beat. (1987, p. 642)[3]

Entrainment leads us to focus our attention to the most salient temporal locations for events; attention is, by its very nature, selective. We are almost always immersed in a rich and, from an information-processing perspective, noisy environment. There is much going on that commands our attention, but only some of the activity and information in our environment—including musical environments—is relevant to us at any give time. In his inimitable fashion, William James put the matter most directly: "Everyone knows what attention is. It is the taking possession by the mind, in clear and vivid form, of one out of what seem several simultaneously possible objects or trains of thought. Focalization, concentration, of consciousness are of its essence" (1890, pp. 403–4). Therefore, when we attend to space and time around us, we do so selectively. Gibson has called this *economical* perception:

It is the ability to avoid distraction—to concentrate on one thing at a time in the face of everything going on in the environment—and yet to accomplish as much knowing as possible. To accomplish this, perceiving must be quick and efficient rather than slow and contemplative. As a result, the information registered about objects and events becomes only what is needed, not all that could be obtained. (1966, p. 286)

Effort and Order

Not only do we respond to regularities that are present in our environment; we also project temporal regularities and order onto our environment. To return to James yet again: "A monotonous succession of sonorous strokes is broken up into rhythms, now of one sort, now of another, by the different accent which we place on different strokes. . . . But we do far more than emphasize things, and unite some, and keep others apart. We actually *ignore* most of the things before us" (1890, p. 284). For James, our subjective sense of rhythmic groups is related to our selective attention. But we do not quite ignore the unemphasized strokes. Rather, we organize them.

Our propensity to impose a sense of accent or grouping on a series of identical tones or clicks has long been known as *subjective rhythmization* (Bolton 1894; Meuman 1894).[4] This is something of a misnomer, for what is really subjective is the listener's sense of differentiation of the stimuli into twos, threes, or fours—

precisely a sense of meter under which the tones or clicks are heard, and thus perhaps subjective *metricization* would be a better term. Be that as it may, musicians and music theorists have also long been aware of subjective rhythmization: in 1787 Heinrich Koch noted how a listener will group a series of six beats in either twos or threes based on "the nature of our sense perception and our power of imagination" (cited in Hasty 1997, p. 27).

Meter is thus more than a response to invariant features of the musical stimulus. In temporal attending, it is useful (and perhaps necessary) for the perceiver to establish a self-generated ground against which the continuing temporal patterns may be discerned. This attending strategy may originate in extrapolations from a local invariant or characteristic rhythmic figure that implies a particular metric schema, but the continuation of a meter is less dependent on subsequent musical invariants than on (a) the listener's ability to generate metric patterns (an ability that may vary with age, talent, training, and enculturation), and (b) the lack of interference from subsequent musical stimuli (interference here meaning the emergence of a pattern of alternate metric cues). Indeed, many passages are metrically neutral, or what I have termed *metrically malleable*.[5] Example 1.1 illustrates this malleability. In 1.1a we have a short series of eighth notes, apart from any particular metric context. In examples 1.1b and 1.1c we see how this snippet can be embedded in $\frac{4}{4}$ and $\frac{6}{8}$ with equal felicity. Note how in $\frac{4}{4}$ (duple meter with binary subdivision) the latent triadic arpeggio within the figure is brought out, while in $\frac{6}{8}$ (duple meter, but with ternary subdivision) a broader stepwise motion becomes more salient (refer to the circled notes in 1.1b and 1.1c). Thus metric context has a strong effect on our sense of the structural (versus ornamental) tones of many melodic patterns. Metric malleability is discussed at greater length in chapter 5.

The effect of metric context on melodic perception has long been known. In 1636, Charles Butler gave the following example (example 1.2). Note that in this older system of mensural notation the open note heads with stems, known as minims (which approximate the modern half note) take different values de-

Example 1.1. Same melodic figure embedded in both $\frac{4}{4}$ and $\frac{6}{8}$. (a) Figure independent of metric context: (b) figure in $\frac{4}{4}$—meter emphasizes G-B-D triadic structure; (c) figure in $\frac{6}{8}$—meter emphasizes G-A-B scale structure.

Example 1.2. Butler's melodic in contrasting metric contexts ("jumping by threes") from Houle (1987), p. 31.

pending on the particular time signature. Thus in describing the third and fourth measures of these two melodies, Butler noted that in the first case the black notes "go jumping by threes," whereas in the second they go by twos, "whereby the melody of the same notes becometh diverse" (cited in Houle 1987, p. 31). Butler recognized how the context established in the opening measures affects the metric construal of the music that follows. This has been documented in experimental studies; Clarke (1987a) found that metrical context influenced discrimination between $\frac{2}{4}$ and $\frac{6}{8}$ meter—that is, the "same" pattern was heard as either $\frac{2}{4}$ or $\frac{6}{8}$, depending on the previous metric cues (see also Large 2000b).[6]

These examples suggest how listeners can impose or maintain a meter even in the absence of any salient surface articulation, that is, without any clear invariants that would group the rhythmic surface one way or another. Yet our efforts after metric order go beyond ambiguous or neutral patterns to passages that openly conflict with an established metric context. A familiar example is that of syncopation. In example 1.3a we have a pattern that, in and of itself, strongly suggests a duple meter with strong beats on the C and D (see circled notes in the example). The first note would normally be heard as a pickup or anacrusis to the following downbeat. This same pattern is embedded in example 1.3b, and the C and D are now heard as syncopations against the prevailing meter. That is, even though relative duration, contour accent, and tonal stability (C is the tonic pitch) fight against it, the metric framework can be maintained rather than shifted. Syncopation depends not only on listeners holding fast to the previously established metric context but also on their selectively construing what they hear, not as new invariants, but rather as subordinate to an estab-

Example 1.3. Syncopation in and out of context. (a) Short-long-short figures independent of metric context (short may sound like an anacrusis); (b) Short-long-short figures function as syncopes in established $\frac{4}{4}$ context.

lished meter. Composers have long counted on (and exploited) our proclivity to maintain an established metric framework, and the force with which we will impose metric order on an uncooperative musical surface.

Musical Meters and Depth of Entrainment

Before I talk further about the nature of metrical entrainment, a few basic points about musical meter must be made. Meter is first and foremost grounded in the perception and production of a pulse or *tactus*. The tactus establishes the continuity of musical motion; without it, no sense of meter is possible. But a tactus, in and of itself, is insufficient for a sense of meter. The tactus establishes a single periodicity, and to be sure, this does give the listener a limited degree of temporal expectancy: something should happen on the next beat. Yet while this is a type of entrainment, if we were to make a representation of this entrainment in metric terms, it would be a series of one-beat "measures":

1, 1, 1, 1, 1 . . .

Musical meters do more than this; consider a simple duple measure:

1, 2, **1**, 2, **1**, 2 . . .

(N.B., here and elsewhere a bold font is used to indicate and/or emphasize the sense of downbeat that occurs on a particular beat in a metrical counting pattern.) If we are at the beginning of such a measure, while we expect something on the next beat (2), our expectations are even greater that a musically significant event will occur on the following downbeat.[7] At minimum, a metrical pattern requires a tactus coordinated with one other level of organization. Yeston makes a similar point: "meter arises from the interaction of two periodic strata, one of which must be on the middleground level" (1976, p. 67). The stipulation offered here differs from Yeston in two important ways. First, Yeston's middleground level corresponds to intervals between successive downbeats, rather than the tactus; this follows from his interest in developing a theory of meter in accordance with a top-down Schenkerian perspective that focuses on tonal relationships. Second, Yeston's characterization of meter as the interaction between quasi-independent rhythmic strata is replaced here by the integration of several strata into single, coherent attentional framework. The treatment of meter as a kind of hierarchic gestalt, while newly argued here, has its antecedents as far back as Mattheson's discussion of *Takte* and *Zeitmass* (see Hasty 1997, pp. 22–25). As I argue later, it is the differentiation of expectation, rather than any tonal or durational criteria, that gives rise to different degrees of metric accentuation, and the subjective sense of a pattern of strong versus weak beats.

Whereas two levels of periodicity are necessary, three or more are preferable, as this provides an attending framework that allow the listener to track rapid, moderate, and relatively slow event onsets, and these correspond to subdivisions of the tactus, the tactus level itself, and a higher-level ordering of beats into measures. This preferred form of meter is related to the *temporal perspective model* of Jones (1987a, 1990a, 1990b, 1992). Her temporal perspective model relates smaller and larger periods of attention to a middle level that she refers to as the *referent* time period. The temporal referent anchors our attentional process, and mediates between analytic attending (awareness of local details) and future-oriented attending (awareness of more global processes and goals). In metric terms, the beat or tactus serves as the referent level. Jones's model thus suggests that beat subdivisions are the product of analytic attending, that is, we grasp them as fractions of a larger span. Conversely, larger levels—measures—are yoked to expectations that derive from the referent level such as anticipating that an important event will occur "in two beats" or "every three beats" (see also Jones & Boltz 1989; London 1990; Monohan 1993; Shaffer 1982).

These three levels are inherent in the standard terminology for Western meters, which distinguishes between two- versus three-beat measures (duple vs. triple) and binary versus ternary beat subdivision (simple vs. compound) as shown in table 1.1. Time signatures for compound meters must finesse the binary-based orthography for durational relationships in modern Western notation—orthographically the relationship from half note to quarter note, or quarter to eighth, is always 2:1. Standard notation for triplet subdivision requires the use of a dot of addition for the beat-unit duration, so that, for example, in $\frac{6}{8}$ the dotted quarter note carries the beat. A common mistake is to presume that the numerator of any time signature refers to the number of beats in a measure; this is usually the case in simple meters but not in compound meters. Most two-tiered meters will comprise an ordering of beats (i.e., a measure), without any subtactus periodicities. Indeed, subtactus levels are often intermittent and over the course of a piece may shift from simple to compound or even drop out altogether.

In many instances, however, additional levels of entrainment, both higher and lower, may be present. Meters may thus be described not only in terms of the organization of their essential levels but also in terms of the presence (or absence) of additional levels of structure. Example 1.4 illustrates this distinction. The melody in example 1.4a moves in half and quarter notes, and invokes a rela-

Table 1.1. Distinctions Between
Two- and Three-Beat Measures

simple duple	simple triple
$\frac{2}{4}$ (and $\frac{4}{4}$)	$\frac{3}{4}$
compound duple	compound triple
$\frac{6}{8}$	$\frac{9}{8}$

Example 1.4. Different "varieties" of $\frac{3}{4}$. (a) Basic $\frac{3}{4}$ with beat and measure levels; (b) additional layers of subdivision.

tively simple meter of just two levels, beats and measures. In example 1.4b the running eighth notes give rise to a richer metrical hierarchy that involves a level of subdivision. Hence, we have two different varieties of $\frac{3}{4}$, and as they give rise to different forms of entrainment, they are in fact *different* meters. It also follows on this view that there is no essential distinction to be made between meter and so-called *hypermeter*. Hypermeter is a term first used by Cone (1968) to refer to levels of metrical structure above the notated measure; hypermeasures are not phrases, although phrase structure and hypermetric structure can and do interact (see Berry 1989; Kramer 1988; Lerdahl & Jackendoff 1983; Lester 1986; Rothstein 1989; Schachter 1987). Yet having several levels of metric structure present above the perceived beat is no more extraordinary than having several levels of subdivision below it.

Dynamic Attending and Accent

A perennial bugbear of music-theoretic accounts of meter is the nature and origin of metrical accent. One of the most attractive aspects of the behavioral approach to meter proposed here is that it finesses many aspects of the accent problem by placing the accentual burden on the entrained listener rather than on the music.

To begin with, not all accents are metrical. Lerdahl and Jackendoff distinguish three varieties of accent: *phenomenal accents* that "give emphasis or stress to a moment in the musical flow . . . such as sforzandi, sudden changes in dynamics or timbre, long notes, leaps . . . and so forth," *structural accents* that are "caused by melodic/harmonic points of gravity in a phrase or section," and *metrical accents* that accrue to a "beat that is relatively strong in its metrical context" (1983, p. 17). Lerdahl and Jackendoff's hierarchic approach to metric accent has precursors in Komar (1971) and Yeston (1976) and has been adopted subsequently by many music theorists. According to the Lerdahl and Jackendoff model, a relatively strong metrical event is one that has greater hierarchic depth than its neighboring events. As they remark: "If a beat at a given level L is also a beat at a larger level, we call it a strong beat of L; if it is not, it is a weak beat of L" (1983, p. 68).

Lerdahl and Jackendoff's approach to meter and metric accent is close to the one developed here, in that they view metrical accent as "a mental construct, inferred from but not identical to the patterns of accentuation at the musical surface" (p. 18). Likewise, they note "once a clear metrical pattern has been established, the listener renounces it only in the face of strongly contradicting evidence" (p. 17), which suggests that they view meter primarily as a form of listener behavior. However, in Lerdahl and Jackendoff's model, metrical accent remains yoked to phenomenal accent: "The listener's cognitive task is to match the given pattern of phenomenal accent as closely as possible to a permissible pattern of metrical accentuation" (p. 18). Yet, as has been noted earlier, metric patterns, which include a sense of metric accent, are not directly dependent on dynamic or agogic accent. A familiar example is the characteristic backbeat emphasis on beats 2 and 4 of a four-beat measure in rock and popular music; these dynamic accents do not displace the metric accents on beats 1 and 3 of the measure. For listeners who are conversant with this style, such dynamic emphasis is not confusing; indeed, it is an idiomatic way of clarifying the metric organization.[8]

What then is a metrical accent? When meter is considered as the listener's entrainment to the musical surface, metric accent becomes a natural fallout of the attending process. Cooper and Meyer famously defined accent as "an event that is marked for consciousness" (1960, p. 8). This may be modified by saying a metrical accent is an event that is marked *by* consciousness (or by subconscious attending processes). One cannot attend to or anticipate events metrically (musical or otherwise) without a mental timekeeper or process that becomes attuned to events in our environment and then directs our behavior accordingly.[9] Large and Jones note:

> Models specifically designed to explain perception and production of rhythmic patterns have proposed differential encoding of successive time intervals in a sequence. . . . Perhaps the most influential is Povel's (1981) clock model. It is a beat-based model: a listener economically encodes time intervals when they form a rhythm sufficient to induce a fixed beat. The beat is mentally represented as a clock grid. (1999, p. 122)

Povel and Essens (1985) extend the clock grid to multiple levels of periodicity creating a hierarchic clock. Such clocks are very good at predicting when future events will occur and generating accentual patterns. Yet, as Large and Jones go on to note: "This prediction comes at a cost. The fixed beat structure of the clock model is not robust enough to [deal with] even small perturbations in a rhythmic pattern" (1999, p. 122).

Povel and Essen's model may be described as *time discrete*, as it first creates an internal representation of an external temporal interval and then uses it as a feed-forward value, spitting out another temporal articulation every so often. As such, the perceiver moves from state to state, where each state includes a representation of past temporal structure as well as the anticipation of future events. Yet as Fraisse (1963) remarked, we do not at one instant hear the "tick-tock" of a clock, and then its "tock-tick," as would be the case in a time-discrete model. Rather, we hear patterns of accented and unaccented beats. Large and Jones's alternative is to develop a time-continuous rather than a time-discrete model for entrainment. A time-continuous model does not move from state to state but varies in a cyclical fashion. It is a resonating system.

Once again, it is striking how earlier music theorists described metric articulation and accent in terms of a time-continuous perspective. For example, Koch (1787/1969) and Sulzer (1792) both use the terms *Ruhepunkt des Geistes* or *Ruhepunkt den Vorstellung* (resting points within the flux of the spirit or imagination) when speaking of the listener's apprehension of rhythmic patterns. Their terminology is related to Batteux's (1747–1750) *repos de l'esprit* (see Christensen & Baker 1995).[10]

A number of dynamical systems models of musical meter have been proposed that treat meter as a system of oscillations (Beek, Peper, et al. 2000; Collyer & Broadbent 1994; Eck, Gasser, et al. 2000; Large 2000a; Large & Kolen 1994; Pressing 1998; Schulze 1989b; Treffner & Turvey 1993;). Large and Jones have described such systems as follows:

> A self-sustaining oscillation has two important features that make it appropriate for modeling the basic process of attentional dynamics. First, it generates periodic activity, an activity that we refer to as an *expectation*. Expectations are similar to the ticks of a clock, with the important exception that an expectation is an active temporal anticipation, not a grid point in a memory code. Second, when coupled to an external rhythm, a self-sustaining oscillation may entrain, or synchronize, to that rhythm. (1999, p. 124)

Metric entrainment can be thought of as involving a number of coordinated and mutually reinforcing oscillations. By tuning its resonance to periodicities in the music, a self-sustaining bank of oscillators is able to match its periods and phases to achieve synchronization with an external rhythm. In figure 1.1, after Large and Jones (1999), the behavior of a single oscillator evolves over time, in this case, representing the listener's evolving sense of a beat. As the beat becomes established in the listener's mind, expectations become both stronger and more temporally focused; this evolution of expectation corresponds to the increasing height and narrowing width of each expectancy peak in figure 1.1.

Of course, musical meters involve more than just a series of beats. Figure 1.2, after Large and Palmer (2001), describes the behavior of a system of internal, self-sustained oscillations that operate at different periods with specific phase

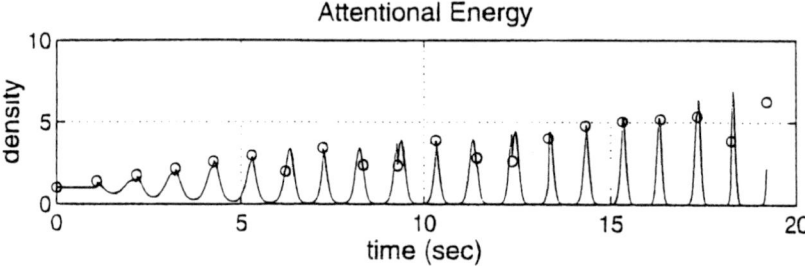

Figure 1.1. Emergence of regular and temporally focused peaks of attention in response to a regular stimulus, after Large and Jones (1999), fig. 12B, p. 134.

and period relationships. The solid line represents the combination of the outputs of a measure-level oscillator (marked by the dashed line) and a beat-level oscillator (marked by the dotted line). Figure 1.2 traces one complete cycle of a $\frac{3}{4}$ measure, although in a somewhat musically unfamiliar fashion, as the downbeat that musically marks the beginning of the measure is placed in the middle of their diagram, as the strongest expectancy peak occurs at the "top dead center" of the phase maps of the component oscillators. This system shows how the listener's expectancy (the solid line) can be modulated in complex ways based on the interactions of the component periods of the metric hierarchy.[11] The sense of accent that accrues to the downbeat of the measure is the result of the mutual reinforcement of the component oscillators. This mutual reinforcement also helps the system continue to self-sustain even when the rhythmic "driving inputs" to the system are absent (e.g., during a sustained note or rest).

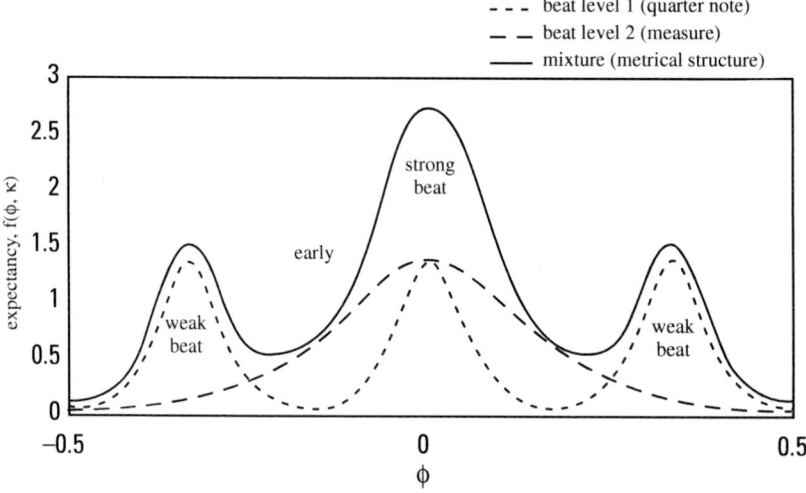

Figure 1.2. Composite and component metric oscillations, after Large and Palmer (2001), fig. 3A (online source)

Not only do oscillating systems generate peaks of attention (and hence metric beats and accents); they also mark particular locations in time. As Hasty points out, durationless time points cannot, in and of themselves, carry any differentiation or accent (1997, p. 17). Schachter similarly remarks "A point of time can never receive an emphasis; only an event that occurs at the point can" (1987, p. 6). If the listener needed to somehow phenomenally grasp time points and differentiate among them, these concerns would indeed be warranted. Yet Schachter also observes that "the metrical accent accrues to a compositional event" (p. 6), and this mapping of metric accent onto phenomenal events accords well with what has been described earlier. A metrical accent occurs when the metrically entrained listener projects a sense of both temporal location and relatively greater salience onto a musical event. In this context, the use of *time point* is not meaningless, nor is its contrast with *time span*. Time points correspond to peaks in attentional energy and mark other phase relationships in the attentional cycle, and consequently time spans may be understood, among other things, as the intervals between successive attentional peaks.

Meter for Listeners and Performers (and Composers)

The approach to meter being developed here is squarely based on the listener's perspective; more precisely, meter involves the perception of an occurrent musical passage. This is different from metric aspects of remembered musical experience (such as simply knowing that a particular song was in triple meter) or from the audiation of musical passages in the "the mind's ear." Moreover, it is presumed that listeners do not normally have access to other, nonauditory information, such as a score or the scansion of song lyrics. Metric audition requires only the musical sounds themselves and the listener's temporal capacities, both innate and learned.

For the performer, the situation is rather different. In many instances, performers will have a printed score before them that specifies both what notes are to be played as well as the metric framework under which they are to be produced. In other instances, especially in the case of classical soloists and small ensembles for jazz, pop, and rock, music is often performed from memory, and of course in oral traditions there are no scores. Whether players use scores or not, what a listener hears on any given occasion is usually well-rehearsed: the performers' skilled musical behavior is the result of hours of practice, both in terms of the general rudiments for their voices or instruments (many of which involve the rehearsal of metric frameworks) and in terms of the specific pieces played.

Unlike the listener, who must extract certain metric invariances from the given musical surface, the performers' task is to set up a pattern of metric invariances that will guide his or her production of the musical surface. Part of an effective performance involves communicating this metric structure to the lis-

Composition for Twelve Instruments
I

Example 1.5. Notated vs. unheard meter in Babbitt's *Composition for 12 instruments,* opening measures.

tener, especially if the musical surface is metrically malleable.[12] In most instances the performer's sense of meter is congruent with that of the listener; as Jones has observed, the result is a common, shared temporal perspective "from which melodic and rhythmic forms may be perceived" (1987, p. 164).[13]

Some contexts, however, especially in the case of avant-garde classical music, do not involve a shared temporal perspective. Example 1.5 is a page from Milton Babbitt's *Composition for Twelve Instruments.* Here the notated quarter-note duration is constant at 84 beats per minute/714 ms IOI, although the number of quarter notes per measure shifts from three to two to four in the excerpt. In order to perform this piece in a coordinated fashion all 12 performers must maintain the quarter note pulse and keep track of the time signatures together. Yet it is highly unlikely that the listener will be able to perceive any sense of beat or measure, given the aperiodic nature of the musical surface. In this example, the notated meter serves as an arbitrary temporal framework for the performers that is opaque to the listener. Indeed, this music is not really metric at all, as it does not afford the listener any possible pattern of temporal invariance.

The composer's metrical perspective may be yet further removed from what the performer sees (and thus does) and what the listener hears. As Babbitt (1962) himself described, composers may use a variety of techniques, some of them derived from the manipulation of pitch relationships in 12-tone music, to generate rhythmic and metric structure. In example 1.5, the metric placement of each note is derived from its position in the 12-tone pitch series, yet the resulting rhythmic surface does not display any aurally obvious relationship to the tone row. Thus, even the performers (and most certainly the listeners) are apt to remain in the dark regarding the composer's metric premises. Such instances of metric opacity are not new to the 20th century; for example, at the height of the

Ars Subtilor of the 14th century, the various combinations and manipulations of mensural rhythm produced equally complex (and for the listener, metrically unintelligible) rhythmic textures. Nonetheless, in most musics, what is desired and usually achieved is a congruence of temporal understanding—the composer intends a certain meter, the performer projects that meter, and the listener grasps it.

Summary and Discussion

In many contexts, we synchronize our attentional energies to the rhythms of the world around us. This synchronization is achieved by latching onto temporal invariants, that is, similar events that occur at regular intervals. Meter is a specifically musical instance of a more general perceptual facility of temporal attunement or entrainment.

In musical contexts, metric attending involves both the discovery of temporal invariants in the music and the projection of temporal invariants onto the music. We actively seek and generate temporal structure through our attending behaviors. The way we attend to the present is strongly affected by our immediate past; once we have established a pattern of temporal attending we tend to maintain it in the face of surprises, noncongruent events, or even contradictory invariants. Music often depends on our making an effort to project and maintain an established meter in passages that involve things like syncopation and hemiola.

Metric entrainment involves a coordinated set of attentional periodicities on different time scales. In the next chapter, we will see there are constraints on these periodicities, but, at a minimum, metrical entrainment requires a tactus coordinated with one other level of organization. Minimal (two-level) meters usually involve a tactus and a superior level; more typically meter involves three or more levels. The notational orthography and nomenclature in western music reflects this: most time signatures signify a tactus level, a level of subdivisions below the tactus, and a particular arrangement of the tactus into measures (most often twos, threes, or fours). These categories by no means exhaust the range of metric possibilities, as there may well be additional levels above the measure and below the first level of subdivision.

Two broad points follow from this observation. First, one may characterize meters in terms of their hierarchic depth—that is, whether a meter involves a rich hierarchy of expectation on many levels at once, or only a limited set of expectations as to when things are going to occur. Second, as the number of metric levels both above and below the beat can and does fluctuate, there is no substantive distinction between meters and so-called hypermeters.

Finally, regarding meter as a form of anticipatory behavior finesses the problem of metrical accent. Rather than seeking a phenomenal basis for metrical accent—whether by brute force in the form of dynamic emphasis, or due to the tonal interpretation of events—metrical accents are generated by the listener via his or her attending process. The degree of metrical accent is correlated with the relative strength and temporal focus of our entrained temporal expectancies. This view of meter and metrical accent also allows one to meaningfully speak about time-points or locations for rhythmic events, as they are marked by peaks of attentional energy.

2

Research on Temporal Perception and its Relevance for Theories of Musical Meter

---

The Upper and Lower Limits of Meter

Not all periodic stimuli afford entrainment—some are too fast, and others are too slow. Rapidly blinking lights can become a blur, and slowly (but regularly) dripping faucets will defeat our attempts to predict when the next drip will fall. This is as true in music as it is in nonmusical contexts, for musicians can play rapid trills or chromatic cascades faster than we can count or even discern them. Likewise in some music, notes or chords may be so widely spaced that we have no sense of a beat or pulse. This is what Heusler (1925) meant in his remark that "rhythm is the organization of time in parts accessible to the senses" (cited in Sachs 1953, p. 15).

The lower limit for meter, that is, the shortest interval that we can hear or perform as an element of rhythmic figure, is about 100 milliseconds (ms). Conversely, the upper limit is around 5 to 6 seconds, a limit set by our capacities to hierarchically integrate successive events into a stable pattern (N.B., unless otherwise noted, the time intervals referred to here are "interonset intervals" [*IOIs*], the time span from articulation to articulation; IOIs will be given in milliseconds or seconds, and where appropriate, tempos or beat rates will be given both in milliseconds (the duration of the beat interval) as well as beats per minute (BPM). These upper and lower bounds can be regarded as a kind of *temporal envelope* for meter. These boundaries are apparent in many different studies of rhythmic perception and performance. What follows is a presentation of some converging evidence for our metric capacities. However, some caveats apply. It is probably impossible to come up with hard and fast values for these boundaries, as well as for other significant thresholds within those boundaries. The values reported later are largely from experiments that employ nonmusical (or what might be charitably regarded as quasi-musical) stimuli and contexts; for the most part this research lacks ecological validity relative to real-life listening situations. Moreover, this research has shown that various thresholds, acuities and so on, are heavily dependent on task, stimulus, context, and so forth. For example, research has convincingly shown that rhythmic perception interacts with pitch (see Hirsh 1990a; 1990b, Jones et al. 1995; Van Noorden 1975).

Another difficulty is that metrical periodicities on each level are subject to *expressive variation*, that is, subtle nuances involving compressions and extensions of otherwise deadpan rhythms, what musicians might call "pushing and pulling the time." These timing nuances serve both structural as well as expressive roles. Although some expressive variations disambiguate metrical structure by indicating which note is on the downbeat, others define the affective or the motional quality of a particular figure. Expressive variations can and do interact with metrical boundaries and thresholds and, as such, they will tend to blur any particular value. Finally, all of the various thresholds and rate limits discussed in this chapter are subject to a high degree of inter-subject variation; the reported values are averages for subject populations, and often these are averages within a wide range of data.

Nonetheless, while the precise value of a metric limit or threshold may be affected by context, its general range and order of magnitude will not. These general ranges will serve as a constraint on metric possibilities and will affect our subjective sense of a rhythmic figure's gestural qualities. While we need to take the absolute values for the thresholds employed here with a large grain of salt, we can still profitably examine how they affect our metric entrainment.

Our first clue for identifying these upper and lower bounds for meter comes from studies of subjective rhythmization. As noted in the previous chapter, subjective rhythmization is our grouping of a series of identical, isochronous stimuli into groups of twos and threes—that is, we hear duplets and triplets, or (at slower rates) a sense of two- or three-beat "measures" even when there are no structural cues for us to do so. Bolton (1894) found a lower limit of 115 ms, and, as the upper limit, 1580 ms for subjective rhythmization. The music theorist Peter Westergaard described the following range of "useful tempos," given in table 2.1 (1975, p. 274. N.B., I have provided IOI equavelents for Westergaard's

Table 2.1. Range of Perceived Tempos

Beats/minute	IOI (ms)	Tempo comment
30	2000	too slow to be useful
42	1414	very slow
60	1000	moderately slow
80	700	moderate
120	500	moderately fast
168	350	very fast
240	250	too fast to be useful

tempos). Westergaard is not talking about subjective rhythmization but the range in which one can perceive a pulse or tactus; for now, let us just note the approximate correspondence between his limits and those found by Bolton.

Why is 100 ms the shortest possible IOI in a metric cycle? Other thresholds for the perception of very short intervals have been noted. Starting with the shortest values, Hirsh (1959) found that a 2 ms separation is required to discern that two tone onsets are present. He also found that a considerably greater interval ($\approx$20 ms) must elapse if the listener is to correctly report the order in which those sounds occurred. Thus, for example, if there are two different tones, one high and the other low, there needs to be at least 20 ms between their onsets in order for the listener to reliably distinguish a "low $\rightarrow$ high" sequence from a "high $\rightarrow$ low."

Hirsh, Monohan, et al. found "listeners can discriminate an interval between two brief sounds with great precision—changes on the order of 5–10 percent can be noticed. This is generally true for intervals down to about 100 ms" (1990, pp. 223–4). The minimum time to allow for the cortical processing of musical elements is also 100 ms (Roderer 1995), and it agrees with Lehiste's observation that the fastest possible vocal articulation of rapidly repeated syllables is around 120 ms (1970, pp. 6–7), as well as Efron's (1973) findings that the shortest perceptual duration was approximately 130 ms, regardless of sensory modality.

In the context of jazz drumming, Friberg and Sundström (2002) found that the absolute duration of the short note in the ride cymbal pattern was constant at 100 ms for medium to fast tempos, thus indicating a performance limit for subdivisions at rapid tempos. In non-musical contexts, Pressing (1998) found that the shortest interval for antiphase tapping was 375 ms (that is, having subjects between beats that were 375 ms apart). Repp (in press) found that the shortest IOI at which musically trained participants could tap in phase with every fourth tone was on average 120 ms (100 ms for the best participants)—thus in this study the maximum tap rate was 480–400 ms. Repp, London, et al. (2004) found that when participants tap to uneven rhythms, the fastest subdivisions were somewhat slower, closer to an average of 170 ms. Thus the limit for these sensorimotor tasks (and, presumably, for the attending tasks that go with them) depends on the complexity of the pattern and the difficulty of the motor behavior. Nonetheless, given this pattern of results from studies of both rhythmic perception and performance, for meter it seems reasonable to propose that the lower limit of the metric envelope is $\approx$100 ms. That is, an IOI of $\approx$100 ms is the shortest possible interval.[1]

Fraisse notes that above 1800 ms subjective rhythmization becomes impossible and that successive sounds are not heard as continuous (1982, p. 156), which prevents us from hearing such sounds in terms of a coordinated motion or movement, and we have already noted the importance of the connection between hearing rhythm and perceiving movement (see also Clarke 1999). This sense of motion in auditory patterns may be related to apparent motion in vision. Wertheimer (1912) found that successive visual stimuli presented within a certain temporal range gave the illusion of motion, and Bregman (1990, pp. 173–84) discusses the parallels between apparent motion in vision and apparent motion in audition in terms of auditory streaming.[2] Gjerdingen (1994) has described a model of apparent motion in music that is sensitive to IOI, pitch proximity, and articulative quality.

Monohan (1993) also notes the 2-second limit on the connectedness of successive events, and this limit also applies to our ability to synchronize with a series of events. For example, Mates, Mueller, et al (1993) found a shift in synchronization strategy at very slow tempos. When an isochronous series of tones is faster than 2400 ms, subjects can synchronize with it, and they produce the characteristic "negative asynchrony error," that is, they anticipate each tone by 20–50 ms (depending on tempo). Above 2400 ms, however, this anticipation disappears, and while subjects can synchronize, the task essentially becomes a reaction time task (Woodrow 1932). Brower (1993) summarized research that shows two seconds as a limit of echoic or sensory memory.

The upper limit for meter is much longer than that for subjective rhythmization. This is because subjective rhythmization studies focus on beat-to-beat intervals, not on hierarchically organized patterns of beats into measures. Woodrow, in a series of extended synchronization and tapping tests, found that:

> There thus appears to be one duration, at around 1.5–2 seconds at which the reproduction of empty intervals, synchronization, and the experiencing of rhythm all begin to become difficult and another duration around 3.4 sec (2–4 sec) which represents the vanishing point of the capacity for synchronization, and (if taken as the duration of a single [poetic] foot) for experiencing rhythm. (1932, pp. 377–8)

The constraint on the scope of larger temporal patterns is related to our sense of the psychological present. Although the idea of the psychological present (or "specious" present) goes back to James (1890), Michon (1978) has more recently characterized it as the time interval in which sensory information and concurrent behavior are to be integrated within the same span of attention. This span of attention may vary; typically 2–3 seconds, its upper limit may reach 5–7 seconds (Pöppel 1972, Michon 1978, Fraisse 1984). The variation reported by these researchers may be related to perceptual context—different rhythmic patterns may afford longer or shorter metric frameworks. And if 2 seconds is the limit for hearing successive events as temporally connected outside of a metric hierarchy, then it makes sense that the absolute value for a measure might be from about 4 to 6 seconds (that is, twice or three times the length of the slowest possible beat).

The Primacy of the Tactus

We can hear a beat or pulse within a range from about 200–250 ms (300–240 BPM) to two seconds (30 BPM). This range for beat perception has been demonstrated in a number of studies. Warren (1993) investigated subjects ability to recognize melodic patterns, and found that they were able to do so within a range of 200–2000 ms for successive note onsets. A similar range also was found in studies that asked subjects to tap to metronomic ticks or to musical excerpts at various tempos, and then observed at what tempos subjects shifted from tapping with every click or note to interpolating taps at very slow tempos or tapping to every other note at very fast tempos (e.g., Duke 1989; Duke, Geringer, et al. 1991). Parncutt (1994), drawing on earlier research and his own experimental studies in which subjects tapped to a variety of rhythmic patterns at different tempos, found a range of pulse perception from 200 to 1800 ms, with a pronounced peak of *maximal pulse salience* around 600 ms (100 BPM).

The special significance of periodicities in the 600–700 ms range has long been known. Early researchers in psychophysics sought to determine an *indifference interval*, that is, a single duration that was judged neither too long nor too short.[3] Wundt (1911) found an average indifference interval of 600 ms, later confirmed by Fraisse (1963). That is, subjects tend to overestimate the duration of intervals less than 600 ms, and underestimate the duration of intervals longer than 600 ms. Another approach investigated spontaneous tempo or natural pace, which often is observed by simply asking subjects to tap with a finger, hand, or foot at a comfortable rate. Although there is a great deal of intersubject variation in these personal tempos, a mean value across subjects also tends toward 600 ms. For example, Semjen, Vorberg, and Schulze (1998) obtained preferred tempo rates from 428.8 ms to 725 ms, with a mean around 565.3 ms (see also Fraisse 1982). Interestingly, Drake, Jones, and Baruch found that preferred tempo seems to change with age with young children having a faster spontaneous tempo, around 400 ms for 4–6-year-olds (2000, p. 266). If personal tempo is kinematically grounded, it makes sense that this change should occur as a reflection in the changing physical dynamics (principally size) of our bodies during different stages of development.

Discussions of tactus by musicians and music theorists go back at least to the late 15th century, when the idea of a basic rhythmic period was correlated with resting pulse (Ramos de Pareia 1482), breathing rate (Gaffurius 1496), or walking period (Buchner 1520)—for a summary, see Brown (1980). Initially, the term tactus referred to the keeping of time by beating with the hand (Adam von Fulda 1490). Many subsequent music theorists have noted the importance of periodicities in the middle of the metric hierarchy. Heinrich Koch (1787) recognized beats (*Taktteil*) as the primary components of the measure (*Takt*), while various subdivisions (*Taktglieder* and *Taktnoten*) are produced by partitions of the beat. Likewise, Hugo Riemann (1903) speaks of a *Grundmaß* within 60–120 bpm, and Cooper and Meyer make note of a "primary rhythmic level" (1960, p. 2). Lerdahl and Jackendoff use the term tactus: "Metrical intuitions about music clearly include one specially designated metrical level, which we are calling the *tactus*. This is the level of beats that is conducted and with which one most naturally coordinates foot-tapping and dance steps" (1983, p. 71). Likewise, Krebs remarks that "in clearly metrical music, one of the metrical interpretive layers generally assumes particular significance for the listener, its pulses becoming reference points for all rhythmic activity in the given work. . . . I refer to this layer as the 'primary metrical layer'" (1999, p. 30).

These discussions of tactus in the music-theoretic literature are remarkably similar to the distinctions proposed by modern psychologists. James's notion of a *referent period* has already been noted in the previous chapter. Clarke notes:

> In music, the primary level of timing, and the level at which some kind of internal clock exerts its influence, is the tactus (that level of the metrical structure at which a listener might tap his/her foot, or a conductor beat time). Subdivisions of the beat (i.e., individual notes) are not directly timed, but are produced by over-learned motor procedures that specify movement patterns that have as their consequence a definite timing profile. The timing properties are thus the consequence of movement rather than a control parameter in their own right: "Note timing is, in effect, embodied in the movement trajectories that produce them" (Shaffer 1984, p. 580). Equally, time periods greater than that of the primary timing level are produced by concatenations of beat periods rather than by means of some higher level clock. (1999, p. 495)

Here Clarke is approaching rhythm and meter from the perspective of motor behavior—how players skillfully control their performances, making the distinction between conscious or studied timing choices versus rhythmic timings that are the result of motor programs for the movements of arms, hands, and fingers. Although it is true that as listeners we are not directly involved in the production of movement trajectories, listening in part involves recovering movement information from the musical surface (see also Iyer 2002; Repp 1998a; Shove & Repp 1995; Todd 1995).

While the tactus level is centrally important, one should keep in mind that metric patterns are hierarchic gestalts. Meters are inherently multi-leveled, even if one of those levels is perceptually privileged. It is worth noting that while our sense of tempo or speed is strongly yoked to the beat level, it is not completely determined by it. Epstein observes that tempo is projected

> as a consequence of the sum of all factors within a piece—the overall sense of a work's themes, rhythms, articulations, "breathing," motion, harmonic progressions, tonal movement, contrapuntal activity. Yet tempo . . . is a reduction of this complex Gestalt into the element of speed per se. (1995, p. 99)

Tempo is a sense of motion that emerges not from any single level of the metric hierarchy but from their collective interaction and interrelationships. Given the wide range in which a tactus may be perceived (200–2000 ms), it often is the case that there are several periodicities present in the musical texture, a number of which could be heard as a tactus. Nonetheless, the tactus, then, is the level that anchors the metric hierarchy.

Perceptual Preferences and Thresholds within the Metric Envelope

Jones's temporal perspective theory (discussed in the previous chapter) claims that there are subjective differences among attentional levels. She has posited that we have a number of distinct "serial integration regions" that correspond to different time scales, each with its characteristic mechanisms and strategies of attending (1992, pp. 100–2). Collyer and Church also noted that "the temporal spectrum encompasses many orders of magnitude of time, a range so large that different mechanisms in different subranges would likely be needed to achieve adequate sensitivity in all of them. . . . the range from 175 ms to 1000 ms is divided into at least two subranges" (1998, p. 85). Likewise, Repp has observed that the same rhythmic pattern "may not be executed in exactly the same way at different tempi, and listeners can find it difficult to match or recognize proportionally scaled rhythmic patterns when the tempo is changed substantially" (1995b, p. 40).

The effect of subjective rhythmic organization may be manifest even when the tempo is held constant or, more precisely, is supposed to remain constant. In a recent study, Meyer and Palmer (2001) found that when performers were directed to shift their attention to different levels within the metrical hierarchy in a series of performances of the same passage, focusing on the eighth notes versus quarters versus half notes, there were systematic shifts in tempo; counting at higher levels led to faster performances, while counting at lower levels led to slower performances. This makes sense, as these strategies will tend to keep the counting rate as close as possible to the middle of the range of maximal pulse salience.

All of this suggests that while temporal relations from 100 ms to 5 to 6 seconds are "accessible to the senses," we do not perform or perceive all durations and durational patterns within this range in the same way. Thus, meter is not only an integrated pattern of temporal attending within a certain range but also involves the integration of subjectively *different kinds of time*, given these perceptual and kinematic differences.

Various studies have suggested that there is a significant threshold around 200–250 ms. The *just noticeable difference* (JND) is one of the basic psychophysical measures of perceptual acuity, and is related to Weber's law: "that two sensations are just noticeably different as long as a given constant ratio obtains between the intensities of their stimuli" (Boring 1942, p. 35). As Allan explains, "according to Weber's law, the just noticeable difference, Δ, between two stimulus durations [d_0 and d_1] is a constant proportion, k, of d_0, the shorter of the two values" (1979, p. 343). Getty (1975, 1976) proposed a generalized form of Weber's law for temporal perception in which the JND between the two successive durations is proportional to their absolute length, plus a constant of minimal discrimination (Allan 1979). The 250 ms threshold crops up in various JND studies for auditory stimuli (for summary, see Dowling & Harwood 1986). For example, Friberg and Sundberg studied judgments regarding the perturbation of an element in a six-tone sequence over a wide range of IOIs (from 100 to 1000 ms), and they found that the absolute JND was found to be approximately constant for IOIs shorter than 240 ms and the relative JND constant for IOIs 240 ms (1995, p. 2524).

Other studies also point to a threshold around 250 ms. Michon (1964) argued that a shift between holistic versus analytic processing occurs around 250 ms, Massaro (1970) reported 250 ms as a limit for auditory backward masking, and Crowder (1993) argued that 250 ms is the limit of a short-term auditory memory (which may play a causal role in some of these other observations). Large (2000) found that "there is some evidence that perceptual categorization [of rhythmic patterns] operates differently depending on the absolute time intervals involved" and this difference was manifest around 250 ms. Finally, Fraisse argued that there are two durational categories in rhythmic patterns: "*short times* [temps courts] of 200 to 300 ms and *long times* [temps longs] of 450 to 900 ms" (1982, p. 167). Although Fraisse's short and long categories do not quite match up with a 250 ms threshold, they are akin to it, as he sets up a kind of temporal no man's land from 300 to 450 ms. Clarke reminds us that, for Fraisse, there were important qualitative differences between short and long times: "Temps longs have the property of true duration according to Fraisse (we are aware, or can become aware, of the passage of time during such an interval), whereas temps courts have the character of collection rather than duration: we have no real sense of the passage of time during each event, but are aware of the manner in which numbers of such intervals group together" (1999, pp. 474–5). Thus, one of the functions of musical meter is to mediate among these qualitatively different durations by integrating them into a coherent attentional framework.

The Special Relationship between Beats and Subdivisions

Recall that while the fastest/shortest IOIs for subjective rhythmization and metric subdivisions occur around 100 ms, the fastest/shortest IOIs for a beat or tactus are around 200–250 ms. The approximate 2:1 relationship between these two limits is suggestive and leads to the following hypothesis: hearing a beat requires at least the *potential* of hearing a subdivision. Thus, if the shortest IOI that is metrically significant is ≈100 ms, then the shortest possible beat will involve two or more subdivision units, and this would be specifically ≥≈200 ms for simple subdivision and ≥≈300 ms for compound subdivision. Indeed, the different results in studies of the lower end of the beat spectrum may be linked to contextual differences between simple versus compound subdivision: the 200 ms threshold stands for simple subdivision, whereas a somewhat longer value is required for compound subdivision (and obviously this also may reflect some variation in the 100 ms threshold itself).

One also could approach this hypothesis from the top down rather than the bottom up: if the shortest beat IOI is 200–250 ms, then the shortest subdivision would be 100–125 ms for simple subdivision or 70–85 ms for compound subdivision, and thus one would tend toward the low end of the former and the high end of the latter. Yet it seems more likely that this relationship is based on a bottom up, rather than a top down constraint. As noted earlier, the 100 ms threshold is related to a number of more basic psychophysical limits on auditory and temporal perception. As a lower limit for any and all metrical relationships, the 100 ms threshold has inherently greater significance than other thresholds. Moreover, simple versus compound subdivision gives rise to a difference in the rhythmic character of the beat itself. Simple subdivision is binary, splitting the beat into two more or less even parts. Compound subdivision undergirds uneven subdivision of the beat, that is, where the beat itself is subdivided into a long element and a short element. For if one infers uneven subdivision, then the compound triplets define the long as two units while the short is but one. There is more to the difference in affect, motion, and expression of simple versus compound beats than just their quantitative aspects (two units for simple vs. three units for compound). But this basic distinction between "twoness" versus "threeness" is an essential part of the character of each.[4]

Here is an illustration of the bottom-up influence of the 100 ms limit. Imagine a perfect duplet, a beat IOI perfectly divided in half (see figure 2.1a). Given 100 ms as the minimum duration for each beat subdivision, the beat IOI for this duplet must be ≥ 200 ms. Now consider what happens as relative durations are made less and less even by shifting the onset of the second note to a later position within the beat span. At first, in figure 2.1b one has a slightly uneven but still duple subdivision, as is the case in rhythmically expressive performances. Note that as the ratio between the two IOIs is now greater than 1:1 (e.g., 1.2:1), the total IOI must be > 200 ms, because the shorter element must span at least 100 ms. This also may explain why the fastest possible beats are often longer than 200 ms, as the typical presence of expressive variation will have these sorts of timing ratios. For example, the 1.2:1 ratio is cashed out as 120 ms + 100 ms = 220 ms total beat IOI. As the onset of the second tone shifts later and later in the beat span, at some point a sense of triplet subdivision emerges.[5] Accompa-

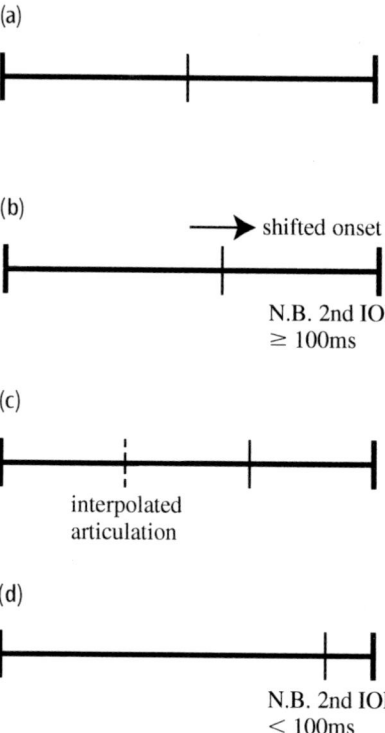

Figure 2.1. Varying subdivisions of a beat span. (a) Perfect duplet; (b) shifted duplet; (c) emergence of sense of triplet; (d) beyond triplet (i.e., short IOI becomes a grace note).

nying the emergence of the triplet will be the emergence of an interpolated articulation of the subdivision (figure 2.1c). It is at this point that we have a sense of a Long (L) element that is categorically distinct from the following Short (S). As the relative duration continues to shift, it will pass through the 2:1 ratio (the "perfect triplet") and on to 4:1, 5:1, and so on. If we insist, as we must, that the "1" remain ≥ 100 ms, note that the beat span IOI will get longer and longer, and we will reach a point at which the S element may be regarded as a component of an even lower level of subdivision. For example, if we have an approximately 5:1 ratio with a total duration of 600 ms, it becomes possible to hear the beat divided in two, and each subdivision further divided into triplets; in other words, the "1" here is the last element of a sextuplet. Conversely, if we allow the "1" to fall below the 100 ms threshold as the relative durations of the L and S shift, it will no longer be heard as a metrical element, though it can be heard as a grace note as in figure 2.1d. Table 2.2 summarizes this metrical thought experiment.

It may be objected that in construing a L–S pattern in terms of compound subdivision I am invoking a response to a durational surface that is peculiar to musicians, given their special training and practice. That is, rather than positing

Table 2.2. Differing Perceptions as Durations Change

Subdivision category	Timing ratio	Comment
perfect duple	1 : 1	deadpan performance; minimum duration of beat is 200 ms
expressive duple	1.2 : 1	expressively varied timing; min. duration of beat must be > 200 ms
expressive triple	1.75 : 1	expressively varied timing; min. duration of beat approaching 300 ms
perfect triple	2 : 1	deadpan performance;
expressive triple	2.3 : 1	expressively varied timing; duration of beat > 300 ms.
quadruple (?)	3 : 1	deadpan or varied—in some contexts heard as "deadpan" quadruplet, in others as expressively varied triplet
???	4 : 1, 5 : 1	when "1" is < 100 ms it may become sub-metrical (i.e., heard as a grace note)

that listeners will interpolate a missing metric element, it is simpler to say that there is a shift from the perception of categorically even to categorically uneven division of the beat span. My response is that the perception of categorical unevenness lies precisely in the listener's sense that the long element has the potential to be further divided, while the short cannot. In many musical textures this objection is moot, as L–S patterns in a melodic line are accompanied by other instruments that explicitly articulate the triplet subdivision. Moreover, if practiced habits of attending are involved in most listening experiences (as is argued at greater length in chapter 9), and these habits may be the product of both formal and informal musical education and enculturation, then most listeners will have experienced the triplet underpinning of uneven subdivision, and can bring that experience to bear on those listening contexts where the triplets are only implied.

If the 100 ms threshold is indeed what drives the lower end of the range of tactus, then one is led to ask if the 200–250 ms threshold is simply a hierarchic artifact. If we are constrained by the ≈100 ms floor for elements in a metrical pattern, and if meter is a hierarchic gestalt such that we entrain not just to a single 100 ms level, or a single 200 ms level, but to both (as well as additional levels), then the 200–250 ms threshold may emerge from the fact that metrical patterns integrate several component periodicities. Such resonance does not mean that the 250 ms threshold lacks salience, at least in some contexts; indeed, it suggests that the richer the metric context, the more salient it becomes. But this does suggest that this particular threshold involves the emergence of the sense of beat, the qualitative aspects of the beat, and, as the beat IOI increases, the latent complexity of the beat, that is, the potential for further levels of subdivision.[6]

Table 2.3 summarizes and extends consideration of the absolute timing constraints on beat and subdivision periodicities and their relationships. The first row of the table is included simply for completeness, for neither beats nor subdivisions

Table 2.3 Absolute Timing Constraints on Beats and Subdivisions

Beat rate	Simple SD	Compound SD
< 200 ms	none	none
200-300 ms	100-150 ms	none
300-500 ms	< 250 ms	< 250 ms
500-750 ms	> 250 ms	< 250 ms
750+ ms	> 250 ms	> 250 ms

are possible at IOIs less than 200 ms. At very fast beat IOIs of 200–300 ms only simple (binary) subdivision is possible; compound subdivision becomes possible only at slightly slower tempos where beat IOIs > ≈ 300 ms. If we presume a temporal threshold around 250 ms, note that it will affect simple versus compound subdivision in different ways, as shown in table 2.3. In the range of 300–500 ms both simple and compound subdivisions are less than 200–250 ms, and, given the 100 ms limit, neither can be further subdivided. However, as the beat gets slower, it becomes possible in the 500–750 ms range for simple subdivisions to be further divided, whereas the triplets cannot. Only when the beat IOI goes beyond about 750 ms can the compound beat also incorporate further subdivision. This means that in the range of maximal pulse salience of 500–750 ms there is a potential difference in hierarchic depth between units of simple versus compound subdivision, as triplets are made of units less than 250 ms, while duplets are made of units longer than 250 ms, and hence could be further subdivided. This might also help explain the subjective differences between simple and compound subdivision in the 500–750 ms beat range: different subdivisions will embody different affective or emotional qualities. Moreover, the differences in the temporal composition of various kinds of subdivision may also explain perceived tempo or motional differences among passages with the same beat-level IOI.

Systematic Interactions between Tempo and Temporal Limits

Having just explored the interaction between tempo as measured by beat-level IOI, beat subdivision, and two absolute perceptual thresholds, we may now take a broader view of tempo and its effect on more extended metrical relationships. Figure 2.2 is a graph of metrically related periodicities; the central node serves as the origin for various branches of the graph. The central node represents the tactus or referent level which directs our understanding of both higher and lower levels, although as noted earlier, at some tempos more than one node might be heard as the tactus. As one moves out from the central tactus, the horizontal branches of the graph carry binary operations, while the vertical

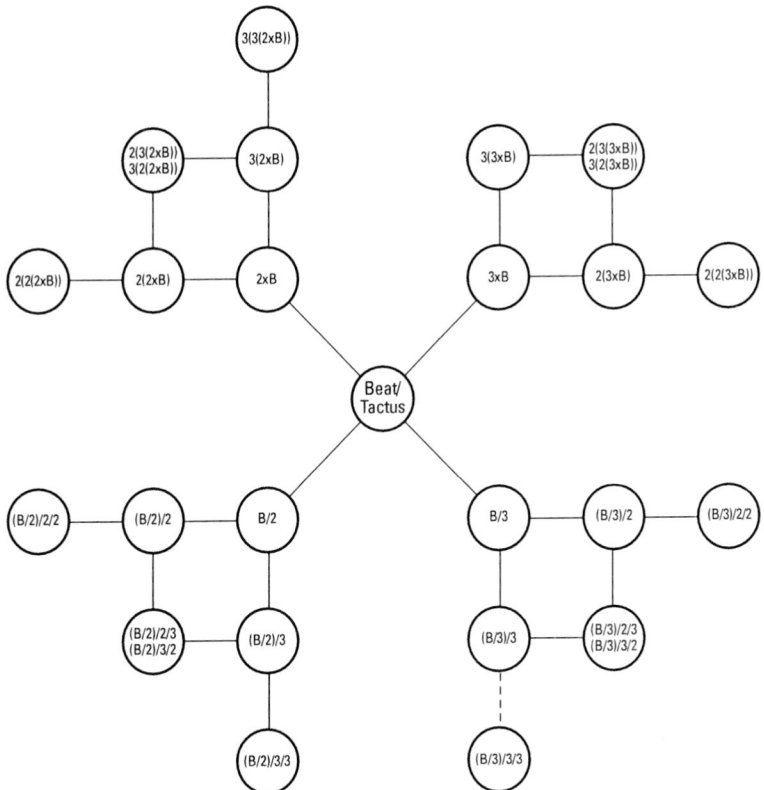

Figure 2.2. Graph of multiply-related metric periodicities.

branches carry ternary operations. Each node is created by multiplicative operations on lower nodes, and nodes that are farther out from the central beat are
hierarchic composites of more central nodes. Thus, for example, the 2(3 (2 × B))
node involves four nested levels of metric structure. Likewise, any subordinate
level below the beat involves nested periodicities up to the beat level itself. In
this graph, there are some nodes that coincide, for example, 2(3 (2 × B)) and
3(2 (2 × B)). Although the absolute value of these two operations is the same
(i.e., both result in a periodicity that is 12 times the duration of the beat interval), their hierarchical arrangements differ.

In figure 2.3, the periodicities of figure 2.2 are relabeled using the most common time signatures in Western music. For convenience, the central beat is represented by a quarter note (a value that lies in the middle of the range of durational orthography, which is probably why quarter-note-based time signatures
are so common). Missing from this graph are the compound time signatures.
This was necessary in order to have a single unit as the central beat. As a result,
compound subdivision has to be represented via the triplet notation, a convention that is used to indicate the ternary subdivision of a quarter note into three

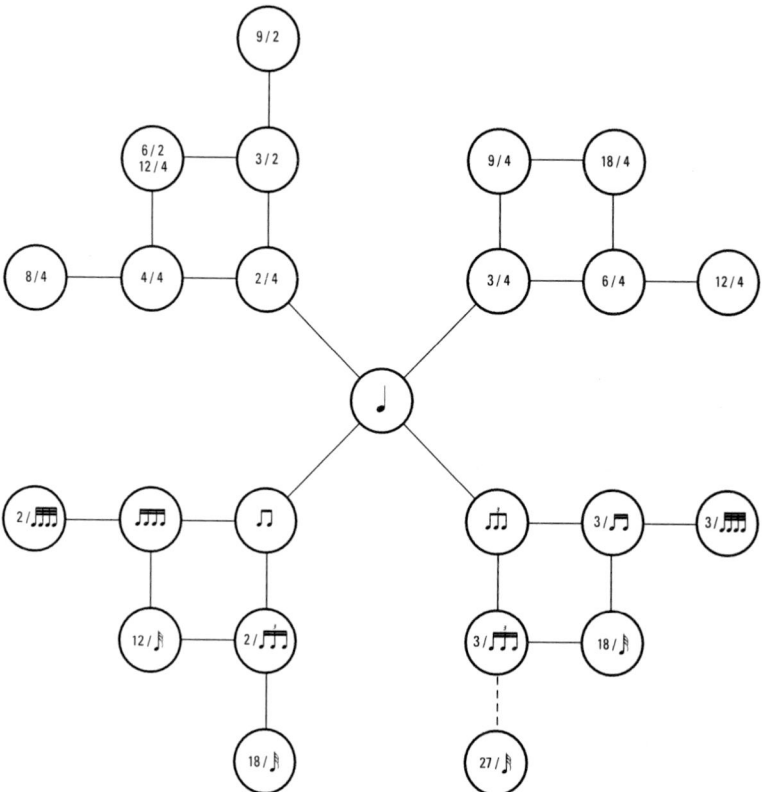

Figure 2.3.   Revision of figure 2.2 using conventional time signatures.

categorically equivalent parts. It can be seen that binary and ternary operations give rise to almost all of the meters found in Western classical music. Nodes above the central beat represent familiar measures, while nodes below the central beat represent layers of subdivision; these will be referred to as *measure* and *subdivision nodes*, respectively. As in figure 2.2, higher-level meters are to be understood as hierarchic composites, so for example, a measure $\frac{9}{4}$ comprises three units of $\frac{3}{4}$, and those $\frac{3}{4}$ units comprise three beat-level units (and, of course, those beats may be further subdivided).

Example 2.1 is a passage from the C-Major Prelude in the first book of Bach's *Well-Tempered Clavier;* Figure 2.4 shows the corresponding region of the metric graph from figure 2.3 that this passage involves; thus a particular meter may be thought of as a subset of the periodicities laid out in figures 2.2 or 2.3. The five layers of metric activity in Bach's Prelude correspond to the five "active" nodes (connected by solid lines) in figure 2.4. That is, in this passage there are metrically active periodicities at the sixteenth-, eighth-, quarter-, half-, and whole-note levels (the last being the entire measure itself); these are given in the familiar dot notation below the staff in example 2.1 (after Komar 1971; Lerdahl & Jackend-

Example 2.1. Metrical structure in the opening measures of Bach's C-major prelude from Book I of the *Well Tempered Clavier.*

off 1983). Over the course of a piece, meters can and often do change—metric levels may come and go, and there may be wholesale shifts of tempo, beat organization, and so forth. But once a meter is established it constrains the formation of subsequent metrical periodicities in metrically continuous contexts. Figure 2.4 shows that, given the $\frac{4}{4}$ periodicity, the most closely related higher level periodicities are either $\frac{8}{4}$ or $\frac{12}{4}$.[7]

Figure 2.2 is a generalized form of metric relationships apart from any particular tempo value for the tactus. Once a tempo for the central beat is chosen, however, one may consider the absolute values of the resulting periodicities in

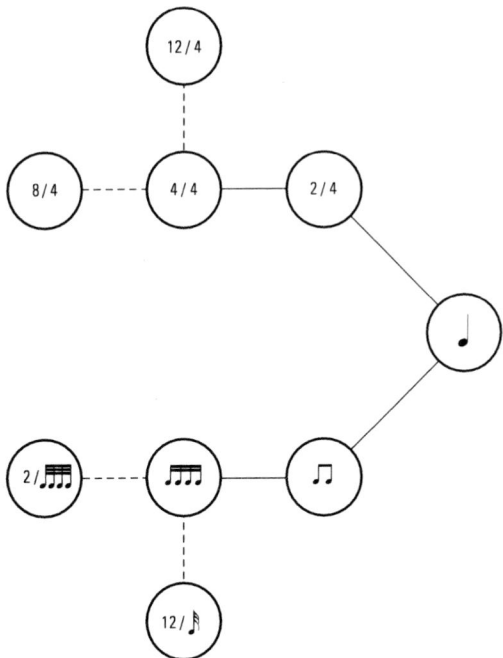

Figure 2.4. Graph of hierarchically- related metric levels in example 2.4; dashed lines indicate possibilities for additional levels above and below those present.

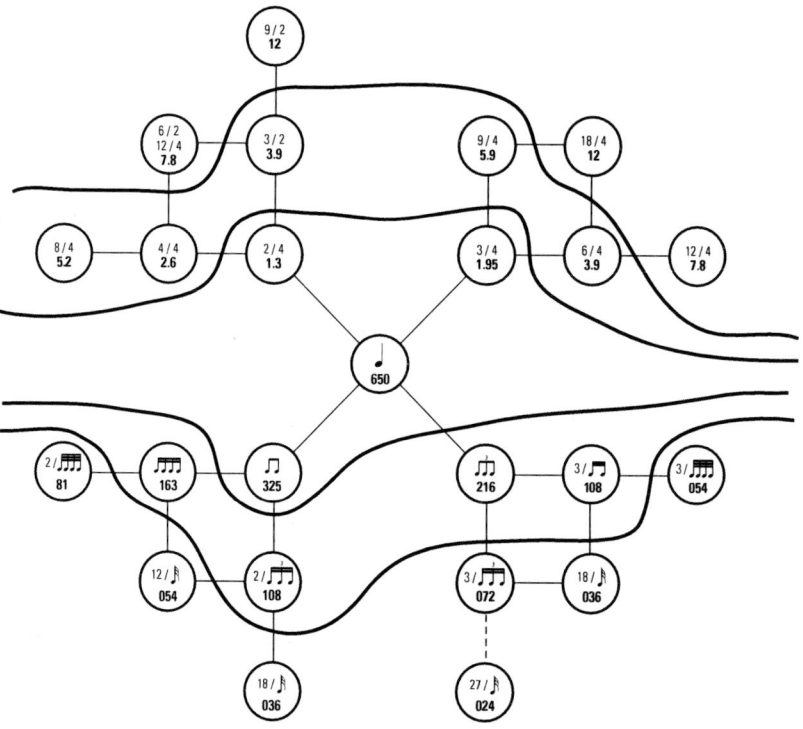

Figure 2.5.   Tempo-dependent revision of figure 2.2 with the central node = 650ms; contour lines indicate various temporal thresholds.

light of the various thresholds discussed earlier. Figure 2.5 shows the result where the central beat rate is set at 92 beats/minute (650 ms IOI). The various metric thresholds at 100 ms, 250 ms, 2 seconds, and 6 seconds are indicated with the contour lines in the example. As can be seen, the longest periodicity is 12 seconds, while the shortest is 24 ms; these as well as many other periodicities lie well outside the metric envelope. If one prunes those nodes that lie outside the limiting thresholds, the graph that remains indicates what metrical relationships are possible at any given tempo. Note also in figure 2.5 that some nodes, while inside the metric envelope, are nonetheless near the proposed thresholds of 100 ms and 6 seconds. Although it may be possible to sustain these layers of meter, it may require more attentional effort as they fall near a perceptual or cognitive limit. As one also might expect, the number of possible configurations is skewed toward 2:1 ratios. At this tempo full measures of both duple or triple time fall under the 2-second threshold, suggesting that downbeats in either meter will seem strongly connected, inviting higher levels of metric structure. As noted earlier, in this tempo range the duple subdivision is longer than 250 ms, while triplet subdivisions are shorter, which may give rise to subjective differences between simple versus compound subdivision.

Several metric family trees at various tempos are given in figure 2.6 (for clarity, any nodes outside the 100 ms to 6-second range have been omitted). Most obviously, there is a shift from many layers of subdivision (and only few layers above the beat) at slow tempos to the opposite configuration at very fast tempos. One also can see that at slow tempos there are rich possibilities for subdivision, including periodicities in both the 100–250 ms range and the 250–600 ms range. Conversely, at very fast tempos there are no subdivisions longer than 250 ms. Thus there are floor effects, which limit the possibilities for subdivision at faster tempos, and ceiling effects, which limit the possibilities for higher levels of meter at slower tempos.

There is another interesting effect of tempo change on the extended metrical hierarchy. As the tempo changes the number of possible hierarchic configurations does not remain constant; these are summarized in table 2.4. The second column in table 2.4 shows the number of nodes present at any given tempo; this number does not remain constant, nor is there any clear pattern or progression relative to tempo change. To get a proper sense of the number of metric possibilities at each tempo, one must consider more than just the number of nodes; their hierarchic relations to the central beat also must be taken into account. This information is given in the third column. Because every metric configuration will involve the central beat and at least one other node above it or below it, in order to determine all of the possible combinations among the beat and related periodicities, one must multiply the number of measure nodes (including the beat) by the number of subdivision nodes (also including the beat) and then subtract one, to eliminate the case of the central beat mapping onto itself. As can be seen, the number of potential meters varies widely, and at times quite abruptly as in the shift from 29 to 41 possible meters as the tempo shifts from 92 to 100 bpm.

The right-hand column in table 2.4 tracks another systemic tempo effect. If we have a strong proclivity toward periodicities in the center of the range of maximal pulse salience, around 600 ms, then perhaps we would tend to prefer attentional frameworks that include such periodicities over those that do not. At some tempos, however, periodicities in this range are wholly absent.[8] Refer again to figure 2.6, bottom panel. At this tempo (MM = 140; 430 ms IOI), given the hierarchical relationships between sub- and supratactus levels, there are *no* periodicities in even a 550–750 ms range. This suggests a (possible) perceptual basis regarding the performer's choice of tempo: one may gravitate toward those tempos that allow for a resonance in the range of maximal salience and avoid those tempos that do not.

Table 2.5 traces the presence of periodicities in the 500–700 ms range across the usable tempo scale, and relates those periodicities to duple versus triple meters. First, periodicities in this preferred range are absent when the tactus lies approximately between 333–500 ms or 700–1000 ms. Second, whenever periodicities in the 500–700 ms range are present, they tend to occur on (a) the beat level, or (b) the level of the measure itself. Ternary "subdivisions" appear on

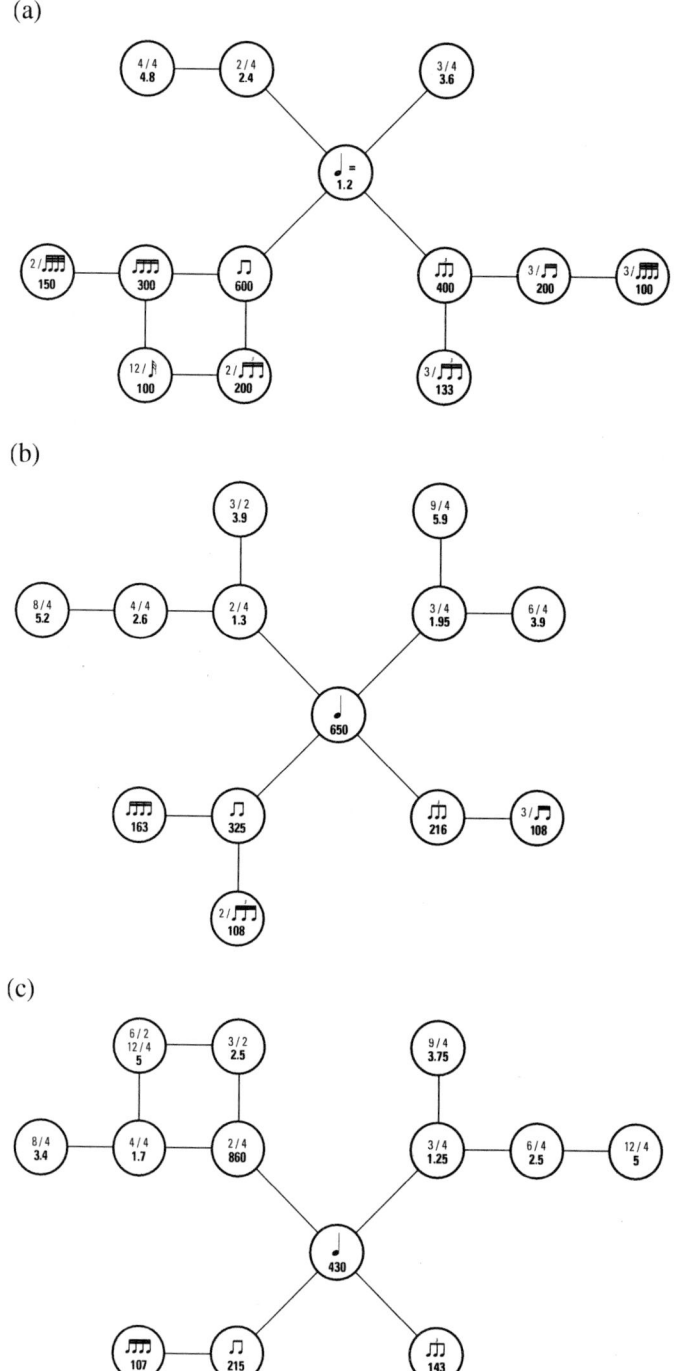

Figure 2.6. Metric "trees" at various tempos; nodes that represent periodicities below 100 ms and above 5 seconds have been omitted. (a) Tactus at 50 beats/minute (1.2 sec); (b) tactus at 92 beats/minute (650ms); (c) tactus at 140 beats/minute (430ms).

Table 2.4. Possible Hierarchic Configurations as Tempo Changes

Duration of the central node in BPM and (ms)	# of nodes within the metric envelope	Measure nodes × Subdivision nodes, −1	Periodicities in the 600–700 ms range?
40 (1500 ms)	12	$3 \times 10 - 1 = 29$	N
50 (1200 ms)	13	$4 \times 10 - 1 = 39$	Y
60 (1000 ms)	11	$4 \times 8 - 1 = 31$	N
72 (833 ms)	11	$6 \times 6 - 1 = 35$	N
80 (750 ms)	11	$6 \times 6 - 1 = 35$	N
86 (700 ms)	11	$6 \times 6 - 1 = 35$	Y
92 (650 ms)	10	$5 \times 6 - 1 = 29$	Y
100 (600 ms)	12	$7 \times 6 - 1 = 41$	Y
108 (555 ms)	11	$8 \times 4 - 1 = 31$	N
120 (500 ms)	11	$8 \times 4 - 1 = 31$	N
140 (428 ms)	13	$10 \times 4 - 1 = 39$	N
160 (375 ms)	13	$10 \times 4 - 1 = 39$	N
180 (333 ms)	12	$10 \times 3 - 1 = 29$	Y
200 (300 ms)	12	$10 \times 3 - 1 = 29$	Y

the chart only at the slowest of tempos, and indeed, are apt to be heard as beats. Likewise, triple measures in the 500–700 ms range are only possible at the edge of the beat range (from 167 to 233 ms). It has long been noted, in both music psychology and in music theory, that humans seem to have a bias toward binary rather than ternary rhythms and meters (Kelly 1989; Kelly & Bock 1988; Kelly & Rubin 1988; Palmer & Kelly 1992; Smith & Cuddy 1989; Todd 1996a, 1996b;

Table 2.5. Periodicities Across the Usable Tempo Scale

Duration of Triple Measure	Duration of Duple Measure	Beat Rate	Duration of Binary SD	Duration of Ternary SD
6000	4000	2000	1000	**667**
5400	3600	1800	900	**600**
4500	3000	1500	750	**500**
3600	2400	1200	**600**	400
3000	2000	1000	**500**	333
2500	1600	832	416	277
2250	1500	750	375	250
2100	1400	**700**	350	233
2000	1300	**650**	325	216
1800	1200	**600**	300	200
1650	1100	**555**	278	185
1500	1000	**500**	250	167
1250	860	430	215	143
1130	750	375	188	125
1000	**660**	333	167	111
900	**600**	300	150	100
750	**500**	250	125	—
600	400	200	100	—

see also Horlacher 1997; London 1996; Schachter 1987). Many sources for this bias have been suggested, such as bipedalism and the walking period, a general preference for symmetry, a greater familiarity with binary rhythms because of enculturation; systemic relationships among metric levels suggest yet another. We are biased against triple meters (and to a lesser extent, triplet subdivision) simply because there are fewer ternary options that lie comfortably within the range of maximal pulse salience.

Summary and Discussion

Metric entrainment can only occur with respect to periodicities in a range from about 100 ms to about 5 or 6 seconds. In addition, we may grasp a sense of beat or tempo in a subrange of 200–250 ms to about 2 seconds, although we have a preference for periodicities around 600 ms. It is perhaps because of these perceptual and cognitive differences among these ranges that, rather than hearing a series of rapid pulses as a string of 12 or 16 articulations, we construe them as groups and meta-groups. Thus we hear a pair of sextuplets or four quadruplets, for example, rather than a single, large group. While this is obviously related to subjective rhythmization, it is more than organizing a stream of pulses into twos and threes. Rather, it is the creation of hierarchically integrated cycles of attention and expectation, cycles that involve multiple levels of structure.

Beats and subdivisions have a special relationship; I have hypothesized that in order to hear a beat there also must be at least a latent sense of subdivision. In this way, the 200–250 ms threshold for beat perception may be related to the 100 ms limit for subdivisions. Likewise, the organization of subtactus levels affects the perceived quality of motion of the beat and higher levels, as subdivisions play an important role in sorting out subtactus perceptions of rhythmic figures. Moreover, if hearing a beat means hearing the potential for its subdivision, and if metric attending minimally involves an ordering of beats (that is, a tactus and at least one superior level), then metric attending in almost all cases will involve three levels of structure.

There is a strong interaction between tempo, that is, the rate of the tactus, and the formal organization of a metric hierarchy. As the tempo changes there may be changes in the perception of the perceived beat (as in figure 2.1). The choice of a particular tempo also limits the scope of metric possibilities; as the tactus changes, other levels are subject to various floor and ceiling effects.

The most speculative point made in this chapter is that qualitative differences between rhythmic figures may be related to the interactions between various thresholds, subdivision type (simple vs. compound) and tempo. These interactions give rise to the subjective differences in musical affect or character between simple versus compound meter (and rhythmic figures cast in those meters) as well as between the same metrical pattern at different tempos. These differences may make more immediate sense to musicians than to psychologists, as they are not necessarily ones that will be manifest in terms of empirical measures such as reaction times, synchronization accuracy, or discrimination thresholds. Instead, they are more likely to be found via listener introspection, or in the kinds of affective or motional descriptions listeners give to rhythms and melodies at particular tempos. It may be possible, however, to test this conjecture experimentally by asking musicians to play various rhythmic figures, prompting them to optimize the tempo to best project a particular affect. Consistency of results in general, as well as correlations with measures of the performer's own natural pace and spontaneous tempos, would give some indication of the role of these various perceptual and cognitive thresholds in shaping musical gesture and meaning.

3

Meter-Rhythm Interactions I: Ground Rules

Meter Functions as a Ground for Rhythmic Figures

The relationship between the rhythmic surface—the real-world timing of musical events—and the listener's metric entrainment is complex. Essentially, however, meter serves as a temporal ground for the perception of rhythmic figures. Although some melodic patterns have a pitch contour and rhythmic pattern that strongly suggest one and only one metric construal, most passages are metrically malleable. As we saw in example 1.2, for instance, it is the metric entrainment that makes the passage "go jumping by threes" rather than by twos.

In a series of experiments on the listeners' ability to change their metric construal of rhythmic figures, Vazan and Schober (2000) made use of a set of computer-generated stimuli, all based on a metrically neutral rhythmic figure: ♪₇♪♪♪₇. Participants were presented with permutations of this pattern in both $\frac{3}{4}$ and $\frac{6}{8}$ metric contexts; six possible serial rotations, created by shifting the downbeat location relative to the figure, were employed so that ♪₇♪♪♪♪₇ becomes ₇♪♪♪₇♪ becomes ♪♪♪₇♪₇, and so on. In one part of the experiment, subjects were given a $\frac{3}{4}$ prompt, then heard a particular rotation of the pattern; subjects were then asked to tap out the beats. They were then given a visual presentation of a metric alternative (either a shift of downbeat or shift to $\frac{6}{8}$) while the aural presentation of the rhythmic figure continued; their task was to tap the beat, which required them to suppress the initial metric prompt. This proved quite difficult, especially if the rhythmic pattern began with a rest. In another part of experiment the tasks were reversed, and subjects were asked to shift the phase of the rhythmic pattern (that is, to shift from one permutation to another) while the underlying meter remained constant. Subjects found this far easier, even when the rhythmic pattern began with a rest. Recasting the meter was far more difficult than recasting the rhythm.[1]

The perception and production of polyrhythms has received a great deal of attention in psychological research. A distinction must be made between polyrhythms and polymeters. A *polyrhythm* refers to any two or more separate rhythmic streams in the musical texture whose periodicities are noninteger multiples. A *polymeter* would involve the presence of two (or more) concurrent metric frameworks. Examples 3.1a and 3.1b show distinct rhythmic streams that are *not* polyrhythms. In 3.1a, the more rapid stream is in a 4:1 ratio with the slower stream. In this case, each stream can be said to articulate a different level of a single, coherent metrical hierarchy. In example 3.1b, the streams have the same basic period but are out of phase; this is known as *hocket* after its characteristic use in medieval polyphony, and these too can be construed in terms of a single metrical framework. Example 3.1c *is* an example of a polyrhythm. In the third and fourth measures, the upper part proceeds in broad duplets against the ongoing quarter notes in the lower part. This is an example of *hemiola*, which involves concurrent periodicities on the beat level in a 2:3 ratio.

Example 3.1c is not a polymeter. The upper part is heard as a rhythmic grouping that chafes against the ongoing triple meter, but the triple meter is nonetheless maintained. If one truly had a polymeter, then one would hear two meters going on at once—the upper stream in a compound duple meter (at a slower tempo), and the lower stream maintaining the established triple meter and tempo.

Researchers concerned with polyrhythm have asked subjects to attend to or

Example 3.1. Faux and true polyrhythms. (a) Metrically nested periodicities; (b) hocketed or interleaved periodicities (composite is metrically stable); (c) hemiola—triplets cast against prevailing duple beats (subdivision values remain constant).

tap along to one stream of a polyrhythm as a test of their attentional focus (Handel 1984; Handel & Oshinsky 1981; Jones, Jagacinski et al. 1995; Klapp, Hill et al. 1985), or to produce polyrhythms as a test of participants' rhythmic ability and accuracy (Grieshaber 1990; Lashley 1951; McGill & Pressing 1997; Peper, Beek et al. 2000; Pressing, Summers et al. 1996; Vorberg & Wing 1996). This research shows that when confronted with complex polyrhythmic stimuli, listeners use one of two metric strategies. They will either (a) extract a composite pattern of all of the rhythmic streams present, and then match it to a suitable metric framework; or (b) focus on one rhythmic stream and entrain to its meter while treating the other rhythmic stream(s) as "noise." The choice of strategy is correlated with the relative tempos of the component streams.[2] These studies also indicate that while on any given presentation we tend to hear a passage under one and only one metric framework, it is also possible to reconstrue the same figure or passage under a different meter on another listening occasion. A polyrhythmic pattern may be heard "in three" or "in four," just as metrically malleable patterns may be set in different metric contexts. This should not surprise anyone familiar with the basic tenets of perception, as the need to maintain a single coherent ground seems to be universal: "The figure-ground dichotomy is fundamental to all perception" (Boring 1942, p. 253). Thus, there is no such thing as a poly*meter*. However, as we shall see in chapter 6, this runs counter to various music-theoretic claims regarding metric dissonance and other instances in which one putatively hears two meters going on at once.

Finding the Meter: Template Matching Versus Period Extraction

When a piece of music starts (or when we cast ourselves into it, as by flipping through songs on a radio dial), we must determine how to metrically respond to it. Jones (1990a) has identified two distinct phases of the rhythmic attending process, (a) *abstraction*, whereby invariant information is inferred from the musical surface; and (b) *generation*, in which listeners use invariants to produce expectations regarding ongoing and future musical events. I have called these phases metric *recognition* versus *continuation* (London 1990), for in many cases inferring a meter does not involve extracting invariant information such as component periodicities, but rather involves matching the musical figure against a repertoire of well-known rhythmic/metric templates. For example, in Western tonal music, an interval of an ascending melodic fourth at the start of a phrase, especially if the first note is shorter than the second, both signifies "sol-do" in terms of scale and key and also marks upbeat and downbeat—it is an anacrustic cliché. Similarly, the "thump-thump" of the kick drum in rock music indicates beats 2 and 4 of the measure. Indeed, these thumps are called the "backbeat" figure. Most listeners have a bevy of metrically familiar templates at their disposal, and in recognizing these commonplace gestures they are readily able to establish metric entrainment. Likewise, once a melodic or rhythmic figure has been metrically defined by its initial presentation(s), we may then use it as a metric cue in its subsequent appearances throughout the remainder of the piece. Lerdahl and Jackendoff acknowledge the influence of intraopus template matching in their very first metric preference rule: "Where two or more [rhythmic] groups or parts of groups can be construed as parallel, they preferably receive parallel metrical structure" (1983, p. 75). Composers are well aware of this, and may rely on such parallels to lead the listener down a metrical garden path (in chapter 6 we shall see how Beethoven does this in the first movement of his Fifth Symphony).

I have been using terms here such as infer, establish, determine, construe, and so forth, with respect to how listeners relate a rhythmic surface to an attentional framework. These terms imply that metric inference or construal requires conscious effort on the listeners' part, but this is not so. For the most part, we reflexively entrain to a rhythmic surface without conscious effort or volition. However, it is also true that listeners, especially musically trained listeners, can often self-consciously reconstrue a rhythmic surface. However, unless specifically indicated, I will use terms such as infer, determine, and so forth, to refer to the automatic and subliminal process of metric entrainment.

In unfamiliar metrical territory we cannot resort to template matching strategies, and in these cases we must proceed by a more general process of extracting the relevant periods from the musical surface and then find the metrical framework that optimizes our attention to them. Here Jones's notion of abstraction is more apt. Likewise, this has been the approach of various computational models for beat or meter "induction" or "extraction" (e.g., Clarke 1985; Desain & Honig 1999; Lee 1991; Longuet-Higgins & Lee 1982). Likewise, Johnson-Laird (1991) has discussed how rhythmic figures may be categorized according to a basic typology such as syncopated versus nonsyncopated rhythmic figures, and this categorization may inform our metric inferences. As I noted in chapter 1, once a tactus and a higher or lower level have been determined, the organization of other levels is highly constrained. Similarly, the differences in absolute value between the IOIs on the subdivision and tactus levels, or tactus and measure levels, aids and abets our metric discovery.

Here is a relatively simple example, the "Ode to Joy" from Beethoven's Ninth Symphony. At a tempo of 78 quarter notes per minute (770 ms IOI), each quarter note articulates a strongly felt tactus or beat. Pairs of quarter notes give rise to a 1540 ms IOI, while ternary patterns would create a 2310 ms IOI. Both of these values are well within the metric envelope, although perhaps we have a slight bias toward the faster IOI of the binary measure. And as example 3.2 shows, the melodic patterning is equivocal regarding duple versus triple organization. The "Ode to Joy's" metrically malleable beginning has the potential to create problems for the listener. However, and as the reader's own experiences of

(a)

(b)

Example 3.2. Beethoven's "Ode to Joy" in different meters. (a) Original version in $\frac{4}{4}$ (common time); (b) alternate version in $\frac{3}{4}$.

this piece may corroborate, we don't hear this melody in triple meter. The performers' expressive variations of timing and dynamics will disambiguate the measure-level organization, making the duple patterning clear. One might also consider this a case of template matching, as this tune is so well known. That is, in the case of a familiar melody, one simply responds in habitual fashion, even if a given performance does not strongly imply a particular metric interpretation.

Tempo makes a big difference in our metric construal of the passage even when its duple organization is not in doubt. Consider the "Ode to Joy" yet again (example 3.3). At the tempo of 78 quarter notes per minute (770 ms IOI) one can comfortably entrain to this passage either in twos or fours, and so at least one other level is also present, marked D (Downbeat) in the example. If the tempo is increased to 138 quarter notes per minute (435 ms IOI), our understanding of the metric hierarchy changes. Each notated quarter note may now seem to occur on a subtactus level. Whereas before we could count either **1**-2-**1**-2-**1**-2 *or* **1**-2-3-4-**1**-2-3-4 at the faster tempo, it seems more natural to count **1**-&-2-&-**1**-&-2-& . . . . Note also that at the faster tempo, the result is a richer metrical hierarchy as there are now three levels of metrical articulation: **1**s (downbeats), 1s and 2s (beats, felt as the tactus), and the "&s" (subdivisions). At different tempos, then, we have different meters. Thus, it is not just that we are trying to determine what periodicities are present in a rhythmic surface. We also are looking for periodicities in particular temporal ranges, and we require that they relate to each other in certain ways.

Thus far I have been considering metric inference solely from the listener's point of view. From the performer's perspective, as noted earlier, things are a bit different. In performance it is not simply useful but necessary for all players and singers to have a clear grasp of the meter from the very start. In rehearsal, performers learn how the melodies and rhythms they play relate to the meter they will use. Even so, performers do not simply start counting with the first note. Solo performers will count internally, a conductor will give a strong upbeat, and a lead performer may count off a measure to establish both tempo and meter. This is not just a practice of Western music. J. H. Kwabena Nketia similarly rec-

Example 3.3. Different metric structures in Beethoven's "Ode to Joy" relative to two performance tempos.

ognizes the practical value of "counting off" in the context of Ghanaian musical performance:

> Where a time line [which clearly articulates the metric pattern] is provided in the form of gong or clap accompaniment it is an invaluable guide to the singer. It adds considerably to the precision and animation of group singing. When a song starts without it, the time is usually somewhat ragged for a bar or two until the regulative beat has been clearly established. On the other hand when the time line is given before the singing starts, the singing is brisk right from the start. (1963b, p. 87)

Keeping the Meter Going

Once the meter is established, our engagement with the musical surface changes. As the music unfolds, rhythmic patterns and articulations serve to confirm and reinforce our current sense of meter. The perceptual task shifts from discovering a pattern of temporal invariants to actively projecting a pattern of beats and measures, with their respective accents, onto the music. And we do so even in the face of contrary durational and dynamic accents as noted with examples 1.1 and 1.3.

We also remain open to the possibility of reconfiguring our expectation according to a new or different pattern of invariance, however. Example 3.4 from Riepel (1752) shows that the listener's metric attending may change as new regularities of harmonic and melodic structure emerge. At the beginning of the example, Riepel indicated that the half-bar level will be most salient, and that listeners will attend to two groups of four half-bar units, as indicated by the small numbers below the staff. At the end of the fourth line, however, a shift takes place, as now the whole measure duration becomes more salient and each measure becomes a member of a four-bar unit, as indicated by the somewhat larger numbers below the staff. The half-bar units of course still persist, but an additional level of structure (the four-bar unit) emerges along with a shift in atten-

Example 3.4. Emergence of a higher level of meter (marked by larger numbers below the staff), from Riepel (vol. 1, 1752), pp. 53–54.

tional focus to higher or longer spans of the metric hierarchy. Conversely, the emergence of rapid subdivision would direct the listener's attention downward to smaller periodicities; this is discussed in conjunction with example 3.6b, from Bach's "Goldberg" Variations, given later.

Composers often orchestrate such attentional shifts through the use of *augmentation*, recasting a melodic motive or theme in longer, often doubled, note values while maintaining a constant beat and measure, or *diminution*, the converse of augmentation, in which a motive or theme is recast in shorter values. Augmentation is more common, with examples ranging from Liszt's recasting of the main theme at the end of his tone poem "Les Preludes" to the Beatles' use of augmentation in the final chorus of their song "Dear Prudence" at the last occurrence of the words "the sun is up, the sky is blue, it's beautiful, and so are you." Changes in rhythmic structure like augmentation are relatively smooth because they do not involve any disruption of the basic beat and beat-orderings; they simply expand or contract the depth of the metric hierarchy.

More radical metric shifts that require more drastic metric reorientation may occur. The shift from a four-beat to a three-beat measure famously occurs in the *ritmo de tre battute* (three-bar rhythm) passages in the second movement of Beethoven's Ninth Symphony, shown in example 3.5. Although notated in $\frac{3}{4}$, the movement is really in a compound duple time with four beats to each true measure with rapid triplet subdivision (*ritmo de quattro battute*). William Caplin (1981) makes the distinction between *notated* versus *expressed* meters—that is, between what we write and what we hear—and this example is a paradigmatic case of this distinction. As $\frac{12}{4}$ or $\frac{12}{8}$ meters were orthographically rare, and given that Beethoven wanted to convey a sense of very rapid tempo, he chose to use the notated measure to indicate the organization of the metric subdivision rather than the beat itself. As Beethoven gave a tempo indication of a dotted half-note = 116 beats per measure (that is, each full measure would be about 535 ms, while each quarter note would be 179 ms), the beat-level periodicity is obvious, as is the expressed meter. Before the passage given in example 3.5, at (notated)

Example 3.5. "Ritmo de tre Battute, Beethoven's 9th Symphony, 2nd mvt., mm. 225–241.

measure 176, there is a fermata which breaks the metric continuity. The fermata is followed by the shift to triple meter (the *ritmo de tre battute*). At notated measure 234, the meter shifts abruptly back to *quattro battute*, this time without any fermata and again maintaining the rapid beat but changing the length of the measure.

Metrically Over- Versus Underdetermined Rhythmic Surfaces

One might presume that if a periodicity is consistently present, we will tend to entrain to it. Yet as a few examples will demonstrate, we need not entrain to each periodicity or potential periodicity present in the musical surface. The question thus arises as to just how much meter a listener will generate in response to a particular rhythmic surface. It is not always easy to determine, either empirically or conceptually, how to answer this question, but a number of examples will illustrate the issues and problems involved. Example 3.6a is the familiar melody "Frère Jacques," an isochronous series of tones at a moderate tempo. Each note articulates the pulse or tactus and the melodic patterning makes the organization of each four-beat measure quite clear. In this case, there is a one-to-one correspondence between the pattern of our expectations and the unfolding of events on the musical surface.

Example 3.6b, from Bach's "Goldberg" Variations, is composed of a stream of rapid notes, only some of which articulate the tactus. When the piece begins the listener does not know if the rapid rhythmic activity will continue and thus reward his or her continued attention at the smallest/most rapid levels of motion. Thus, at the start, there are "too many notes," or, to put it another way, this passage is metrically overdetermined. In discovering the beat and measure levels, the listener's task is to filter out the extra information. The example indicates how one might hear the passage, at first generating expectancies relative to the quarter- or eighth-note levels, but not for each sixteenth note. However, as the piece continues, and the ongoing presence of the running sixteenths seems secure, it then becomes possible and useful to expect a continuous level of sixteenth-note subdivision. To put it another way, the consistency of the rapid articulations justifies heightened expectations at that very short metric level. As levels of meter emerge in example 3.6b, they are first provisional (as indicated by the parentheses) and then stabilize.

Example 3.6c, the opening measures of Beethoven's Piano Sonata Op. 2, No. 3, presents the opposite problem. As is indicated by the dots below the staff, at the very beginning only the half-note periodicity is clear; all of the other metrical levels are underdetermined. The mixture of durational values and rests makes it difficult to entrain to anything shorter than the notated quarter note.

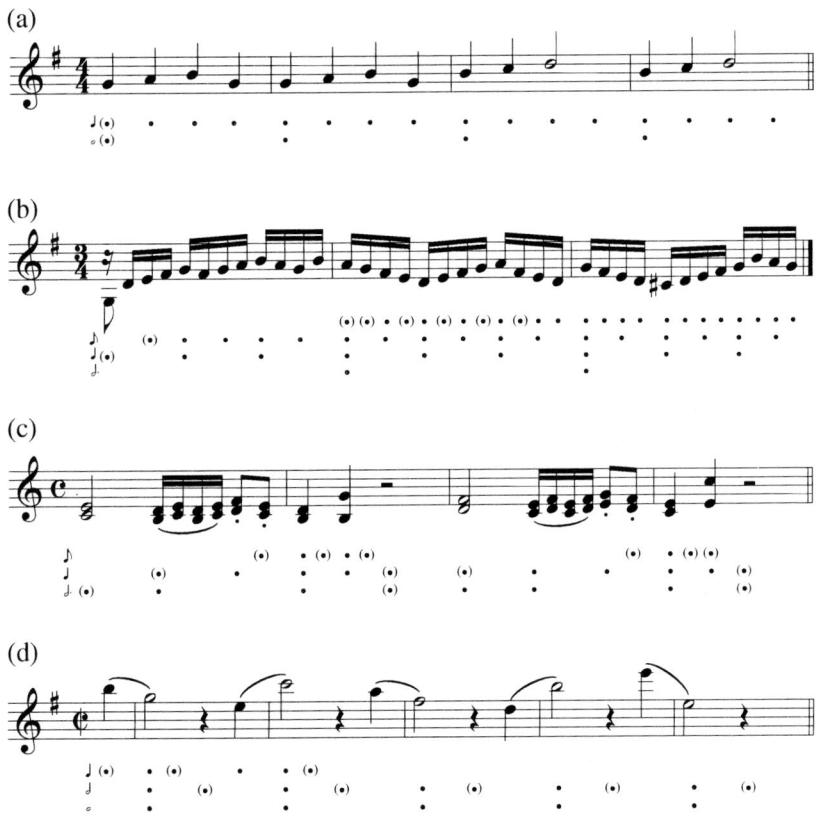

Example 3.6. Metrically over- and under-determined rhythmic surfaces. (a) Frère Jacques; (b) J. S. Bach, Goldberg Variations, var. 5; (c) Beethoven, Piano Sonata Op. 2, no. 3, first mvt.; (d) Brahms Symphony No. 4, first mvt.

The eighth- and sixteenth-note passages are simply too intermittent, and so it is highly unlikely that listeners would latch on to these levels. In the second measure, the quarter-note invariance begins to emerge, but even it may not be sustained by the listener.

Example 3.6d, the opening melody from Brahms's Fourth Symphony, presents yet another problem. When taken by itself, apart from the accompaniment in the lower strings, this melody does not articulate the tactus level. The ¢ or "cut time" signature indicates a performance tempo in which the half note carries the beat, and this piece is typically performed at a tempo of half note about 90 BPM (660 ms IOI). On the one hand, the quarter notes, which serve as anacruses to the following half notes, are too brief to carry the tactus; they articulate a subtactus level. On the other hand, they are also intermittent, and their lack of continuity stymies the establishment of a quarter-note level of the meter, that is, a level of beat subdivisions. Therefore, in this melody one cannot generate the tactus from the bottom up. In hearing this melody (again, apart from any accompaniment) it seems likely that most listeners will interpolate the missing beats that occur on the second half note of each measure; these are indicated by the dots below the staff. To set up a stable meter in this instance, listeners will have to generate a periodicity—indeed, the tactus itself—that is not phenomenally present in the music.[3]

Chapter Summary and Discussion

I have examined the nature of the interactions between musical sounds and the listener's ability to establish and continue to hear a metric framework for interpreting those sounds. First and foremost, meter functions as a ground for the perception of rhythmic figures, and as such may influence the figural organization of an otherwise neutral or metrically malleable melodic pattern. While some patterns strongly evoke but a single construal, metrically malleable patterns may evoke more than one metric framework. However, on any given perceptual occasion a musical figure can be metrically construed in only one way. Similarly, once a metric context has been established, this context will often disambiguate metrically malleable figures. In more complex rhythmic textures there are often several rhythmic streams or figures present, and in some cases not all of them can be readily accommodated within a single meter. In those cases, one of the figures will dominate, serving to ground the listener's metric construal, while the other figure is interpreted against it. While it is thus possible to speak of these instances as polyrhythms, it does not make perceptual sense to claim that they involve or evoke polymeters.

It is worth noting that just as rhythmic patterns evoke metric responses in the listener, at the same time the listener's metric entrainment can give rise to a rhythmic figure, a stream of even yet accentually differentiated inter-onset intervals such as the **1-&-2-&-1-&-2** counting pattern noted in conjunction with the "Ode to Joy" example. Yet this figure—a stream of even but accentually differentiated durations—should not be confused with the meter itself. Meter controls our temporal behavior, and it is that behavior, whether in the form of internal entrainment or externalized tapping or other performance, that gives shape to the ensuing rhythm. This is the crucial distinction between meter and rhythm: meter inheres in our attentional and motor control behaviors, while rhythm inheres in the phenomenal manifestations of sound patterns in time.

Thus far, we have discussed musical patterns whose rhythmic organization more or less directly corresponds to a particular metric pattern (although in some passages, perhaps more than one metrical pattern). But very often a musical surface will require that the listener interpolate one or more beats, or sort out which articulations correspond to beats versus subdivisions between beats.

Given the primacy of the tactus level, a rhythmic surface can be said to be metrically underdetermined if there are more beat articulations than there are surface articulations. Likewise, a rhythmic surface is metrically overdetermined if there are too many surface articulations, such that not all of them can or will correspond to beat locations. These conditions obtain both when we have well-known metric templates and when we do not.

4

Metric Representations and
Metric Well-Formedness

Picturing Meter

Traditional Western musical notation is a continuous graph of pitch and time, with pitch (scale steps) on the vertical axis and time (relative durations) on the horizontal axis. Essentially, each musical score represents these primary musical parameters as a long ribbon with recurring patterns of pitch and duration rendered in similar orthographies. What is never fully notated in our familiar system of staves, rests, noteheads, stems, and beams is meter. To be sure, there are usually time signatures and barlines to give the performer some guidance. But what is indicated within or sometimes across each bar is a pattern of durations, and while the score may make patterns of rhythmic grouping visible through the use of beams, slurs, and note spacing, meter—the felt pattern of beats (and other levels)—remains invisible.[1] Yet metric analysis has a long history and this history includes the development of various kinds of analytic notation, that is, various attempts to make meter visible.

In almost all cases, analytic representations of meter are yoked to musical notation. We have already seen a few examples of how a metric analysis can be laid over an existing score, from Riepel's use of numbers below the staff (example 3.4) to the patterns of dots that represented subdivisions, beats, and measures in Beethoven's "Ode to Joy" (example 3.3). One of the oldest traditions in rhythmic (as opposed to metric) analysis involves the use of markers for accented and unaccented notes, borrowed from poetic scansion. One often finds poetic feet such as iamb, trochee, and dactyl used for the taxonomy of various types of musical rhythms; studies of "rhythmopoeia" were common in 17th and 18th century musical discourse (see Houle 1987, pp. 62–77). Example 4.1 is taken from Koch (1787), while example 4.2 , from Cooper and Meyer (1960), is a more recent instance of this form of analysis.

ober in den Zweyvierteltact eingekleidet:

Example 4.1. Same melodic figure (with same rhythmic scansion) notated in $\frac{2}{2}$ vs. $\frac{2}{4}$, from Koch (vol. 2, 1787), p. 297.

It should be emphasized that these analyses describe the rhythmic and not the metric organization of various musical gestures and passages. Nonetheless, they relate to meter in at least two important ways. First, on lower, if not the lowest, levels of analysis, one usually finds that the rhythmic accents correspond to beats and downbeats—thus a rhythmic accent is often functionally equivalent to metric accent. Second, in passages in which accent is not cued by duration, dynamic stress, and so on, the accentual relationships among notes and rhythmic groups are often determined by the prevailing meter: in these cases metrical context determines rhythmic accent. Thus these rhythmic analyses also imply particular metrical analyses. Rhythmopoetic analyses are also good examples of what Povel has called patterns "in time," as opposed to patterns "of time" (Povel 1984, p. 315; see also Handel 1989, pp. 400–10). Patterns in time involve durations, their order, and the way they group together. In example 4.2 great care is taken to show how larger patterns in time are hierarchic composites. Povel (1981) has proposed a similarly hierarchic representation in figure 4.1 employing a more explicit tree-diagram for a series of durations. While Povel's main point is to show how the same rhythmic pattern may be organized differently, his tree diagrams are an alternative way of showing different metric construals of the same series of IOIs.

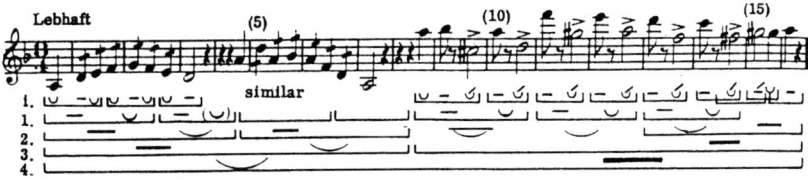

Example 4.2. Analysis of nested rhythmic levels in the opening measures of the Scherzo of Schumann's 4th Symphony, from Cooper and Meyer (1960), ex. 115, p. 102. Reprinted with the kind permission of The University of Chicago Press, ©1960 by the University of Chicago.

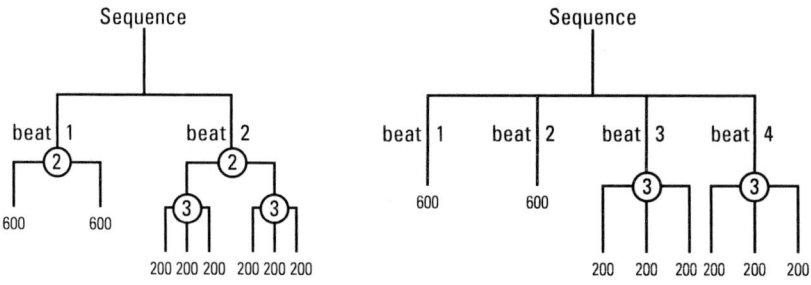

internal beat 1200 msec.   internal beat 600 msec.

Figure 4.1.   Two different metrical tree diagrams for the same sequence of IOIs, after Povel (1981), fig. 5, p. 16.

As we move from rhythmic to metric representations, we move from patterns in time to patterns of time. Lerdahl and Jackendoff's dot notation is the metric representation that is perhaps best known to researchers in music perception and cognition; it has become ubiquitous in musical analysis as well.[2] Lerdahl and Jackendoff align a grid of time points with the musical staff, such that each musical articulation aligns with at least one dot as shown in example 4.3. Note that in this analysis Lerdahl and Jackendoff claim that (a) at the outset, the listener will interpolate a level of meter in between the opening IOIs; (b) a faster levels will emerge and then continue in measures 5 and 8, respectively; and (c) the rapid flurry of notes at the end of measure 6 does not give rise to another, ongoing level of meter. All of these points are indicative of meter's independence from the musical surface (but note also Lerdahl and Jackendoff's remarks regarding "reading meter off the surface," given in chapter 1). The use of dot notation has been criticized in that it seems to imply (or may actually express) that these points are perceived by the listener, that points of time are phenomenal entities of one's musical experience (e.g., Kramer 1988). While this does not necessarily follow from the dot notation itself (and indeed, the interpolated beats in example 2.1 are an illustration of how and why they do not), others have sought to represent musical meter as a time-continuous rather than as a time-discrete function.

Hasty (1997) attempts to approach both meter and rhythm as time-continuous

Example 4.3.   Metric analysis of the opening measures of the finale of Mozart's 41st Symphony IV, after Lerdahl and Jackendoff (1983), ex. 4.8, p. 73.

aspects of our musical experience, in support of his contention that temporal becoming—a continuous durational unfolding—is the basic substrate for musical rhythm. Hasty's main enterprise is to show how a time-continuous perception of rhythm gives rise to and interacts with an always-evolving sense of meter. However, his diagrams of meter are rooted in 19th-century rhythmic theory, especially Moritz Hauptmann (see Hasty 1997, pp. 100–2) and, unfortunately, these diagrams are inherently time-discrete. As such, the articulation of one duration then gives rise to the projection of a similar unit, and in analytic practice Hasty's metric representations move from state to state. In his written analyses Hasty labors mightily to escape this aspect of his representation. Roeder (1998), in an online review of Hasty, wrote a java-script implementation of Hasty's representation that finesses some of the time-discrete aspects of Hasty's representation, but even in Roeder's real-time implementation of Hasty's model, the articulation of a note onset (the click of a mouse, in this case) gives rise to a discrete change in metric field.

Zuckerkandl (1956) describes metric patterns as waves with a continuous ebb and flow of virtual motion. Example 4.4 shows this in the opening measures of Chopin's A-Major Polonaise. Zuckerkandl's diagrams are much like the characterization of meter as a continuous ebb and flow of attentional energy developed by Large (1994), Large and Jones (1999), and Large and Palmer (2002) discussed in chapter 1. In example 4.5, an analysis of the scherzo from Mendelssohn's *Midsummer Night's Dream*, Zuckerkandl indicates how a metric wave may be broken down into several component frequencies. Zuckerkandl's breakdown of the metric wave is much like Large and Palmer's multiple oscillator model for entrainment (see figure 1.2). Unlike Zuckerkandl's diagram, figure 1.2 is not a description of some virtual motion but represents the modulation of the listener's attentional energy.

temporal succession
of tones
metric wave
rhythm

Example 4.4. Metric "wave" analysis of the opening measures of Chopin's A-major polonaise, after Zuckerkandl (1956), p. 171.

Example 4.5. Composite metric wave, opening measures of the Scherzo from Mendelssohn's *Midsummer Night's Dream*, after Zuckerkandl (1956), p. 178.

Cyclical Representations of Meter

If a meter is a stable, recurring pattern of attentional energy, it makes sense to represent this pattern with a circle, for in this way certain aspects of metrical structure will become apparent while at the same time freeing our representation of meter from any particular musical surface. Figure 4.2 is a cyclical representation of a simple three-beat measure. In the cyclical diagrams for meter developed here, time flows clockwise and the position of each metric articulation—in this case, just a series of beats—is marked by a dot on the circumference of the circle. Figure 4.2 embodies two levels of meter, the intervals from beat to beat and the total time-span of the cycle, that is, one measure. Each dot on the circle marks a peak of attentional energy and the 12:00 position marks the location of the downbeat. Cyclical representations do not give an explicit measure of the

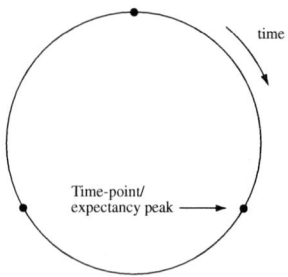

Figure 4.2. Basic 3-beat metric cycle.

relative strength or amplitude of each attentional peak, although the alignment of component cycles (as shown later) does give an implicit weighting to attentional or accentual strength at each position, much in the same way the vertical alignment of dots indicates relative metric accent in Lerdahl and Jackendoff's diagrams in example 4.3. Although dots as markers for attentional peaks will have some temporal spread, I will refer to them as time-points in the sense that they serve to mark determinate temporal locations. This representation of the metric cycle is continuous, and while the locations for each attentional peak are built into the structure of the cycle, they are subject to continuous timing modification and adjustment, while the overall arrangement of the cycle remains stable.

Although it may seem (at least to music theorists) somewhat novel to construe meter as a pattern of attentional peaks, if meter is regarded as a pattern of accented and unaccented beats, and if one acknowledges that accented events are "marked for consciousness in some way" (Cooper & Meyer 1960, p. 8), then this approach is not really so different from its music theoretic predecessors. Cyclical representations relate attentional models to more musically familiar notions of meter and will allow us to see the hierarchically emergent features of particular metric patterns. They also will give us a context in which to develop a set of metric well-formedness constraints.

Most metric contexts are more complex than figure 4.2. The next two examples, while still simple, show how quickly metric complexity may arise. Example 4.6 gives the first phrase of the familiar melody "Twinkle, Twinkle, Little Star" along with a pair of variations; Figure 4.3 diagrams the metric structure of each variation. In figure 4.3a, note that in addition to the four-beat cycle, a half-bar cycle is also present, drawn as an ellipse to show segments of the subcycle (from beat 1 to 3 and back again). A terminological note is needed here: a

(a)

(b)

(c)

Example 4.6. Variations on "Twinkle, Twinkle, Little Star" (composed by the author). (a) Theme; (b) duple variation; (c) triplet variation.

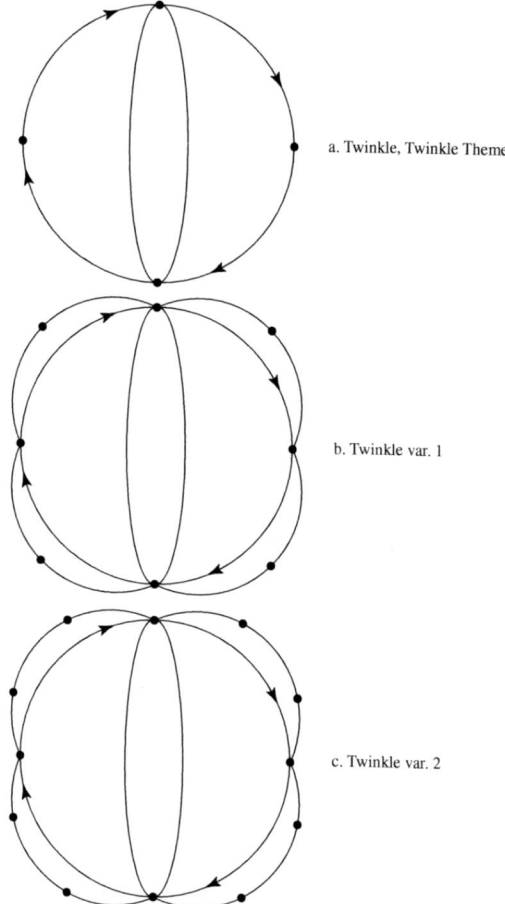

a. Twinkle, Twinkle Theme

b. Twinkle var. 1

c. Twinkle var. 2

Figure 4.3. Metric diagrams corresponding to example 4.6. (a) "Twinkle, Twinkle" theme; (b) Duple variation; (c) Triplet variation.

meter is often, if not usually, a metacycle, that is, a set of hierarchically coordinated component cycles. But as seen in figure 4.2, sometimes a meter consists of just a single cycle. Thus the term *cycle* will be used here to refer to a meter inclusive of all of its component cycles. When I wish to refer to a particular component cycle, they will be referred to as such, or by use of terms such as "beat-cycle," "8 cycle," and so on, as defined later.

To continue with the "Twinkle" variations, at the start of the first variation the binary subdivision triggers the appropriate attending behavior, and hence the meter is enriched, as in figure 4.3b. In figure 4.3c, the binary metric subdivision is supplanted by triplet subdivision. As figures 4.3a, 4.3b, and 4.3c refer to different sections of a continuous piece of music, we can see how some levels and meters can come and go, while others are maintained over its course. In this case, the continuity of the four-beat and half-bar cycles is preserved from variation to variation while the subdivision levels change. From one point of view, a meter can be thought to include *all* of the possible periodicities, both active and inactive, that relate to some core set of periodicities that remain constant. As such, a meter may be regarded as a dynamic system that has various modes of excitation or resonance. From that perspective, figures 4.3a, 4.3b, and 4.3c simply describe different resonating states of the same system. One might diagram such a system as in figure 4.4. Here the core periodicities that form the four-beat cycle are drawn with solid lines, while other potential cycles are given in dashed lines. Only some of these component cycles can be active at any one time (e.g., one cannot have both simple and compound subdivision active concurrently, as noted in chapter 3).

As noted in chapter 1, it is customary to think of all of example 4.6 as being in the same meter; on this view figure 4.4 can account for all of the metric possibilities that may arise in such a passage. Yet, as also noted in chapter 1, each variation gives rise to rather different attending behaviors, a different sense of motion, gesture, and so forth. Thus, I regard each as metrically distinct. To be sure, some of these states may be closely related, and at times we may use diagrams such as figure 4.4 to show how closely related meters may interrelate. Normally, however, the metric diagrams presented here represent the particular attentional state that emerges at a particular point in the listening experience.

Figure 4.5 is a reworking of figure 4.3b; rather than placing the subdivisions as "petals" around the four-beat cycle, here the subdivisions are placed on the rim of the circle and other levels are drawn within it. The beat IOIs are marked by the diamond that connects every other time point on the outer circle. While figures 4.3b and 4.5 are topologically equivalent, drawing the metric cycle in the manner of figure 4.5 allows us to see how the total number of elements in the

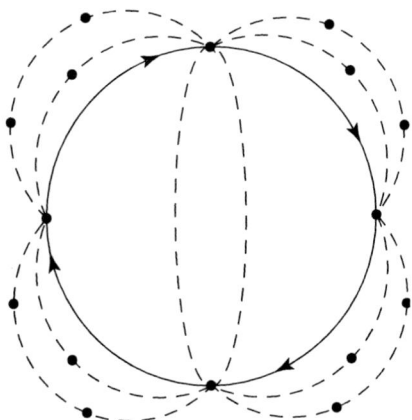

Figure 4.4.   4-beat metric cycle with various potential subdivision and half-measure levels.

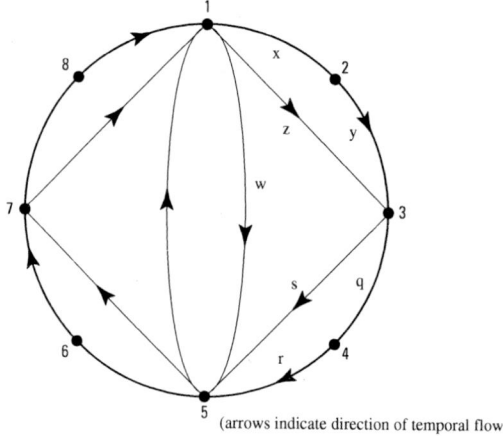

(arrows indicate direction of temporal flow

Figure 4.5.   Redrawing of figure 4.4 as an 8-cycle.

cycle acts as a fundamental constraint on metric structure. It also makes clear the particular ways in which a set of attentional periodicities must coordinate. In discussing of metric well-formedness, I will use diagrams like figure 4.5 in which the shortest or fastest periodicity anchors the formal definition of the other cycles. In other contexts, as when dealing with shifting subdivisions, representations such as figures 4.3 or 4.4 will be more useful.

A metric pattern can first be labeled based on the total number of elements or time points it involves. This will be referred to as the *N-cycle* of the meter, and the particular value for N will be referred to as the *cardinality* of the cycle. The N-cycle appears by other names in some discussions of non-western musics. Nketia speaks of the "density referent" for the integer unit or IOI for the construction of the N-cycle, and then proceeds to classify African rhythms according to N-cycles of particular cardinalities (1974, p. 127; see also chapters 5 and 6). In Hindustani (northern) and Karnatic (southern) Indian music, various tālas are defined by an additive sequence of mātrā (roughly "beats," although they may or may not be subdivided), and these sequences are sometimes organized by the cardinality of the sequence. Figure 4.5 is an *8-cycle,* but notice that it also involves other cycles, including a cycle of four beats and a cycle of two *half-measures.*[3] Note that in example 4.3, when there is a shift from simple to compound subdivision, there is a change from an 8-cycle to a *12-cycle.* Because most meters include at least one level of subdivision, the N-cycle is usually not the tactus. The interior cycles will be referred to as *subcycles,* and the cycle that carries the tactus will be referred to as the *beat cycle.* Note that the beat cycle can be the N-cycle as in figure 4.3a, but it is usually a subcycle.

The cyclical metric diagrams require coordination among periodic attending processes, as each cycle must "nest" neatly within cycles of higher cardinality. This nesting also reflects hierarchic timing constraints. Each line segment from time point to time point represents a particular IOI between attentional peaks on a given component cycle. In order to maintain coordination among an N-cycle and its subcycles, each IOI must equal the sum of its lower-level components; in figure 4.5, this means that the IOIs represented by $x + y = z$; $q + r = s$; $z + s = w$; and so forth.

Each component cycle has some degree of temporal elasticity both because the attentional peaks have some amount of temporal spread and because dynamic attending involves adaptive error correction (Large & Jones 1999). However, this elasticity is constrained by (a) the stability of the IOIs in the musical signal—the more regular the musical surface, the more focused the attentional pulse (see Large & Kolen 1994); and (b) the number of levels involved at a particular point in the metric cycle. That is, one presumes that time points which only articulate IOIs on the N-cycle are less constrained and more elastic than those which are involved in several subcycles.

What Is Metric "Well-formedness"?

Music theorists have long debated which meters are permissible and which impermissible. For example, in the late 18th and 19th centuries, theorists such as Kirnberger, Fétis, or Hauptmann told students of composition that a five beat measure was, at best, to be avoided, and, at worst, impossible (Arlin 2000, p. 278). The basis for these judgments varied from a natural bias toward symmetry and binary relationships often ascribed to respiration and the "principle of systole and diastole" (see London 1990) to the perceptual problems that malformed meters present, such as Weber's claim that five-beat measures are "far less agreeable to our ear" (cited in Arlin 2000, p. 278). Hauptmann claimed that a five or seven beat measure was simply inconceivable (1881, p. 267), although, in claiming that it was not conceivable, he conceived it.

Two things should be kept in mind when considering these historical sources on metric well-formedness. The first is that they are almost always highly prescriptive: they make claims about how meter *ought* to be. Indeed, many of these sources are student composition manuals, and metric prescription is part and parcel of their pedagogical orientation. Second, their prescriptions are drawn from the authors' native musical practice, such as 19th-century Viennese classical music in the case of Hauptmann and Weber. Only in recent years have theories of meter taken cross-stylistic and cross-cultural differences into account (see London 1991; Temperley 2001).

More recently, which is to say ever since Lerdahl and Jackendoff's *A Generative Theory of Tonal Music* (1983), it has become commonplace to couch these sorts of theoretical discussions in terms of a set of well-formedness rules or conditions. Indeed, a comprehensive set of well-formedness rules in and of themselves can comprise a theory of meter. Nonetheless, there are several senses of well-formedness in musical and music theoretic discussions of meter, and these need to be teased out. *Stylistic well-formedness* indicates the kinds of metric formations that tend to appear in a particular stylistic or cultural context. In this case, "well-formed" really means "typical." Of stylistic well-formedness, little more needs to be said other than the rejoinder that one should not mistake what is typical in a particular cultural context to be musically universal (though typical structures will of course reflect cognitive constraints that often have similar effects in different styles).

Notational well-formedness is more interesting; this term refers to what is possible or permissible within the context of a particular notational system. First, what has been "notate-able" in Western written musical tradition has evolved over the years. Whereas the use of some time signatures such as $\frac{3}{2}$ and $\frac{2}{2}$, as well as $\frac{4}{16}$, has become less common, others including $\frac{5}{4}$ and $\frac{7}{4}$, as well as "additive" signatures such as $\frac{2+2+3}{8}$ have become legitimate. Changing notational license is not only motivated by changing musical practice—in order to write down a new rhythmic idea, the notational system is forced to evolve—but also invites further changes in musical practice. The use of additive time signatures is a case in point: once they were used for indicating the metric construal of certain rhythmic figures, it became apparent that they could be used for others as well. A second point regarding notational well-formedness is that the rules of notation do capture some more theoretical aspects of metric well-formedness. Time signatures since around 1600 are given in the form of a fraction, X/Y. X indicates the number of beats in a measure (in simple time), or it indicates the number of subdivision units in a measure (in compound time). X must be an integer > 1 (i.e., a measure must have at least two beats), and one cannot have fractional beat values. Y indicates the beat or subdivision unit, and these values are restricted by convention and orthographic necessity—one would not, for example, use an excessively long note for Y, as that limits the possibility for notating durations longer than a beat in length. Thus the conventions of notation presume that (a) measures contain two or more beats, (b) they do not include fractional beats, and (c) in most instances the meter is relatively stable such that the framework established in the first measure via the time signature carries over to subsequent measures.

Theoretical well-formedness defines the range of musically possible meters apart from their notational particulars. Theoretical notions of metric well-formedness try to explicate the kinds of temporal regularities captured by notation, as well as those that are only implicit in musical notation and musical practice. Lerdahl and Jackendoff's (1983) metrical well-formedness rules (MWFRs) are a good case in point:

MWFR 1: Every attack point [on the musical surface] must be associated with a beat at the smallest metric level present at that point in the piece (p. 72).
MWFR 2: Every beat at a given level music must also be a beat at all smaller levels present at that point in the piece (p. 72).

MWFR 3: At each metrical level, strong beats are spaced either two or three beats apart (p. 69).

MWFR 4: The tactus and immediately larger metrical levels must consist of beats equally spaced throughout the piece. At subtactus metrical levels, weak beats must be equally spaced between the surrounding strong beats (p. 72).

These MWFRs, along with other primitives such as beat, tactus, and strong beat that they define elsewhere, circumscribe a set of permissible metrical structures. The MWFRs are supplemented by a set of *metrical preference rules* or MPRs). These preference rules adjudicate between competing metrical parsings of a given passage. For example:

MPR 1: (Parallelism) Where two or more groups or parts of groups can be construed as parallel, they preferably receive parallel metrical structure (p. 75).

MPR 2: (Strong Beat Early) Weakly prefer a metrical structure in which the strongest beat in a group appears relatively early in a group (p. 76).

Unlike the stylistic or notational well-formedness rules that indicate what a performer or composer can or cannot *do*, Lerdahl and Jackendoff's MWFRs delimit what one can and cannot *hear*, metrically speaking, in listening to a particular passage. Their MPRs adjudicate between conflicting metrical construals of a passage if and when such conflicts occur. The MPRs also can be used to justify a music theorist's choices in positing a particular analysis of a musical passage, that is, as to why one analytic "reading" of a passage might be musically better or otherwise more defensible.

While MWFRs 1 and 2 are universal, MWFRs 3 and 4 are idiom-specific (p. 4), though Lerdahl and Jackendoff take them to hold quite broadly in Western music. Both the tactus and the level above it must be isochronous (MWFR 4), although subtactus levels need not be—for example, one can embed the occasional triplet in the context of an otherwise binary subdivision. Tactus is not formally defined, though it is associated with a kinematic response to the music (p. 71). MWFR 3 prevents adjacent accented beats. While Lerdahl and Jackendoff treat MWFR 3 as idiom-specific, later I will argue that this is a more general or universal aspect of metric well-formedness, as this constraint helps preserve the stability of each hierarchic level. Lerdahl and Jackendoff correlate metrical strength with hierarchical persistence and depth: "if a beat is felt to be strong at a particular level, it is also a beat at the next larger level" (p. 19). Thus, Lerdahl and Jackendoff's MWFRs relate the norms of Western musical practice to more universal constraints on metrical hierarchies.

In the following section I give a set of metric well-formedness constraints that, like Lerdahl and Jackendoff's MPRs, are listener-based. While they are related to musical practice and also have formal considerations, they are grounded in the psychology of perception rather than musical practice. It is perhaps worth pointing out that from the perspective of empirical research in rhythmic perception and performance, one does not need any well-formedness rules at all. Rather, one may simply list the tapping patterns that subjects either can or cannot reproduce; the perturbations that they can or cannot notice, the durational patterns that they can or cannot judge as the same or different. While certain psychophysical and motor limits may become apparent, one need not posit a general set of well-formedness rules in order to interpret one's data. Indeed, most psychologists are properly reluctant make more general claims, as it is clear that many of these results are highly context-dependent.

A Set of Metric Well-formedness Constraints

The set of well-formedness principles proposed here are constraints rather than prescriptive rules since my aim is to stake out the widest possible range of meters found in both Western and non-Western musical practice. No set of preference rules is given, for as we have already seen, very often there is no single, correct metrical construal for a given rhythm. Because the primary constraints on meter are viewed as psychological rather than stylistic, a number of the well-formedness constraints include specific psychological and cognitive limits, as discussed in chapter 2. Cyclical representations of meter provide a context for the following metric *Well-Formedness Constraints* (WFCs):

WFC 1: The IOIs between the time points on the N-cycle must be categorically equivalent. That is, they must be nominally isochronous and must be at least ≈ 100 ms.

WFC 2: Each cycle—the N-cycle and all subcycles—must be continuous, that is, they must form a closed loop.

WFC 3: The N-cycle and all subcycles must begin and end at the same temporal location, that is, they must all be in phase.

WFC 4: The N-cycle and all subcycles must all span the same amount of time, that is, all cumulative periods must be equivalent. The maximum span for any cycle may not be greater than ≈5 seconds.

WFC 5: Each subcycle must connect nonadjacent time points on the next lowest cycle. For example, each successive segment of the beat cycle must skip over at least one time-point on the N-cycle.

By grounding metrical patterns with an isochronous N-cycle, WFC 1 serves to ensure that the overall metric pattern is "regular enough" to permit a stable attending behavior.[4] It also establishes the absolute value of the metric floor. WFCs 2, 3, and 4 collectively ensure formal coordination among the component cycles of the metric pattern. WFC 4 also establishes the metric ceiling. WFC 5 ensures the hierarchic integrity of the meter, insuring that each level involves attentional periodicities that are of the same order of magnitude. In other words,

WFC 5 ensures that one does not mix up beats and subdivisions on the same cycle. WFC 5 is expressed in the form of a drawing rule. That is, in order to draw a representation of a metric pattern, one would start with the N-cycle, and then fill in successive subcycles according to it.

Figure 4.6 contains a number of hypothetical cases, each showing what would happen when a particular WFC is violated. In figure 4.6a, the IOIs on the N-cycle are wildly nonisochronous. As a result, while the beat-cycle it contains follows all of the other WFCs, including WFC 5, the resulting "beats" are radically uneven in terms of the value of their relative IOIs, and indeed, the "beat" from time-point 1 to time-point 3 is shorter than the "subdivisions" from time-points 3-4 or 4-5, rendering the distinctions among metric levels meaningless. A similar problem occurs in figure 4.6e, which shows a violation of WFC 5 in the context of a well-formed N-cycle. Here the resulting IOIs form a 2-1-2-1-2 pattern. The problem here is not that we have a pattern of uneven beats but in the specific relation between them. The problem is this: here a short beat is half the duration of a long beat, and so each short is equivalent to a unit of subdivision for the long. As in figure 4.6a, the distinction between a subdivision and a beat is rendered meaningless.[5]

Figure 4.6b contains a discontinuous subcycle that violates WFC 2. Whereas its N-cycle is continuous and coherent, the subcycle it contains is incomplete, indicating a sense of rupture or displacement in the attending and expectation on that level. Note that unless the N-cycle is also broken, some sense of continuity will remain. Hence there is a nominal continuation of the subcycle, as indicated by the dotted line. In this way the continuity of each component cycle of a meter ensures the hierarchic integrity of the whole. This also shows that metric rupture, when it occurs, is an all or nothing affair. To break the sense of the beat-cycle, one has to break the continuity of higher and lower levels as well.

In figure 4.6c, the 2-4-6-8 subcycle connecting the even time-points of the N-cycle is out of phase with the N-cycle and the half-measure cycle. As a result, the cycles do not properly nest in violation of WFC3. Moreover, if one of the time points on the 2-4-6-8 beat-cycle functions as a downbeat (i.e., represents greater attentional salience than the others), then the resultant pattern would have two downbeats. Figure 4.6d illustrates a violation of WFC 4, a time span violation. Given the 8-cycle (as N-cycle) and a beat unit consisting of three N-cycle IOIs, the result is the rather pretty but metrically malformed diagram. As it takes three iterations of the N-cycle in order for the two cycles to phase align, the result is a subcycle that cannot nest in the N-cycle.

Timing Constraints and Metrical Types

We now have a means of categorizing various metric structures. A *metrical type* can be specified by (a) the cardinality of its N-cycle, and (b) the arrangement of

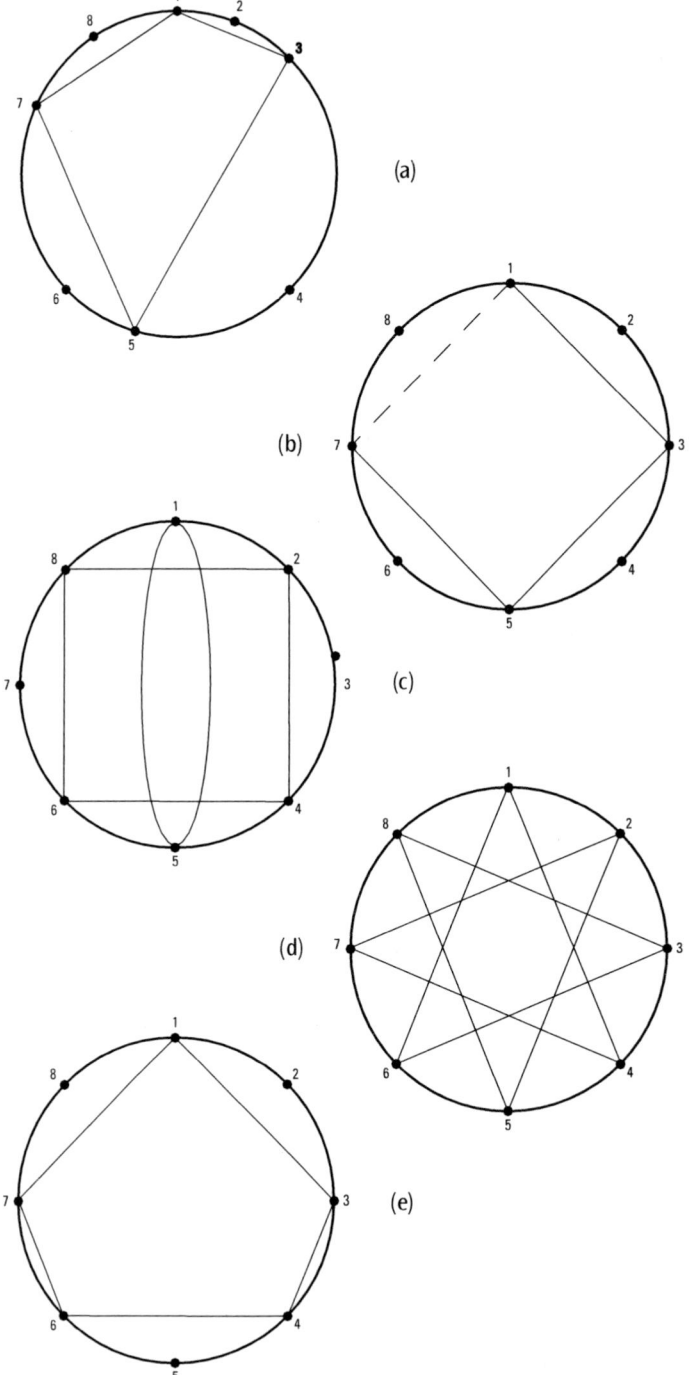

Figure 4.6. Examples of violations of well-formedness constraints. (a) Violates WFC 1 (N-cycle is non-isochronous); (b) violates WFC 2 (sub-cycle is not closed/continuous); (c) violates WFC 3 (sub-cycles are not coordinated); (d) violates WFC 4 (sub-cycle's total duration exceeds that of N-cycle); (e) violates WFC 5 (sub-cycle connects adjacent time-points on the N-cycle).

its component subcycles. If we label each time-point on the N-cycle, we can readily specify the organization of each subcycle. Thus, figure 4.5 is an *8-cycle* with 1-3-5-7 and 1-5 subcycles.[6] Metrical types may be further individuated based on the absolute value of the IOIs of its N-cycle and component cycles. That is, the upper and lower limits of meter and other metric thresholds discussed in chapter 2 may be considered in the construction of both simple and more complex metric cycles. The lower limit requires that time points on the N-cycle must be at least ≈100 ms apart. Likewise, the upper limit means that the cumulative span for the N-cycle cannot be more than ≈5 seconds. These two requirements work in tandem because, for example, as the basic interval on an 8-cycle approaches 650 ms, the cumulative time-span begins to exceed the 5-second limit. Conversely, if the N-cycle has a cumulative time-span of about 3 seconds, for example, and the shortest possible interval is ≈100 ms, then there is a maximum of 30–32 elements that might appear on the N-cycle.

Let us take our trusty 8-cycle (with 1-3-5-7 and 1-5 subcycles) and see how incremental increases in tempo interact with the various temporal thresholds discussed in chapter 2; a set of cyclical timings for the 8-cycle is given in table 4.1. The values in table 4.1 represent average IOIs, with the understanding that in actual practice these will often be subject to a degree of expressive variation. Since our concern here is the approximate location of various temporal thresholds, average IOIs will suffice (the effect of expressive variation on metric cycles is discussed in chapter 9). In table 4.1 the bold font marks the temporal thresholds (here arbitrarily pegged at 250 ms, 600 ms, and 2000 ms, for clarity's sake). Given the hierarchic relationships among cycles (that is, among metric levels), each subcycle involves IOIs within a certain range, which means that certain thresholds are only relevant to certain subcycles. While these thresholds do not line up perfectly from column to column, a number of them are close—for example, the 250 ms threshold for the N-cycle roughly aligns with the 600 ms threshold for subcycle one and the 2-second threshold for the total span. As has

Table 4.1. Cyclical Timings For the 8-Cycle

N-cycle IOI	Sub-cycle 1	Sub-cycle 2	Total Span
100	200	400	800
125	**250**	500	1000
150	300	**600**	1200
175	350	700	1400
200	400	800	1600
225	450	900	1800
250	500	1000	**2000**
300	**600**	1200	2400
350	700	1400	2800
400	800	1600	3200
500	1000	**2000**	4000
600	1200	2400	4800
650	1300	2600	5200

been emphasized, these thresholds are not absolute, but dependent on context, and so it may be more accurate to look at these intercolumn alignments as defining transition zones from one temporal range to another. In terms of the N-cycle, these zones occur between 125–150 ms, 250–300 ms, and 500–600 ms, indicated by the dashed lines in table 4.1. As such, table 4.1 shows that there are four tempo-dependent varieties of the 8-cycle. We may thus say that there are four *tempo-metrical types* of an 8-cycle with 1-3-5-7 and 1-5 subcycles. This does not mean that each tempo-metrical type is defined in terms of the level that is heard as the tactus, such that at the slowest tempos the tactus is heard on the N-cycle and, as the tempo increases, it then shifts to subcycle 1, and so on. As Meyer and Palmer (2001) have shown, performers and listeners have some flexibility as to which level they may hear as a tactus in a sufficiently rich metric context, especially at moderate tempos.

Summary and Discussion

This chapter developed a time-continuous representation for meter in which each representation captures a particular resonating state of a dynamic entrainment process. These representations employ a circular mapping that mutually coordinates each component cycle to create a well-formed metrical gestalt. This mode of representation is primarily concerned with the temporal location of attentional peaks on each subcycle, although peaks of relatively greater salience are involved in a greater number of subcycles. While I have emphasized that meter is a fluid attentional process, and not a "crystallized" structure (as is often given in traditional music theory), these representations do seem to be akin to traditional metric analyses in that they are static abstractions from real-time processes. This is a fair enough assessment, for any printed two-dimensional picture of musical meter will have to be a kind of snapshot of a dynamic process. I would emphasize, however, that what is important here is not the structure per se, but the set of relationships (and the constraints under which the relationships may occur) that these metric diagrams aim to capture.

This chapter also introduced a number of important terms:

Metrical cycle: the coordinated set of periodicities (as well as their graphic representation) that make up a particular attentional state, typically involving beats, beat subdivisions, and measures.

N-cycle: the lowest/fastest level of meter present; typically a level of subdivision that functions as a constraint on the formal organization of higher levels of metric structure. Particular values of N can be given such that one can speak of 8-cycles, 12-cycles, and so forth.

Subcycle: any level of metrical structure above the N-cycle; subcycle refers to their representation as pathways within the typically circular representation of the N-cycle.

Beat-cycle: the level of the meter that carries the tactus. This may be the N-cycle, but more often is a subcycle. IOIs for the beat-cycle strongly tend toward the 500–700 ms range, as noted in chapter 2.

Half measure: For meters whose beat-cycle is of cardinality 4 or greater, it may be possible to have additional layers of meter (that is, additional attentional periods) that are approximately half of the total IOI for the entire metric cycle.

Metrical type: A description of all of the cycles that comprise a particular meter based on their cardinality and arrangement, such as a meter based on an 8-cycle, with a 1-3-5-7 beat-cycle and a 1-5 half-measure (see figure 4.5).

Tempo-metrical type: A means of distinguishing among metrical types based on the absolute value of the IOIs of their component cycles. Distinctions can be made based upon the IOI of a given component cycle relative to various temporal thresholds.

The point has been made that there are different varieties of standard meters such as $\frac{3}{4}$, of $\frac{4}{4}$, and so forth. It is now clearer that these different varieties may be considered both in terms of metrical types and tempo-metrical types and, as will be discussed in chapter 9, even further differentiated by characteristic expressive variations within a tempo-metrical type. This means that every standard meter subsumes a good number of tempo-metrical types but not an extraordinarily large number. While the resulting metric taxonomy is moderately large, it is hardly infinite.

The idea of metric well-formedness has been explored and distinctions between stylistic, notational, and theoretical well-formedness have been drawn. While stylistic and notational well-formedness are rooted in specific cultural traditions of performance and notation, theoretical well-formedness is not. Theoretical well-formedness delimits the range of musically possible meters and also explicates some notions of well-formedness that are implicit in musical notation and practice. In light of the discussion given earlier, more can now be said about theoretical well-formedness. Its roots are two: (1) the psychological limits on temporal attending and entrainment, and (2) the formal requirements for hierarchically coherent patterns of attending. The well-formedness constraints presented in this chapter combine these two aspects of theoretical well-formedness, and as such, they should be applicable to a wide variety of musical and cultural contexts. Indeed, my aim has been that they should function more or less as metric universals, such that any metric pattern that is considered well-formed according to stylistic criteria will also meet the WFCs.

In terms of their formal structure, the WFCs are cast in terms of both bottom up (WFCs 1, 5) as well as top down (WFCs 3, 4) aspects of cycle formation. In addition, one can see how there are constraints related to periodicity (WFCs 1,

4), phase relationships among subcycles (WFCs 2, 3, 4), nesting relationships (WFC 5) and symmetry (WFC 1). Collectively, the WFCs create and maintain the hierarchic integrity of the meter.

Finally, by grounding the WFCs in relationships derived from the N-cycle, the approach developed gives the metric foreground its due. Most theories of rhythm and meter have focused on the formation of measures and larger units. But the metric foreground—that is to say, the subdivision levels of the beat—has an equally significant import on our metrical attending and hence the meaning and motional qualities of a musical gesture.

5

Meter-Rhythm Interactions II: Problems

Metric Malleability and Metric Ambiguity

Metric malleability, the property that many melodic or rhythmic patterns may be heard in more than one metric context, was illustrated by the very first examples presented in this book (examples 1.1 and 1.2); example 5.1 is another case, a longer melodic sequence which can fit comfortably in either $\frac{2}{4}$ or $\frac{3}{4}$. Note that in this example the organization of the lower metric levels is the same in both. Indeed, one might reasonably claim that both are based on a 12-cycle, with the first having a 1-5-9 subcycle, whereas the second has a 1-7 subcycle. Example 5.2 (after Sloboda 1983) illustrates a different type of metric malleability. Here both versions share the same tempo-metrical type but differ in terms of their downbeat placement—that is, in terms of the phase relation between the metric framework and the melodic surface. Finally, example 5.3 involves $\frac{4}{4}$ versus $\frac{9}{8}$ organization of an undulating stream of eighth notes. Note that while the $\frac{4}{4}$ version highlights the unfolding of the G Major triad (circled in the example) and involves a motivic repetition from the first to the second bar (bracketed), the $\frac{9}{8}$ version features a motivic repetition on a larger scale (from measures one to three, bracketed in the example). Both versions of example 5.3 display hierarchically well-formed melodic patterns. Yet in the $\frac{4}{4}$ passage there is an 8-cycle with a quarter-note beat (1-3-5-7 subcycle), while in the $\frac{9}{8}$ there is a 9-cycle with a dotted quarter-note beat (1-4-7 subcycle). As a result, these two differ not only in terms of meter, but also in terms of tempo, given the different IOIs on their beat cycles.

In deadpan performances of examples 5.1–5.3 it may be possible for different listeners to latch on to different meters. In those performances, these malleable melodies *are* metrically ambiguous. However, when malleable melodies are performed by musicians who see them notated in a particular meter, the performer's use of expressive variations of timing and dynamics will usually serve

(a)

(b)

Example 5.1. $\frac{2}{4}$ vs. $\frac{3}{4}$ settings of "same" melody (composed by the author). (a) $\frac{2}{4}$ version; (b) $\frac{3}{4}$ version.

to disambiguate them. For example, the use of characteristic patterns of dynamic stress and timing will make clear whether or not the first note is an upbeat in example 5.2, which was precisely what Sloboda found. Likewise, if a deadpan performance of one of these examples were to appear in an established metrical context, in all likelihood the listener would maintain the established metrical context. Therefore, it is not quite right to simply claim that malleable melodies are metrically *ambiguous*—they may be, but only under certain contextual and performance conditions. Hence my use of the term *metrically malleable* for these kinds of rhythmic surfaces. Examples 5.1–5.3 also suggest that metrically malleable melodies must be used with care in studies of rhythm and meter perception and performance.

Conflicting Cues and Metric Dissonance

The examples of metric malleability discussed earlier involve a single melodic line, but musical textures usually involve more than one layer of activity, such as a melody line over an accompaniment. These may be played by different instruments or instrumental groups, and their timbral differences can help to delineate different rhythmic layers. Indeed, the art of counterpoint is to produce a musical texture in which each part has a distinct shape and musical identity,

Example 5.2. "Same" melodic pattern, but shifted relative to downbeat, after Sloboda (1983) fig. 1, p. 383. (a) First note as anacrusis; (b) First note on the downbeat.

(a)

versus

(b)

Example 5.3. $\frac{4}{4}$ vs. $\frac{9}{8}$ settings of the "same" melody, involving shifts of beat and measure IOIs (composed by the author). (a) $\frac{4}{4}$ version; (b) $\frac{9}{8}$ version.

even without timbral distinctions among parts. It is in these more complex textures that one typically finds metric ambiguity and metric dissonance, and for that reason they differ from the multiple-metric-construals-of-a-single-figure sort of ambiguity discussed earlier. A number of music theorists have proposed that some musical passages may involve two (or more) coexisting metric frameworks. Rothstein, for example, says:

> A shadow meter is a secondary meter formed by a series of regularly recurring accents, when those accents do not coincide with the accents of the prevailing meter (or hypermeter). . . . Of course, regular counterstresses need not seriously undermine an established meter . . . but in [the] example, supposedly a paragon of *Ur*-simplicity there *are actually two meters* in conflict with each other. (1995, p. 167; emphasis added)

The term "shadow meter" originates with Samarotto: "The main meter, the meter as written, casts a shadow, as it were, on a subsidiary, displaced meter, which we are drawn to hear as real until it dissolves" (1999, p. 235). Music theorists have also described conflicting metrical cues in terms of "metric dissonance" (Cohn 1992; Grave 1995; Krebs 1987, 1999; Yeston 1976), a term that implies the presence of two conflicting metric structures. Krebs (1999) gives a thorough history and a detailed taxonomy of the concept of metric dissonance. He notes that these dissonances involve the nonalignment of two (or more) layers of rhythmic activity, and that this nonalignment can involve phase offsets ("displacement dissonance") or different periodicities ("grouping dissonance").

Example 5.4 is the passage from Beethoven's song cycle *An die ferne Geliebte*, Op. 98, No. 6, the very example in which Rothstein claims that there are actually two meters in conflict. Figure 5.1 is a diagram of this metric conflict. One meter is congruent with the notated bar, the other displaced by a beat.[1] The notated meter is projected by the piano with its harmonic and figural organization, while the shadow meter is projected in the voice part, both by phonetic stresses in the German text and by the use of relatively long durations (note how the shadow downbeats usually occur as a shorter note—usually a sixteenth—moves

Example 5.4. Example of "shadow meter" in Beethoven's *An die ferne Geliebte*, Op. 98, no. 6, after Rothstein (1995), ex. 1, p. 168.

to a longer one). Rothstein is clearly onto something regarding relationships among the rhythmic layers in this passage and our metric construal of them.

In Example 5.5, the opening of the Minuet movement from Mozart's G minor Symphony, K. 550, we find a more blatant set of conflicting metrical layers. Triple meter (here $\frac{3}{4}$) is normative for the Minuet. As Cohn's analysis in the example shows, while the low strings and bassoon project two measures of $\frac{3}{4}$, the violins and flutes strongly suggest three measures of $\frac{2}{4}$ (1992, p. 15). This is an instance of hemiola, but on the level of downbeats rather than beats. The prob-

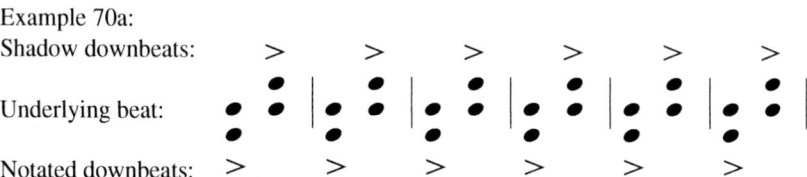

Example 70a:
Shadow downbeats:

Underlying beat:

Notated downbeats:

Figure 5.1.　Alignment of notated vs. shadow downbeats in example 5.4

lem is that Mozart *begins* this minuet with a hemiola, making it difficult (although perhaps not too difficult) to set up the normative triple-meter context in the first place. Eventually, $\frac{3}{4}$ does emerge as the clear winner, but the hemiola figure continues to reappear, clouding the listener's ongoing sense of metric order.

While both Cohn and Rothstein have found musically rich examples of the noncongruence between a durational surface and its metric context (or possible contexts), as was noted in chapter 3 it is problematic to claim that these durational surfaces give rise to conflicting meters. If one has two meters in conflict with each other, then from a cognitive point of view one is saying that the listener is simultaneously using two distinct attending strategies—that is, that she or he is maintaining multiple grounds for the construal of melodic figures. To be clear, it may well be possible for different performers in an ensemble to be hearing and thinking in terms of different meters; indeed, there are many scores that call for the musicians to do just that. A famous example occurs in the finale of act I of Mozart's *Don Giovanni*, where three onstage orchestras play in $\frac{3}{4}$, $\frac{2}{4}$, and $\frac{3}{8}$ at the same time. Even so, one cannot claim that because the flute is counting in $\frac{6}{8}$ and the violin in $\frac{3}{2}$, the listener can/will hear the resultant music polymetrically.

This is not to say that the idea of metrical dissonance is not an apt one, at least metaphorically. Harmonically, a dissonant structure on the surface level involves the presence of tones that grate against (in terms of harmonic function and auditory roughness) an otherwise consonant or stable harmonic structure. Harmonic dissonances may be simultaneous, such as the clashes of tritones and sevenths in a dominant chord, or they may be successive, such as the presence

Example 5.5.　Duple versus triple meter at the beginning of the Minuet from Mozart's 40th Symphony, after Cohn (1992) ex. 3, p. 15.

of a leading tone that resolves to a tonic pitch in an established tonal context. Likewise, the dissonant metric structures listed by Krebs (1999) may be regarded as noncongruences between a pattern of metric entrainment and a pattern of events in the world. Such dissonances have a metrical aspect in that their very regularity threatens to displace the existing pattern of entrainment and on some occasions, they may do so. But hearing a pattern of contrasting organization against the context of an ongoing pattern of attentional invariance is not the same thing as generating two patterns of attentional invariance at the same time. Construing metric dissonance in this way does not entail hearing two meters at once, any more than grasping a harmonic dissonance requires hearing two keys at once.[2] Recall also the discussion of polyrhythms in chapter 3, in which I noted that when confronted with such patterns, listeners will either (a) extract a composite pattern of all of the rhythmic streams present, or (b) focus one rhythmic stream and entrain to its meter while ignoring the metric implication of the other rhythmic streams. Thus, in the Beethoven and Mozart examples given earlier, listeners may focus on either layer of activity, using it as the basis for their metric construal, or they may derive a composite pattern from the two layers of rhythmic articulation.

If a listener makes use of a composite pattern, however, it may often have interesting metric results, as it does in both of these cases. In figure 5.2 , an analysis of the Beethoven passage, when the two metric streams are folded together the result is an accent on every beat—as if each beat were a downbeat. Because this cannot be so according to WFC 5, the effect of folding the two streams together is to efface the sense of measure entirely. To be sure, a listener could simply hold to the primary meter as it has been already well established and hear the shadow patterning as counterstresses that chafe against but do not displace the established meter. But if the shadow meter is really as robust as Rothstein claims, then a collapse of higher metrical levels seems most likely. Figure 5.3 gives a composite patterning of two rhythmic layers in Mozart's Minuetto, and the result is a 2-(1-1)-2-3 pattern. This actually suggests a non-isochronous meter, a 2-2-2-3 pattern. Although I am quite sympathetic to such a construal, in most performances the tempo is probably not quite brisk enough for the half-note and dotted half-note durations to be heard as beats. While the 2-(1-1)-2 composite may initially suggest $\frac{2}{4}, \frac{3}{4}$ wins out by about measure 7.

Whatever strategies listeners may use when confronted with passages such

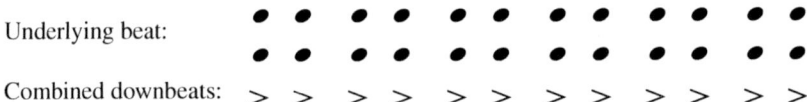

Figure 5.2.   Collapse of the sense of measure due to aggregate effect of notated and shadow downbeats in example 5.4.

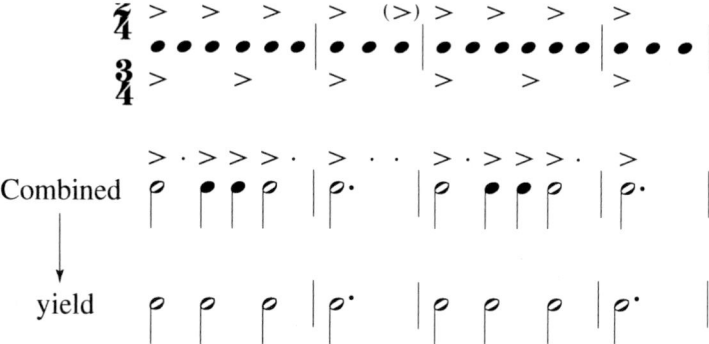

Figure 5.3. Composite effect of $\frac{2}{4}$ and $\frac{3}{4}$ metric accents in example 5.5.

as examples 5.4 and 5.5, they differ from examples 5.1–5.3 in that they involve multiple figures, each with its own, strongly projected metrical implications. While these contexts do create metric ambiguities—in that there are a number of distinct, well-formed meters under which the passages may be construed— the source of their ambiguity does not spring from the fact that each layer can have multiple construals. Indeed, if they could, in all likelihood the metric dissonance would evaporate. Rather, it is because the metric implications of each layer are strong and incommensurate that metric difficulties arise.

The presence of conflicting cues in different layers of a musical texture is found in the music of many cultures. Locke (1998) notes five possible "downbeat" locations that may arise in listening to the West African Gahu rhythm (discussed in chapter 7). Unlike Western music, in African drumming performances these complex rhythmic textures are repeated many times, and thus the pattern of conflicting cues persists longer than in the case of a local hemiola. This persistence gives the listener the opportunity, once he or she has latched onto a particular metrical framework, to then reconstrue the meter. Locke has aptly termed this reconstrual a "gestalt flip" (1998, p. 24). We can do this in much the same way we can visually reconstrue visual figures such as Wittgenstein's famously ambiguous duck/rabbit figure or the perspectival orientation of a Necker cube, as the characteristic repetition of rhythmic patterns in African drumming performances keeps them in our perceptual field long enough to allow both an initial perception, and then subsequent reorientation that leads to a different percept.

Finally, one may draw a distinction between contexts that are metrically *ambiguous* versus those that are metrically *vague*. If a passage has no discernable periodic organization at all, it is simply nonmetric (as in Babbitt's *Composition for Twelve Instruments* example 1.5). By contrast, in metrically vague situations there is a discernable sense of regularity, but the listener is stymied when he or she tries to construe any particular metrical organization. Consider a pattern of very long and very short notes (eighth note = 300 ms duration):

♩. ♪♪♩ ♪♪♩ ♪♪ (etc.)

Here it is unclear whether the listener must interpolate two missing beats to form a four-beat measure, as is somewhat implied by the notation, or if they should interpolate just a single beat, forming a two-beat measure. At the given tempo, the dotted half note is 1800 ms long—far too long for a beat, while at 300 ms eighths are too short to be beats. It is true that the eighth-note pair, if played in strict tempo, would suggest a 600 ms beat period, but this periodicity is not immediately reinforced, and will die away over the long span of the following dotted half note. In such cases, there is no palpable sense of beat or pulse that would allow the listener to instantiate a basic cycle or any subcycles; the figure is *metrically vague*.[3]

Here, then, is a taxonomy of metric ambiguity:

Unambiguous metric contexts involve pitch/durational patterns that strongly tend to project a single meter and are readily maintained by the listener, even in a deadpan performance.

Latently ambiguous metric contexts involve metrically malleable pitch/durational patterns that have the potential for ambiguity, but these are usually disambiguated by the use of expressive variations in performance.

Truly ambiguous metric contexts involve pitch/durational patterns that give rise to different metric construals on different listening occasions. This includes polyrhythms in certain tempo ranges, complex textures in which different voices/layers project different metric organizations, as well as metrically malleable passages in a deadpan performance. Each construal is nonetheless determinate: on each occasion a listener will hear the passage in terms of a particular metrical organization.

Vague metric contexts involve the absence of one or more normative levels of metrical structure. In contrast to a metrically ambiguous context in which there are two or more plausible and determinate patterns of metric organization, in a metrically vague context, no determinate pattern ever emerges.

Contextual Mismatches: Syncopations, Hemiolas, and Loud Rests

In contrast to instances of full-blown metric ambiguity, there may be short-term mismatches between an established meter and a rhythmic figure in which, over the course of a measure or two, the listener encounters a pattern whose durational accent, periodicity, and pattern of dynamic emphasis conflicts with the pattern of metrical periodicity and accent. We have already noted one variety of mismatch, the hemiola. Syncopation is another variety of this sort of mismatch (see ex. 1.3b), in which the durational periods on the surface are out of phase with those of a related metric subcycle. Yet another mismatch involves "loud rests" as illustrated in example 5.6 (after London 1993). The $\frac{3}{8}$ meter is well established in the opening bars, so the lack of an articulation on the downbeat of measure eight is quite a surprise. The metric surprise is aided by the melody and harmony. Following a clear antecedent phrase that ends on a half-cadence on an implied dominant chord (D), in measure 8 we expect the consequent phrase to end on a full cadence on an implied tonic chord (G). This harmonic expectation includes our sense that the melody will arrive on the note G on the downbeat of measure 8, given the "sol-la-ti" melodic figure in measure 7. But the expected melodic G never arrives—instead, we have an eighth-note rest, and then B, and while the B fulfills the harmonic requirement (it is a member of the tonic triad), it only heightens our sense of G's absence.[4]

Krebs (1987, 1999) uses the term "indirect dissonance" to describe another sort of mismatch. These arise because of the successive rather than simultaneous presentation of rhythmic surfaces with different metrical implications. As Krebs has noted, "[an] indirect dissonance exists because of our tendency as listeners to maintain an established pulse for a short time after it is discontinued in actuality" (1999, p. 45). Thus, in contrast to the direct dissonance of example 5.6, in an indirect dissonance "the first interpretive level [i.e., a metric subcycle] is not immediately effaced upon the appearance of the second, but is continued in the listener's mind. The attacks of the imagined continuation of the first level do not coincide with the actually sounding attacks of the second, resulting in a sense of collision" (1987, p. 105). In order for there to be this sense of a collision, as Krebs has aptly put it, two conditions must obtain. First, the listener has to interpolate a metrical articulation on a subcycle that is not phenomenally present in the music. Most typically this is a beat articulation, although more dramatic interpolations may involve higher-level subcycles. At the same time, the surface figure must contain various cues for an alternate metrical construal, such as a change in the period of one or more levels of the meter or a shift of the phase of one or more levels of the meter. One effect of these mismatches is that listeners may become more aware of their metric sensibilities and activities, as they must exert more effort to maintain an attentional framework.

Example 5.6. Melody containing an "accented rest" (composed by the author).

Summary and Discussion

The nature of metric ambiguity is clarified in this chapter. In some cases, metric ambiguity may stem from the metric malleability of a melodic or rhythmic figure, especially if expressive timing and dynamic cues are absent. A metrically malleable figure is likely to be unambiguous if it appears in an established metric context, though in other cases, the same figure can be metrically ambiguous. This ambiguity is marked by the presence of two or more competing, well-formed rhythmic patterns, each grounded on a different (though well-formed) metric construal. Such metrically ambiguous passages allow for a determinate metrical construal on any given listening. Metrically ambiguous contexts differ from those which are metrically vague, which, while metrically regular, do not allow the listener to extract beat and subdivision periods and thus foil the establishment of the basic metric cycle and subcycles.

Oftentimes a passage may contradict the established metric context. If the contradiction is consistent, and continues long enough, it may force listeners to abandon their initial pattern of entrainment and reconstrue the metric context, perhaps by a shift of phase, beat period, measure period, or some combination. Alternatively, the conflicting cues may have a lesser impact, in that some established levels of meter may be effaced, while other levels remain, as in the excerpt from *An die ferne Geliebte.* Many contradictions are merely local, as in hemiola, loud rests, and the like. These local perturbations depend on the presence of an established metric framework for their musical effect. Indeed, they often make the listener more aware of their role in creating meter, as they must "feel a beat that isn't there" or otherwise have a palpable sense of the conflict between the music's rhythms and their own metrical entrainment.

There is a difference in metrical ambiguities in Western versus non-Western musics (and some Western minimalist music). In contexts involving the continued repetition of a dense, multilayered rhythmic pattern, as is common in some forms of African drumming, the continued repetition allows listeners the opportunity to metrically reconstrue the pattern. This may happen several times during the course of a performance. This is different from ambiguous rhythms in Western musical contexts. Given their relatively short presentation, ambiguous rhythms in Western music usually afford only one metric construal on any given listening occasion.

Finally, this chapter examined the notion of metric dissonance. Although this term makes some sense as a metaphorical extension of the concept and experience of dissonance from the harmonic to the metrical/rhythmic domain, claims that such dissonances derive from the listener hearing two meters at once are without a sound psychological basis.

6

Metric Flux in Beethoven's Fifth

Some Preliminaries

The first movement of Beethoven's Fifth Symphony is perhaps the most famous piece of Western classical music; indeed, it is in many respects *the* icon for Western art music. It can be heard in concert halls and as a cell-phone ringtone; it is used in movie scores and television commercials. Yet the symphony still retains great expressive power and aesthetic significance in spite of its ubiquity. Although much of the movement's energy and drama stems from its motivic materials and tonal design—from the opening motive that supposedly symbolizes fate knocking on the door, to the appearance of a new theme at the very end of the work in the coda section—here it is argued that its sweep and power owe just as much to its metrical design.

Epstein cites a common view, that "once established on the level of measure, metric structure in this repertoire [i.e., Western classical music from the 18th and 19th centuries] tends not to change. . . . It seems likely, therefore, that an experienced listener would assume an ongoing, invariant meter once it has initially been determined, rather than continually process and redefine it as a work runs its course" (1995, p. 43). Epstein is partly correct, in that certain aspects of meter, such as the basic beat period and measure, usually do not change. Yet other aspects of meter can and do fluctuate. Meter may shift from relatively rich patterns of expectation with several additional levels of structure above and below the beat and measure to patterns of expectation that are relatively sparse, a bare bones series of beats. Thus while some periodicities remain invariant, other periodicities on the musical surface may come and go, and such shifts from thick to thin meters may be as dramatic, if not more dramatic, than changes in the basic pattern of beats (see also Nauert 1997, pp. 62–64, on active vs. inactive metric levels).

In Beethoven's Fifth there is a great tension between extreme continuity below the level of the tactus (quadruplet subdivisions are almost always present, and the few times they are absent are highly significant) versus discontinuity on the tactus and higher levels. This is a piece that keeps starting and stopping, lurching forward and careening to a halt. Beethoven never allows the listener to settle into a particular meter, but is constantly adding and subtracting metric levels. In other words, just when the meter appears to have settled down, it changes.

Before plunging into the analysis, several points need to be made. The first is the distinction between *notated* versus *expressed* meter (as discussed earlier). In this piece, the tactus is at the level of the half-note, so that each written measure represents a single beat. The meter we hear, however, involves two, four, or eight notated bars. The second point is that for most of this piece, the boundaries of rhythmic groups and measures are out of phase. The famous fate motive, which is the main motivic idea for the piece, consists of three short notes that serve as a pickup to a much longer note. That longer note almost always falls on the beat, and often this motive serves to mark the downbeat as well. Beethoven can and does exploit its significance as an intraopus template, one that cues (or ought to cue) a particular metrical orientation. A third point, especially for readers who are not music theorists, is in regard to the claims that I make in the analyses given here. A musical analysis is grounded in the way one hears the music—in this case, my introspective sense of my metric engagement with the music. Whereas I believe that most of what I say has intersubjective validity, some observations may, of course, be peculiar to my experience of the piece. Nonetheless, I assume my experience of the piece is broadly representative. Finally, although I will often speak about the meter in a given measure (or the meter emerging at a given measure), this is to be understood as a shorthand for "the meter that arises in response to the rhythmic patternings present at measure X."

My main concern is the emergence of various levels of meter above the notated measure, that is, above the tactus level. For expediency, metric levels are indicated with brackets, rather than "dot" notation, but these brackets should not be confused with grouping analysis. Rather, by using dashed versus solid brackets, I am able to indicate latent or emerging versus established levels of metric structure, respectively. For we do not entrain to a metric period the first time it is present in the rhythmic surface of the music—we have to hear it at least once in order to grasp it. Likewise, a level may persist for a while even though cues for that level of structure may be absent, given our internal metric inertia. Anacruses are marked with a curved arrow, where the arrow points to the anchoring beat.

The analysis here will first walk through the piece, lingering over particular sections where appropriate. Then more general points will be made with respect to metric pacing and metric form, that is, the large-scale strategies Beethoven uses in arranging different varieties of meter. To save space and make reading easier, examples have been reduced from full orchestral score to a simple treble/bass staff with instrumentation noted where appropriate.

Starting and Stopping: The First Theme and Exposition

The first five measures show, in miniature, what the metric game will be in this movement: discontinuity (see ex. 6.1). The short notes launch the piece with decisive motion, but the fermata then halts it. These short notes are too fast to be the tactus, but it is clear that the tempo will be fast. The piece starts up again in measure 3, and again, it is a false start. Beethoven's notational details are worth scrutiny here. The first fermata is a single measure; it is often possible to count through it, so that the beat level becomes attenuated, but doesn't break. However, the second fermata is attached to an extra measure, and this is a strong hint to the conductor and performers to make the second fermata longer than the first, and indeed, long enough (greater than 1500–2000 ms) to stifle the emerging sense of pulse. Moreover, as a result of the extra-long fermata there is a metric gap—the pulse train has stopped, and it doesn't palpably resume until the downbeat of measure seven, as the pickup notes lead to, but do not articulate, a beat. Thus measure six does not have a downbeat—it is a notational conceit, but it is not heard.[1] This is the legacy of the opening measures: (1) strongly imply motion and then jam on the brakes, and (2) imprint a metric template whose very short notes are all heard as metrically unaccented relative to the following long note that articulates the beat.

The meter finally gets going in the following measures as two- and four-beat levels emerge. For as the motive in the strings unfolds, we hear a half-half-whole note figure, arpegiating tonic, and then dominant triads (mm. 6–10 and mm. 11–14). This figure consistently marks off two- and four-beat metric levels, and they then emerge in our metrical entrainment. These levels are called into ques-

Example 6.1. Beethoven's Fifth Symphony, mvt. I, mm. 1–21.

tion in measure 21 with reprise of the opening fermatas. When the music resumes in measure 26 (after another metric gap in m. 25), the cascading figures do not really articulate a two-beat level, so we hear just an undivided four-beat measure. While we have the potential for an eight-beat level to emerge, it is not to be. As can be seeing in example 6.2, in measures 34–37, a two-beat level clearly returns (while the four-beat level continues). But then the four-beat level, which had persisted without difficulty, hits mud at measure 44. Starting in measure 38, the ascending scalewise sequence undermines both the two- and four-bar levels—there is no pattern of grouping that reinforces the meter; it must persist in the listener's ear on its own. Whereas the two-beat level can be maintained, at measure 44 the *forte* outbursts, change of motive, registral peaks, melodic contour, and harmonic rhythm all effectively shift the phase of the four-beat measure, enabled by our metric attenuation.

Four-beat measures continue, though again without a two-beat level, until measure 56. Once again, the surface of the music is broken by silences. But in measures 56–59 there are no fermatas, and the meter continues on through the rests to the horn call that announces the second theme (ex. 6.3). There is some metric ambiguity here, as the downbeat location/phase orientation of the violin figure in measures 63–66 (echoed in the clarinet at mm. 67–70) is uncertain. While one can hear both two- and four-beat metrical levels, it is unclear whether they simply start at measure 63, which would make the horn call a truncated three-beat measure, or if measure 63 functions as pickup to measure 64, with grouping and meter again out of phase. The latter, more conservative hearing is given in example 6.3: the phase orientation from measure 60 is maintained on the four-beat and two-beat levels.

Example 6.2.   Beethoven's Fifth Symphony, mvt. I, mm. 32–47.

Example 6.3. Beethoven's Fifth Symphony, mvt. I, mm. 56–70.

The rhythmic activity then lessens somewhat, as the second theme is not undergirded with constant eighth note quadruplets, but the basses (which keep presenting the fate figure) reinforce the subdivision just enough to keep it going in the listener's mind. Thus there is a sense of quadruplet underpinning to the beat throughout this section. At measure 83, the eighth notes become more pervasive; at the same time, the four-beat level is again attenuated, and dies out by measure 88 (ex. 6.4). Four-beat patterns reemerge at measure 95, and, indeed,

Example 6.4.   Beethoven's Fifth Symphony, mvt. I, mm. 79–95.

an eight-beat level seems to be settling in as well, giving a sense of stability and security to the closing theme.

Metric Crisis: The Development

After the repeat of the exposition, we launch into the development section, and it begins with a metric rupture much like the very start of the movement. The four-beat measures then resume, and eight-beat measures may emerge, starting at measure 138. Not surprisingly this does not pan out, and even the four-beat level is soon in trouble (ex. 6.5). First, there is a rhythmic stutter at measures 176–80. Following the emphatic repeated eighth notes in measures 171–74, we are desperate for a downbeat (note the use of a shortened version of the anacrustic fate figure). The violins then try to set matters aright at measure 180, but the lower strings counter with an offbeat/syncopated entry at measure 182. There is, however, a subtle reinforcement of a four-beat metric level with the F♯ in the low strings in m. 184, as it is the first bass note that occurs on the beat (that is, the notated downbeat) we have heard since measure 179.

As the development continues, the eighth notes in the music are rapidly evaporating, and then quarters are gone, such that by measure 196 there is nothing but half notes (ex. 6.6). This is a moment of high tension, not only dissonant and harmonically remote, but also metrically most tenuous. For the quadruplet subdivision of the beat that had been almost constant is now gone. Two- and four-beat measures are clearly present, but just as before at measures

Example 6.5.   Beethoven's Fifth Symphony, mvt. I, mm. 175–90.

Example 6.6. Beethoven's Fifth Symphony, mvt. I, mm. 195–216.

63–64, the phase orientation of the measure is unclear: is the downbeat at measure 199, or measure 200? While the principal motive at measure 195 strongly points to measure 196 as a downbeat, the harmonic resolutions and melodic inflections give structural accents to measures 197 and 199. Indeed, we are in a metric fog at this point, and while one can impose either metric orientation, Beethoven then further calls one's metric sense into question at measure 210, breaking up the motive into single half-notes (alternating between strings and winds). Imbrie has aptly described the effect of this passage:

> The motives have been liquidated; the texture has been radically simplified and now consists of the raw alternation of chords between winds and strings; the harmonies seem to have traveled far from the home tonic. . . . The rhythms, too, I believe, have been deployed throughout the preceding measures in such a way as to prepare the ear gradually for the metrical dislocation. Both the preparation and dislocation are accomplished through metrical ambiguity on a large scale. (1973, p. 57)

The upshot of the conflicting metric orientations is that they cancel each other out, much like those in the passage from Beethoven's *An die ferne Geliebte* (ex. 5.4). While in the song subdivisions still were present underneath the beat, and there one could readily maintain one sense of measure (or another), here there is no ongoing sense of downbeat and no subdivisions; we are down to a bare pulse, weak and thready. In some sense, at this point there is no meter, as there are neither subdivisions of the beat nor patternings of beats into larger measures. Not surprisingly, in performance this is often the slowest passage in the movement, as the very lifeblood of the tactus has been drained away.

The Recapitulation and Coda—But It's Not Over Yet

At measure 228, the fate motive returns, marking measure 229 as a downbeat, and we are relieved to be able to start hearing two- and four-beat levels, but this leads us right to . . . the recapitulation, which, of course, starts by stopping with the fermatas at measures 249 and 252. Another dramatic pause occurs in measure 268 with the (in)famous oboe mini-cadenza; this is marked *adagio*, and is often performed without a discernable sense of pulse. The recapitulation then proceeds as did the exposition until measure 374, where Beethoven launches into an extended coda with a constant barrage of *forte* and *fortissimo* eighth notes. Two-beat and four-beat levels continue through measure 386, where Beethoven writes out a number of rests including an extra measure of rest at measure 389 (ex. 6.7). The result is a bit of a stutter, cued not by any event in the music but by the absence of an expected pickup figure in measure 389 or downbeat articulation in measure 390. The *fortissimo* pickup figure that *does* occur in measure 390 jarringly shifts the location of the downbeat (this is an especially clear example of the kind of metric collision Krebs described as an indirect dissonance). Two- and four-beat levels resume, although the two-beat level is attenuated over measures 399–406, with the two-beat level dropping out at that point.

Example 6.7.   Beethoven's Fifth Symphony, mvt. I, mm. 382–95.

Example 6.8. Beethoven's Fifth Symphony, mvt. I, mm. 423–39.

The entrance of the new theme at measure 423 restores metric stability, as the two- and four-beat levels are again secure (ex. 6.8). Indeed, it seems that a latent eight-beat level might finally emerge. But the sequential patterns run on too long and fail to reinforce the four-beat level at measures 431–40. Order is then restored at measures 339–440, and the four-beat level reemerges at measure 441. Indeed, the eight-beat level finally does emerge at measure 449. But this soon evaporates, as we come again to the fermata figures from the opening of the movement—in their most emphatic statement yet—at measures 475–82 (the opening pickup notes have been drawn out for four measures here, mm. 475–78, leading to a downbeat at m. 479). From here on, however, the metric organization is utterly regular, with clear two- and four-beat levels. In light of what has come before, this is almost banal.

The very ending also involves a bit of metric mischief, as it is possible to hear a "missing beat," that is, a measure that Beethoven left unnotated (ex. 6.9). If the listener maintains the regular meter through the end, he or she will interpolate an extra downbeat, and thus instantiate an extra "measure 503" consisting of a rest. Hearing the ending this way depends on maintaining the tempo through the end of movement, as even a modest ritardando may be enough to put the brakes on our metric entrainment, such that we would not project an extra beat following the final chord. In either case, the result is a closing gesture that is both highly overstated and strangely unconvincing—which, I would argue, is precisely the effect Beethoven was aiming for.

Example 6.9.   Beethoven's Fifth Symphony, mvt. I, mm. 483–end.

Summary and Discussion

Meter is not static but constantly changes in this movement. Whereas Krebs (1999) has described the way that metrical dissonance can fluctuate over the course of a piece, here the fluctuations of metric "consonance" have been described. The primary indicator of the metric flux in this movement is the presence or absence of subdivision.

The quadruplet subdivisions give a lot of energy and continuity to the tactus level, thus enhancing the dramatic impact when the tactus is broken by fermatas or extended rests. They also enhance the effects of phase or downbeat shifts, as the finely textured subdivisions give us a very precise sense of where the beats and downbeats ought to be. Conversely, for the most part there are only a limited number of levels above the beat. Although two-beat measures are present most of the time (though not always), it is significant where and when locally stable four-beat and eight-beat periodicities emerge, and how the emergence of those levels compares with the absence of subdivisions. Meter is thickest and most secure at the end of the exposition, recapitulation, and coda—thus, metric stability is correlated with high-level formal closure.

Conversely, the point of the highest tonal and dramatic tension is coeval with the near-elimination of meter, and almost of the tactus as well. With only a pulse in measures 210–28, we are at a loss to predict the patterning of future events. Without subdivision, we lack a sense of the gestural quality of that pulse and rhythms that embody it. For while a pulse provides a modicum of temporal anticipation, it is anticipation at its most anxious. Though we can still anticipate from beat to beat, we are very much in the dark, so to speak, as to when we may expect events on a larger scale. We have no sense of rhythmic groups or gestures longer than a beat, so not only do we lack a sense of *when* significant events will occur, we have no idea of what they will be (two-beat? three-beat? four-beat?). In this movement, meter and metric fluctuation plays an equal role with harmony and melody in creating large-scale processes of tension and release and shaping its larger form.

One reason for tracking the metric changes through this piece is that elsewhere this book concentrates on meter in steady states, that is, the nature of a particular pattern of attending, the constraints on its structure, and so forth. The Beethoven analysis acknowledges how supple and fluid meter can be. Now, of course, the ways in which one meter can morph into another are highly constrained—a two-beat level, once established, will naturally accommodate higher levels of four, six, or eight beats, but not five beats, for example. These are relationships that are detailed in the tree diagrams given at the end of chapter 2.

The comings and goings of metric levels in this movement from Beethoven's Fifth Symphony are an index of the listener's sense of motion and continuity. This movement is atypical in that Beethoven, at various points, completely breaks the thread of the tactus, and at the moment of highest tension in the development, breaks the continuity of metric cycle, eliminating a sense of downbeat. This movement is often used as a textbook example of a sonata-form movement in a minor key, and textbooks note both how it follows as well as how it alters the thematic and tonal conventions of the sonata form archetype (e.g., presenting the second theme in the recapitulation in the parallel major, rather than tonic minor key; introducing a new theme in the coda, and so forth). By the same token, this movement involves both conservative and radical uses of meter, establishing dense and rapid continuity—all those quadruplets—only to keep bringing it to a dramatic halt.

7

Non-Isochronous Meters

Isochronous and Nonisochronous meters

Although the well-formedness constraints (WFCs) presented in chapter 5 require the N-cycle to be isochronous, they do not require subcycles to be isochronous. This means that well-formed meters may have non-isochronous beat patterns. Consider two meters based on a 9-cycle. Figure 7.1 demonstrates an isochronous beat pattern with three beats, symmetrically spaced over the course of the 9-cycle; this is compound triple meter. Figure 7.2 involves four beats, but four does not divide into nine without a remainder and the result is an uneven series of beats. However, this example, unlike figure 4.6e, does not violate any WFCs, including WFC 5. There is no confusion of subdivisions and beats in figure 7.2; rather, each subdivision is an integer unit of the N-cycle and beats are composed of either two or three N-cycle intervals. Example 7.1 is a well-known jazz tune, Dave Brubeck's "Blue Rondo a la Turk," which is cast in the meter given in figure 7.2. I will use the term *NI-meters* to refer to meters with non-isochonous beat patters, in contrast to *I-meters*.[1] Depending on the context I will refer to the beats in an NI-meter either as a series of Shorts and Longs (e.g., S-S-S-L), or in terms of their specific composition in N-cycle units (e.g., 2-2-2-3). Just as we have noted that I-meters are hierarchic gestalts, so, too, are NI-meters. Thus, neither I-meters or NI-meters are additive or multiplicative; these are terms that apply more to systems of rhythmic notation than to the structure of patterns of entrainment.

According to the WFCs, the 9-cycle may be partitioned into two other three-beat subcycles: 2-3-4 and its variant 3-2-4.[2] Neither of these represent beat-cycles (although they may of course represent a recurring pattern of surface durations). The question is why not? First, consider the 2-3-4 pattern, and an analogous case in an I-meter based on an 8-cycle, a 2-2-4 pattern (figs. 7.3a and 7.3b).

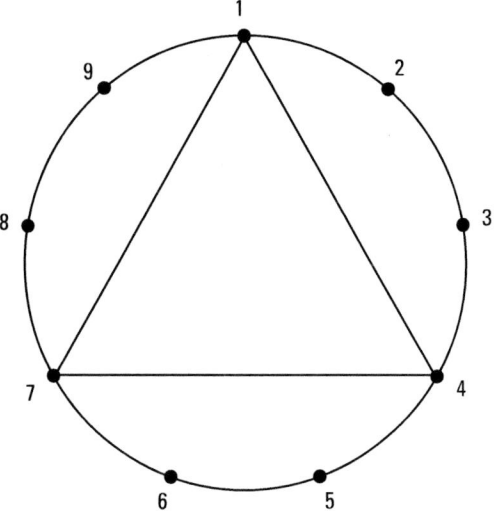

Figure 7.1.　9-cycle with 3-beat sub-cycle (isochronous beats).

In figure 7.3b, which could undergird a durational surface of two quarter-notes followed by a half, we would readily interpolate the "missing" beat over the course of the half note's duration. Missing is written in scare quotes here, because if the four-beat meter is well established, this beat is of course not missing at all. In the case of I-meters, one might simply justify this interpolation by the need to maintain isochrony on the beat level. This same sort of interpolative pro-

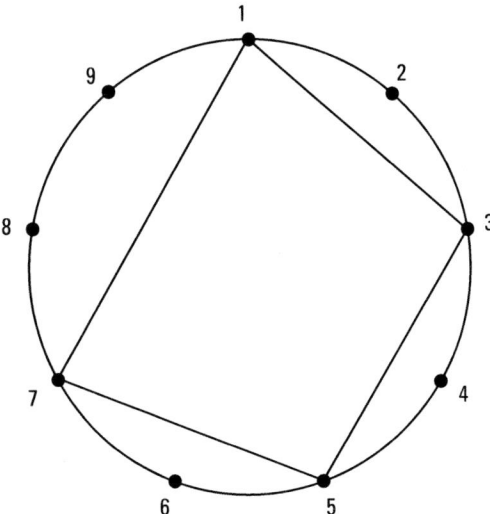

Figure 7.2.　9-cycle with 4-beat sub-cycle (non-isochronous 2-2-2-3 beat pattern).

Example 7.1. Opening measures of Brubeck's "Blue Rondo al a Turk" (2-2-2-3 beat cycle).

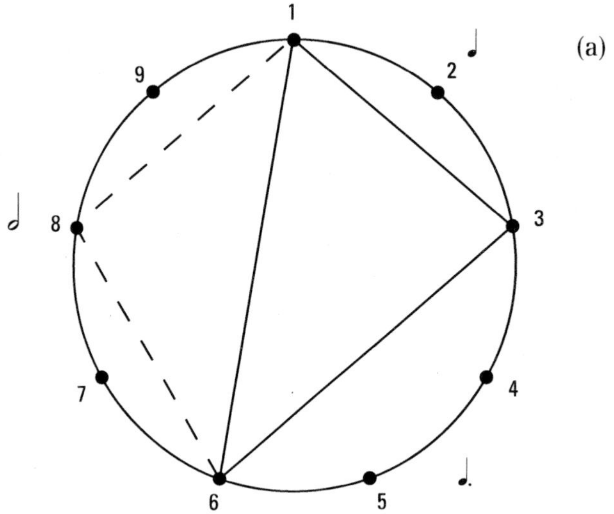

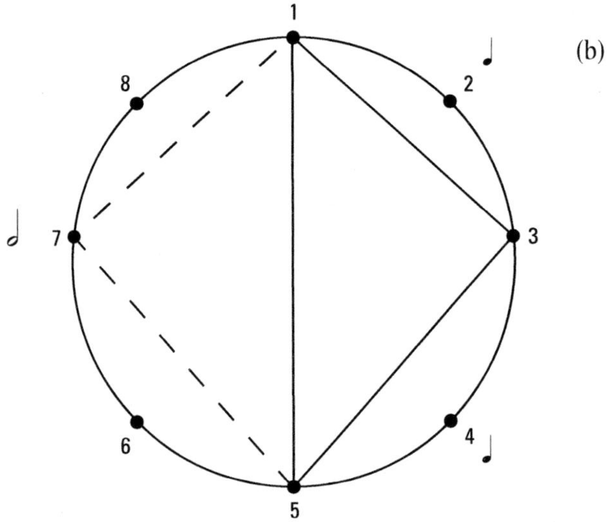

Figure 7.3. Beat interpolation in analogous NI-and I-metric contexts. (a) Beat interpolation with ♩♩♩ rhythmic pattern; (b) beat interpolation with ♩♩♩ rhythmic pattern.

cess of feeding forward an ongoing beat interval would not hold in the case of NI-meters, but one immediately gets a sense of how the two cases are related. What is needed is a principle of metric well-formedness that will hold for both I- and NI-meters and lead to similar interpolations in analogous cases.

Now it might be argued that the "4" segment in figure 7.3a would devolve to 2 + 2, as the duple unit heard earlier would or could somehow persist in the listener's perception and anticipation. Alternatively, one could specify that subcycles should only involve two or three elements; this is the approach taken by Lerdahl and Jackendoff whose MWFR 3 asserts, "At each metrical level, strong beats are spaced either two or three beats apart" (1983, p. 69). Although the "two or three" rule would work in many instances, there may be attentional patterns that involve patterns of four or five elements, such as a meter that is based on an N-cycle of 10 beats and has two subcycles of five beats each. Various ad hoc rules to permit these structures, but not others, would then be needed.

An Additional WFC: Maximal Evenness

To avoid such ad hoc rules, one may turn to a global constraint on the spacing of higher level time points relative to the N-cycle: the principle of *maximal evenness*. The principal of maximal evenness was developed in the study of scales and pitch-class sets (Clough & Douthett, 1991). A maximally even pattern is one in which a subset of *M*-elements are spaced as far apart as possible on a circle that represents their *N*-element superset. By definition, (a) the N-cycle is maximally even, and likewise (b) every cycle in an I-meter is maximally even. Because isochrony on every metric level is often stipulated as a metric well-formedness condition (see, e.g., Lerdahl & Jackendoff 1983, MWFR 4, p. 72), considerations of maximal evenness usually do not even arise for discussion. In his more recent work, Lerdahl acknowledges the relevance of maximal evenness as a metric well-formedness constraint, as he models metric well-formedness directly from scalar and tonal prototypes (2001, p. 286). Here I will explicitly include it as an additional WFC:

WFC 6 (version 1): All subcycles must be maximally even.

This is a first approximation of WFC 6; it will be further refined in the next chapter. As a result of maximal evenness, the number of beats in a measure depends on the cardinality of the N-cycle. In the case of a 9-cycle, if one has three beats, maximal evenness requires that those beats be spaced isochronously. Hence the 2-3-4 pattern fails WFC 6. Hearkening back to the five-beat meter mentioned earlier, maximal evenness allows for a five-beat pattern in the context of a 10-cycle, presuming each beat involves two units of subdivision.

In more general terms, given an N-cycle of cardinality N and a subcycle of cardinality M (by definition, M < N), if M is a factor of N, then the maximally even subcycle of cardinality M must be isochronous. If one has four beats in a 9-cycle, however, one cannot space them isochronously; the best one can do, vis-à-vis maximal evenness, is to space the four beats 2-2-2-3 subdivisions apart.[3] Maximal evenness ensures that a pattern of beats will be as evenly spaced as possible, given WFC 1. This reinforces the importance of the relationship between the beat and subdivision levels in a metric pattern. The presence of subdivision in an NI-meter lets us know that the beats, although uneven, are still as evenly spaced as possible. Knowing how many elements of subdivision each beat contains also lets us know that the beats are categorically equivalent (i.e., that there is only one specific beat-cycle IOI), or that they are not. It is also perhaps for this reason that in most music that involves an NI-meter, the N-cycle (i.e., the beat subdivision) tends to be phenomenally and continuously present, providing a constant underpinning for the uneven beats.

Maximal evenness leads us to consider another parallel with constraints on scale structure. Balzano (1980) noted that a scale is *coherent* if all of its seconds are smaller than all of its thirds, all of its thirds are smaller than its fourths, and so forth. Rahn (1991) refines this notion of coherence by developing the concepts of *difference, ambiguity,* and *contradiction* to explain certain features of well-formed scales and scale systems (see also Carey 2000). Keep in mind that there are two ways to account for melodic intervals in Western music, either (a) as a kind of absolute value expressed in terms of semitones, or (b) as intervals relative to some scale. So, for example, we can describe the interval C–E in the context of the C major scale as a third, as it is composed of two steps of the scale, C→D and D→E. Rahn notes that in many scales (and not just Western scales) there are *generic* intervals as well as different *specific* interval sizes. Yet there is more to it than just the conventions by which we designate various varieties of generic intervals such as major versus minor thirds.

Rahn explains his special notion of *difference* this way: "In the diatonic collection, C–E and D–F have single generic size of two scale degrees (insofar as they are so-called 'thirds'), but they have different specific sizes: four semitones for C–E and three semitones for D–F" (1991, p. 35). Note that difference here is yoked to the particular intervallic structure of the scale, and hence what counts as a step in the scale. When one has more than one variety of step, there are going to be different varieties of skips.

Ambiguity is related to difference. In the distinction between F–B and B–F in a diatonic collection, both have the same specific size (six semitones), but different generic sizes, three and four scale degrees, as the first is an augmented fourth while the second a diminished fifth. It is because the scale steps involve different specific sizes the tritone can be measured in two different ways, depending on the direction of the scale. *Contradiction* is a more severe discrepancy between specific and generic intervals. Rahn gives the example of a scale made of the following tones: C, D♯, E, F, G♭, A, B. Of this scale, he notes that here "D♯–F is smaller than G♭–A in terms of semitones, but D♯–F is bigger than G♭–A in terms of scale degrees" (1991, p. 36). Thus a contradiction involves two intervals, one of which is larger in terms of scale degrees than another, but smaller in terms of semitones.

The nominal isochrony of the N-cycle allows it to define the specific intervals of any and all generic intervals that form higher level metric periodicities. In the case of I-meters, where all levels involve isochronous periodicities, all of the generic intervals such as beats, measures, and so on comprise one and the same number of specific intervals. All beats are made up of the same number and kind of subdivisions, all measures contain the same number and kind of beats, and so forth. As a result, in graphs of I-meters the subcycles all display rotational symmetry with respect to the N-cycle, forming isosceles triangles, squares, regular pentagons, and so forth. As the N-cycle must be isochronous, it is analogous to the chromatic scale relative to diatonic subsets of the total chromatic (this has obvious parallels to the different levels of the "basic tonal space" proposed by Lerdahl, 2001). Hence beat intervals are analogous to steps of a scale. Unlike scales, however, and to avoid confusion between beats and beat subdivisions, WFC 5 requires that a *metric step* involve at least two chromatic units on the N-cycle. I-meters are like scales with only one specific step interval such as the whole tone scale. NI-meters, by contrast, are like scales with two specific step intervals such as the pentatonic (but *not* the diatonic scale).

The combination of WFC 1 (N-cycle isochrony), plus WFC 6 (maximal evenness) and WFC 5 ensures that meters (and especially NI-meters) will not contain ambiguities and contradictions. Returning to the 2-3-4 pattern, if we were to consider both the "2" and the "4" to be beats, we would then have the situation where doubling the "2" unit, which putatively would create a higher level metric structure, instead creates a unit equal to another beat span. Another way, a binary subdivision of the longest beat creates two units that are equal to the shortest beat ($4 \div 2$). Thus, the specific beat intervals "2" and "4" give rise to an ambiguity.

Maximal evenness in the beat-cycle has implications for symmetry at higher levels of metrical structure when the beat-cycle is composed of four or more beats. That is, beat-cycles of cardinality ≥ 4 constrain the way in which the metric cycle as a whole may be partitioned into two *half-measures*, and the half-measures themselves may be examined in terms of their maximal evenness. Thus, if the cardinality of the N-cycle is even, then a *perfect half measure* is one half of the N-cycle, and will involve $N \div 2$ elements. If an N-cycle is odd, then the best possible half measures involve $(N - 1) \div 2$ and $[(N - 1) \div 2] + 1$ elements, respectively. For example, if $N = 13$, then the maximally even half measures involve 6 and 7 elements, respectively.[4]

Perceptual Motivations for Maximal Evenness

Maximal evenness ensures that a pattern of beats (or any other level of metrical structure) will avoid differences, ambiguities, and contradictions, which are all problems for a well-formed metrical hierarchy. More important, perhaps, there is also a perceptual motivation for maximal evenness. First, maximal evenness ensures that even when IOIs of a subcycle are of categorically different durations, they will still fall within the same approximate temporal range. Second, maximally even meters give rise to optimal allocations of attentional energy.

Let us use an empty N-cycle to define a span of time or temporal window (fig. 7.4). Now suppose that four events will occur within this span of time; the events may or may not be isochronously timed. Knowing only this—that four events will occur within a certain span of time—what would be the best possible allocation of our attentional energy? We can indicate various allocations by the placement of dots on the N-cycle. In figure 7.4b, we expect four events, but our attention is clustered in one temporal region of the cycle. Although this might be optimal in a few cases where the pattern of event onsets is always similarly clustered, for the most part, this attentional allocation will cause us to miss more than we might catch. For our attentional expectations involve a tradeoff between when things have happened in the past versus when we expect them to happen in the future. A purely stimulus-driven attentional mechanism, while effective when confronted with slavishly regular rhythmic patterns, leaves us ill equipped to deal with rhythmic novelty, both musical and nonmusical. In figure 7.4c, attentional peaks are spread evenly throughout the window, signifying that we are listening for four events at more or less equal intervals within the time span defined by the cycle. Even if those events should cluster, this distribution of attention makes it likely that at least some of them will be given a relatively high level of attention because they will occur on or about an attentional peak. Moreover, in maintaining the maximally even attentional pattern, we also are prepared to attend to events at other locations in the cycle if and when they occur.

Metric regularity thus makes us better prepared for rhythmic variety. Maximally even attentional patterns make good perceptual sense even when the events in the environment are not perfectly regular, as it provides the best attentional net to catch a given number of events per unit of time.

Why Are Most NI Beats in a 2:3 Ratio?

NI-meters, by definition, involve two or more specific classes of a generic *beat-class*, the metric analog to the notion of interval class in the previous discussion of scale theory. In various musics that use NI-meters, most involve short and long beats composed, respectively, of two versus three subdivision elements, although occasionally a three versus four relationship may occur. A consideration

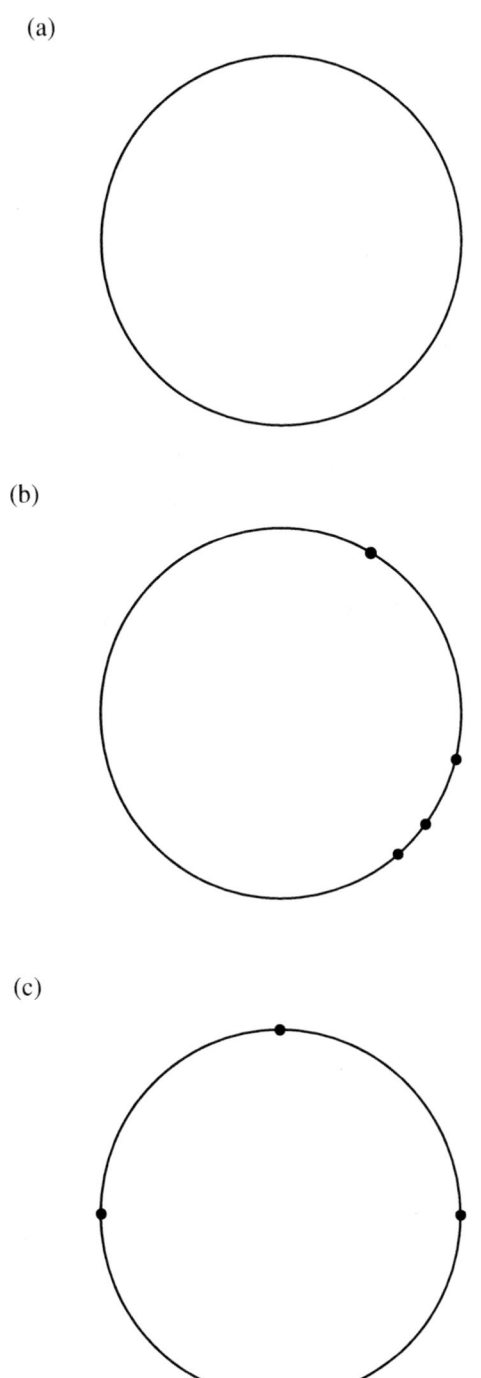

Figure 7.4. Distributions of attentional peaks within a metric cycle. (a) Empty N-cycle; (b) A poor allocation of attentional energy; (c) A much better allocation of attentional energy.

of some of the basic timing constraints on beat-to-beat relationships will show why NI beats tend not to involve nonadjacent integer ratios, and hence why 2:3 and 3:4 beat relationships are prevalent.[5]

First, if one speaks of a pair of NI beats with a particular relationship, such as 4:5, this presumes that a lower level of subdivision is also salient, for such subdivisions define the sense of "4" versus "5." For all practical purposes a beat cannot involve more than seven to nine subdivision units. Given the typical range in which subdivisions occur (between the 100 ms floor for N-cycle IOIs to about 300 ms), as the number of subdivisions per beat increases the beats themselves simply get too long. Moreover, if one wanted to have a long beat composed of seven to nine subdivisions, it is imperative that the listener *not* interpolate an intervening level. For example, if one wants to have a beat that is based on an octuplet and at a tempo where the N-cycle IOI is 150 ms, the surface rhythm must scrupulously avoid any cues that would lead the listener to hear the pattern in shorter IOIs such as 4 + 4 (note here that the fours will be at 600 ms, that is, near the center of the range of maximal pulse salience). Even in the absence of any cues from the musical surface, it is still possible that the listener may interpolate an intervening level due to subjective rhythmization. Moreover, such octuplet beats will be 1200 ms long—getting near the edge of the range for beat perception. Even a sextuplet with a similar N-cycle IOI would be 900 ms. Indeed, it is telling that the practical limit for subdivision in Western musical practice is the sextuplet.[6]

In cases where the ratio between the S–L beats is of the form $J:J + 1$ (where J is a positive integer), this ratio rapidly approximates a 1:1 relationship as J increases. At all but the slowest tempos, any $J:J + 1$ pair of beats beyond a 4:5 ratio is apt to sound like a nominally isochronous pair of beats with some rubato or expressive variation; in such cases the $J:J + 1$ relationship may only be apparent if every subdivision is phenomenally present in the musical texture. And if the tempo is slow enough to make the 4:5 ratio salient, for example where IOIs on the N-cycle are ≥ 150 ms, the listener is apt to interpolate an intervening level of metric articulations, creating a 2-2-2-3 or 2-2-3-2 pattern—in other words, decomposing the fours and fives into twos and threes. Conversely, as the tempo increases, the IOIs of the N-cycle may go beyond the lower perceptual limit for intervals on the N-cycle, rendering the 4:5 ratio meaningless. For example, one could not really speak of a 4:5 relationship in which the absolute values of the beats were 260 ms and 325 ms, as this would require that the N-cycle be comprised of 65 ms IOIs, which is well beneath the 100 ms metric floor.

By contrast, if the relationship between an S–L pair involves a ratio between nonadjacent integers, of the form $J:J + N$ (where $1 < N < J$), as the non-adjacency grows the value of J approaches the value of N. Thus if $J \approx N$, then it becomes likely that the putative L will decompose into two Ss. For example, if one posits a 4:7 relationship, $J = 4$ and $N = 3$ (i.e., J and N are roughly commensurate), it is likely that the 7 will decompose into 4 + 3. While we still have two beat-classes, they are of the relationship 4:3.

Finally, when the S−L pair involves a ratio of the form J:J + N, in which N ≥ J problems of ambiguity or contradiction arise. To avoid contradiction, we can stipulate that for a well-formed pair of beat-classes N cannot be > J. When confronted with a surface pattern in which J = N, the "L" will decompose into J + J and the result is an I-meter. For example, if the S:L ratio between surface durations is 3:6, the 6 will split into 3 + 3. When confronted with a surface pattern where N > J, the "L" will decompose into J and N-J. For example, if the S:L beat ratio is supposedly 2:5, the 5 will decompose to 2 + 3. Once again, we have two beat-classes, here 2:3. Note also that in those cases where the beat relationship J:J + N where N > 1, and given the upper limit on beat length (J + N ≤ 9), as one does the arithmetic one sees how the decomposition of the long beat (J + N) yields either a single specific beat-class (an I-meter) or a pair of beat-classes of the form J:J + 1.

The 1:1 and 1:2 ratios stake out limiting conditions on S−L relationships for beats in NI-meters. Moreover, as one takes both combinatoric properties and perceptual limits into account, we see why NI beats tend toward 2:3 or 3:4 ratios. For with a 2:3 or 3:4 relationship, both short and long beats are of the same order of magnitude in duration, categorically distinct, and are not hemmed in by perceptual limits on subdivision or overall beat duration.

The 100 ms floor for the N-cycle is also a reason why one rarely finds metric patterns with more than two specific beat-classes. Recall that earlier we saw in the 2-3-4 pattern (fig. 7.3a) that there is an ambiguity involving the shortest versus longest beats, as a binary subdivision of the longest beat (4) creates two units that are equal to the shortest beat (2). If the pattern of Short−Medium− Long beats is instead based on a 3:4:5 or a 4:5:6 relationship this ambiguity does not arise, but other problems emerge instead. When one has three specific beat-classes, in all but the fastest tempos the duration of the L of the S−M−L triple quickly goes over the absolute limit on beat length. For example, if the N-cycle IOI is ≈ 200 ms, a 4:5:6 set of beat-classes involves absolute values of 800, 1000, and 1200 ms for the respective beats. The longest interval here, 1200 ms, is twice the value of the center of the range of maximal pulse salience, and just as in the octuplet described earlier, there is a natural tendency for the listener to divide it into two shorter beats of 600 ms each (i.e., 3-3). This decomposition redefines the beat-classes into a 3:4:5 relationship.

It is clear, then, that establishing a meter with three specific beat-classes is a perceptually difficult task, as various constraints lead one to reduce the three beat-classes to two. This is also true for SDs (Repp, Windsor, & Desain, 2002). It also seems clear that if one would have three specific beat-classes, they would tend to fall into 3:4:5 or 4:5:6 relationships in order to avoid ambiguities and contradictions between the shortest and longest beat-classes. Moreover, the L of each of these S–M–L sets would have to have a high degree of rhythmic integrity, marked by the coherence of the rhythmic surface, in order to prevent it from decomposing to shorter units. And all of this is only possible at relatively rapid tempos, for as the N-cycle IOI increases, there is a natural tendency for the beat IOI to subdivide, with a concomitant shift of the sense of beat to a lower level. When this happens, each putative beat-class will decompose into smaller beat-classes.

NI-meters and Tempo

Like I-meters, NI-meters may be differentiated according to metrical type and tempo-metrical type, as defined in chapter 4. Indeed, NI-meters may be especially sensitive to tempo effects in the formation of their beat-cycles and higher subcycles. Table 7.1 shows the timing relationships among NI-beats (here, just the 2:3 ratio) at various tempos. First, unlike table 2.5, here there is no clear alignment between thresholds on the N-cycle and beat-cycles; thus there are no obvious transition zones from one tempo-metrical type to another. Nonetheless three ranges are roughly evident in table 7.1: (a) where N-cycle IOIs are less than 150 ms and hence both L and S beats fall below the 500–700 ms range; (b) where N-cycle IOIs are between 150–250 ms and Ls fall within the 500–700 ms range; and (c) N-cycle IOIs are > 250 ms, and the Ss fall within the 500–700 ms range. This suggests that there may be at least three tempo-metrical types for NI-meters, and that these exist independent of the particular cardinality of the N-cycle, number of subcycles over and above the beat-cycle, and so forth.

At the very shortest IOIs (N-cycle IOI = 100 ms), Ls and Ss fall on different sides of the 250 ms threshold. As the IOI on the N-cycle moves above 125 ms, the L and S beats both move above 250 ms. Thus there is a very narrow range in which the 250 ms threshold might be exploited. However, at such rapid tempos

Table 7.1 Timing Relationships Among NI-Beats at Various Tempos

N-cycle IOI	Long Beat Interval	Short Beat Interval
100 ms	300 ms	200 ms
125 ms	375 ms	250 ms
150 ms	450 ms	300 ms
175 ms	**525 ms**	350 ms
200 ms	**600 ms**	400 ms
225 ms	**675 ms**	450 ms
250 ms	750 ms	**500 ms**
275 ms	825 ms	**550 ms**
300 ms	900 ms	**600 ms**
350 ms	1050 ms	**700 ms**
400 ms	1200 ms	800 ms

it is likely that a higher level of meter might be heard as the tactus, especially if that level is isochronous, as $S + L = 500$ ms, and a 300 ms–200 ms L–S might then be heard as a binary subdivision of an expressively varied beat. Conversely, when IOIs on the N-cycle are greater than 400 ms, the durations of both L and S beats moves beyond the range of maximal pulse salience (>1200 and >800 ms, respectively). Therefore, NI-meters may be more strongly constrained by tempo than I-meters.

Accent in NI-meters

In an I-meter all the beats are (nominally) isochronous, so there is no need to relate downbeat location to beat length. In the case of NI-meters, however, orientation relative to the downbeat does make a difference for distinguishing, for example, S–S–S–L organization from S–S–L–S. There are four distinct permutations or phase relationships for this pattern relative to the downbeat that are analogous to what music theorists often refer to as *rotations* of a series of pitches or pitch-classes in discussions of melodic patterns. An example of four possible rotations of pitches would be:

C–D–E–D ⇒ D–E–D–C ⇒ E–D–C–D ⇒ D–C–D–E

one more rotation takes us back to C–D–E–D. As S–S–S–L, S–S–L–S, S–L–S–S, and L–S–S–S represent four ways of aurally construing this NI-cycle, these phase rotations should be regarded as metrically distinct variants of a given beat-cycle; they are NI subtypes of the basic S–S–S–L metrical type.

This example points out an important difference between I-meters and NI-meters with regard to the phenomenal manifestation of the downbeat within a meter. In his discussion of the basic metric aspects of the Gahu rhythm in the music of the Ewe-speaking people of West Africa, the drummer and ethnographer David Locke contrasts western and African senses of metric accent. Having shown how one may notate a basic Gahu pattern in $\frac{4}{4}$ time, as it is based on a 16-cycle, he cautions the reader:

> Clearly, Gahu seems to be in $\frac{4}{4}$ time, but this time signature implies inappropriate conventions of accentuation—strongest accent to the first stress [beat], secondary accent to the third stress. . . . It might be closer to an African conception to regard the beats as . . . an unaccented organizational device, for in fact each beat receives an equal accent. (1998, p. 19)

He calls this kind of accentless meter "African $\frac{4}{4}$" (p. 23). Importantly, Locke also observes that the gankogui (bell) pattern—additively 3-3-4-4-2—functions as the "rhythmic core" of Gahu drumming (p. 15; see also Nketia 1974, pp. 131–2;

Example 7.2.   The "time" of Gahu, after Locke (1998), p. 36.

Rahn 1987, p. 25; Arom 1991, p. 211). Example 7.2 is a score of the three central percussion parts in Gahu drumming: the gankogui, axtase (gourd rattle), and kaganu (high-pitched drum); collectively, they perform what Locke terms "the time" of Gahu music (1998, p. 36). Locke also shows that the bell pattern can take any of five different phase positions against the backdrop of African $\frac{4}{4}$. In example 7.3 the placement of the note onsets remains constant within the notated measure, but Locke uses different beamings to show how the metrical (phase) relationships change (p. 23). Elsewhere, he makes clear that this is not

Example 7.3.   Metric variants of the gankogui time line, after Locke (1998), p. 23.

just a matter of grouping, but how one's subjective sense of the downbeat and on-beat versus off-beat location can shift over the course of listening to a Gahu performance. This is another instance of the gestalt flip noted in chapter 5.

Leaving aside until chapter 8 Locke's claim that the gankogui pattern involves three beat-classes, what is important here is that (a) the Gankogui pattern involves a series of NI beats, and (b) those intervals are not symmetrically distributed within the N-cycle. In terms of the arrangement of S–M–L beat-classes, the following sequence will emerge in performance:

...M M L L S M M L L S M M L L S M M L L S M M L L S...

It is clear that there is a five element sequence, *even if one is not certain which element stands as the downbeat.* As Arom notes, "When the sounds in a rhythmic figure [cycle] have no accents and do not contrast in tone colour, segmentation is only possible with respect to alternating durations, i.e., on the basis of how the values resemble or differ from each other, and how they are grouped together" (1991, p. 236). And this is what happens here: one does not require any accent such as dynamic stress, timbral or textural differentiation, and so on, to discern that this series is based on the repetition of a five-beat pattern. Consider the analogous case in the context of an I meter, where there is but a single specific beat-class (B):

...B B B B B B B B B B B B B B B B B B B B B B B B B...

Without accent, there is not any sense of metric differentiation, and hence there isn't any inherent beat-cycle *at all*, although subjective rhythmization can, and most likely will, give rise to a subjective sense of meter. It is precisely because "the time" of Gahu may involve a NI series of beats that Locke can speak of accentless meter in a meaningful way.

Of course, when we listen to the Gankogui, we latch on to the sequence in a certain way and we subjectively metricize the pattern according to one of the five possible orientations given in example 7.3 and thus construe one of the note onsets as the downbeat. While I may latch on to the first M, you may latch on to the first L, and so in listening we each have our own sense of the metric organization. Note, however, that you and I are more in agreement than disagreement. We have the same overall measure period and pattern of beat periods; we differ only with respect to the subjective sense of accent at each beat. I hasten to add that this also may cause us to disagree as to the motional and affective qualities of the rhythmic gesture because we place different events at the center of the ebb and flow of the musical motion. Suffice to say, however, that patterns like the Gahu rhythm, although metrically equivocal, have enough temporal structure to allow listeners to respond to them in similar if not identical fashion. Moreover, their responses will be close enough to permit coordinated rhythmic behaviors like clapping, dancing, or speaking even though their individual metric frameworks will have different downbeat orientations.

In contrast, if there is a symmetrical distribution of Longs and Shorts within a cycle—for example, a 14-cycle that contains a 2-2-3-2-2-3 beat-cycle—one cannot recover the cardinality of the N-cycle from pattern of Ls and Ss:

...S S L S S L S S L S S L S S L S S L S S L S S L...

All that is apparent here is the S–S–L repetition. In order for the higher level patterning to emerge, if it is not simply the result of a higher level of subjective rhythmization, the same sorts of expressive differentiation of timing and dynamics that occurs in the context of I-meters must be applied to the units in this pattern.

Summary and Discussion

The WFCs developed in chapter 5 allow for NI-meters. With the addition of WFC 6, the principle of maximal evenness, we have a set of well-formedness criteria that should apply to most of the world's musics. These WFCs render moot the distinction between additive and multiplicative meters, terms that are better understood as applying to limitations on systems of metric notation rather than meter itself.

The principle of maximal evenness creates symmetrical or quasi-symmetrical relationships among elements in a spatially arrayed or ordered set. In the temporal domain, maximal evenness emerges as a global constraint on metric pattern formation that is cashed out in different ways in isochronous and non-isochronous contexts, but that fulfills similar formal and perceptual functions in both. From a perceptual standpoint, maximal evenness ensures that our attentional energies are effectively distributed over the time course of a metric cycle, so that we can efficiently attend to and differentiate among events of varying salience.

In borrowing concepts such as maximal evenness from scale theory, we must be cognizant of both the similarities and differences between the pitch and time domains. Metric beats are not perfect analogs to scale steps, for as we have seen meters are subject to additional constraints that keep subdivision and beat levels distinct. Another important difference between scales and meters is that while we can speak of skips relative to a scale, we do not have similar skips relative to a meter. This is because, once established, a meter keeps cycling through and articulating each beat whether or not the beats are articulated by the unfolding rhythmic surface. While we readily interpolate beats into a long surface duration, we do not analogously interpolate missing tones into a melodic skip.

As in the case of I-meters, various temporal thresholds, especially the 100 ms and 250 ms thresholds, have a strong influence on the range of possible NI-metrical types. When one crunches the numbers with various beat-class ratios at different tempos, it becomes rapidly apparent that these limits on subdivision may be the principal reason why non-isochronous beats tend toward a 2:3 ratio. Likewise, changes in tempo give rise to different NI tempo-metrical types, given the ways various thresholds align for subdivisions, beats, and measures. These thresholds do not display the same sorts of systematic interaction as in the context of I-meters, but in some ways NI-meters may be more constrained by tempo, especially tempo ceilings (i.e., they cannot get very slow) than I-meters.

While I-meters and NI-meters obey a common set of WFCs, and are similarly constrained by other perceptual and cognitive thresholds, there are a number of important differences in the ways they operate. Although I-meters may or may not have a level of subdivision phenomenally present in the musical texture, NI-meters almost always do. There are several reasons for this. First, this means that the categorical difference between long versus short beats is explicitly articulated in the musical texture. This prevents confusion, as the absolute values of these uneven beats are often similar to the timings that occur when I-meters are performed with a high degree of rubato, or with phrase-final lengthening of durations. Second, NI-meters typically involve faster tempos, and so having subdivisions perking away in the musical texture is a means of pumping energy into the resonating system of entrainment (see Large & London 2002).

NI-meters also give rise to a different sense of accentuation than I-meters, as an NI-meter will have a number of distinct rotations of its beat pattern. A series of NI-beats immediately presents a higher level periodicity to the listener without necessarily distinguishing one of them as a downbeat. It is for this reason that some have spoken of accentless meters, or that African and other non-Western meters function in an inherently different way from Western musical meter. Temperley (2001, p. 289) has cautioned against overstating the differences between western and non-Western meters, and I heartily agree. The kinds of downbeat reorientations noted earlier may occur in some Western musical contexts, from minimalist pieces to popular dance music. As we will see in chapter 9, expressive variations seem to function in a manner quite similar to the patterning of long and short beats in NI-meters. Likewise, once a listener has latched onto a particular metrical orientation in a NI-meter, he or she then *does* hear a sense of accent, the accent that accrues to the head of the metric cycle as it is heard. This is quite akin to the sense of accent that accrues to particular beats in the case of subjective rhythmization.

8

NI-Meters in Theory and Practice

N-cycle Cardinality and Beat-cycle Formation

The N-cycle is a powerful constraint on metric structure and complexity. It is especially useful to talk about how a beat-cycle relates to its N-cycle, given the well-formedness constraints developed in chapters 4 and 7. This chapter systematically examines all of the beat patterns that can occur within N-cycles of particular cardinalities. In the case of I-meters, almost any nested set of subcycles can describe the organization of an attentional pattern, provided their IOIs fall within certain temporal limits. In the case of NI meters, however, we must also take the relationship between the various specific classes of beat and higher intervals, as well as their particular ordering, into account.

For starters, if the N-cycle is not the beat-cycle but a level of subdivision, then the cardinality of the N-cycle must be ≥ 4, as each beat will involve at minimum two units of subdivision and each measure will have at least two beats. The "next largest" I-meter will involve a 6-cycle, either a duple meter with triplet subdivision or a triple meter with duplet subdivision. The cardinality of the N-cycle in more complex I-meters increases multiplicatively, following the relationships diagrammed at the end of chapter 2. If N is even, the maximum number of beats any such N-cycle may contain is $N \div 2$, because each beat involves at least two intervals on the N-cycle. If N is odd, first recall that according to WFC 5 one cannot have beats that are equal to a unit of subdivision. As a result, in calculating the maximum number of beats an N-cycle can contain, one cannot have a remainder of a single unit of subdivision, and so the upper limit on the number of beats within an odd N-cycle is $(N - 1) \div 2$. In odd N-cycles such upper limit beat-cycles will necessarily be non-isochronous and of the form $(2\text{-}2\text{-}2 \ldots -3)$, that is, a string of short beats ending with a single long. In the following discussion I will presume that the N-cycle is the only level of subdivision present. It is of course possible to have several levels of subdivision, and in those cases it is not the N-cycle that acts as a constraint on beat-cycle formation but a subcycle above it.

When the cardinality of the N-cycle is a prime number >3, the beat-cycle must be non-isochronous, as primes cannot be divided into twos, threes, and so on. Here are a few examples:

5-cycle = 2-3
7-cycle = 2-2-3
11-cycle = (3-3)-3-2; (3-3)-2-3; (2-2-2)-3-2; (2-2-2)-2-3; 3-4-4
13-cycle = (3-3)-3-2-2; (3-3)-2-3-2; (2-2-2)-3-2-2; 3-3-3-4

Parentheses have been included to show similarities among various metrical types as well as to clarify some of the half-measure distinctions, for example, between (3-3)-3-2 and (3-3)-2-3. Note also that the lists for the 11- and 13-cycles are not exhaustive.

NI-meters may of course also be constructed in the context of nonprime N-cycles:

8-cycle = 3-3-2
9-cycle = 3-2-2-2;
10-cycle = 3-2-3-2
12-cycle = 3-3-2-2-2 or 2-3-2-3-2
16-cycle = 3-3-3-3-4; 3-2-3-3-2-3

In the following pages, every possible beat-cycle in the 8-, 12-, and 16-cycles will be discussed, followed by consideration of NI-meters in a number of other N-cycles, including some with prime values of N. For the nonprime NI-meters, many examples will be drawn from various African musics, based on the work of Rahn (1987), Nketia (1963a, 1963b, 1974), Arom (1991), and Agawu (1995). These examples are often in the form of *time-lines*, that is, rhythmic patterns that are commonly performed by various instruments in African drum ensembles and in African song accompaniments. Very often these patterns function as a rhythmic ostinato for an extended stretch of a musical performance, and we will be concerned with the metric implications of each.

Examples and discussions of NI-meters based on prime N-cycles will be drawn from Indian music, based on the work of Morris (2000, 2001). The use of both Western and non-Western musical examples is primarily illustrative, and while one aim is to show the broad applicability of the metric theory developed here, this is by no means an exhaustive treatment of NI-meters in non-Western musics.

NI Meters and NI Rhythms

As with considerations of maximal evenness, scale theory provides a useful approach regarding the relationship between NI-meters and the rhythmic surfaces that give rise to them. Rahn (1991) discusses under- and overdetermined collections of pitches and their relation to a well-formed scale. We can see how rhythmic figures whose metric construal requires the interpolation of a beat are analogous to a gapped collection of pitches, such as:

C _ E F G A B

In a tonal context, the question posed by this collection is, "What diatonic scale is most likely the 'parent' collection (superset) for these six pitch classes?" The answer will relate the gapped collection to a particular diatonic scale and tonal center. To find the answer, Rahn applies the criteria for well-formed scales that minimize ambiguities and contradictions, such that the best scalar context for this pitch-class collection is the one that leads to the most well-formed scale. Table 8.1 lists the possible candidates to fill the gap between C and E; the winner is D because it creates a scale without ambiguities or contradictions (see Rahn 1991, p. 45, fig. 6). Note that Db and D♯ create manifold problems of scalar well-formedness. Rahn also shows how in some cases there may be more than one solution to the problem of a gapped collection, as in the example of the C D E F G A _ collection, in which the interpolation of either B♮ or B♭ will create a well-formed diatonic scale.

Beat interpolation involves similar considerations of metric well-formedness, as the listener relates the pattern of surface durations to a meter that minimizes, if not wholly eliminates, ambiguity. Recall that unlike scales, meters cannot tolerate any contradiction (in the special sense defined by Rahn et. al), as contradiction

Table 8.1. Possible Scales that fill the Gap Between C and E

Gapped collection	Filled collection	Resulting contradictions (c) and ambiguities (a)
C _ E F G A B	C D E F G A B	none
	C Db E F G A B	B- **Db** vs. F-G, G-A, and A-B (a);
		B- **Db** vs. **Db** -E (c)
		Db-E vs. E-G and A-C (a);
		A- **Db** vs. **Db** -F, F-A, and G-B (a);
		Db -G vs. G- **Db** (a) etc.
	C D# E F G A B	**D#**-F vs. F-G, G-A, and A-B (a)
		D#-F vs. C-**D#** (c)
		C-**D#** vs. E-G and A-C (a)
		D#-G vs. F-A, G-B, and B-**D#** (a)
		A-**D#** vs. **D#**-A (a) etc.

gives rise to a fatal confusion of metric levels. As we saw in chapters 3 and 7, some instances of metrically gapped rhythms are unproblematic:

𝅗𝅥 𝅘𝅥𝅘𝅥 𝅗𝅥 𝅘𝅥𝅘𝅥 (etc).

When performed at a tempo of a quarter note = 600 ms (100 bpm), the half note is obviously too long to be a beat, and the interpolation of the missing beat allows for the formation of an isochronous four-beat cycle. A different organizational problem occurs in the following pattern:

𝅘𝅥 𝅘𝅥 𝅘𝅥𝅮𝅘𝅥𝅮𝅘𝅥𝅮𝅘𝅥𝅮 𝅘𝅥 𝅘𝅥𝅮𝅘𝅥𝅮𝅘𝅥𝅮 (etc.)

If the quarter notes have an IOI around 600 ms, they are clearly beats, although we are initially unsure of their subdivision. The duple subdivision becomes quickly obvious in the second half of the nascent measure, and soon thereafter the 8-cycle and four-beat subcycle becomes apparent and readily established in the listener's mind. Note here the importance of the absolute values of the IOIs. As various metric levels tend to occur in certain ranges (e.g., subdivisions are ≤ 250 ms, beats are maximally salient around 600 ms, etc.), and as there is a reasonably small number of tempo-metrical types, the task of recognizing the meter is not too onerous.

As a general rule, the interpolation of a missing element of a subcycle in the context of an I-meter is unproblematic. However, NI-meters present thornier problems of interpolation and indeed, these examples present problems that are more analogous to Rahn's underdetermined pitch-class collections. Figure 8.1 gives the metrical analysis of a 𝅘𝅥𝅘𝅥𝅘𝅥𝅗𝅥 durational sequence (see Rahn 1987). As I will discuss the interaction between a durational surface and the listener's metric construal of it, durations will be represented in musical notation: 𝅘𝅥𝅮, 𝅘𝅥, 𝅘𝅥., 𝅗𝅥, and so forth, while metric patterns will be represented with numbers (e.g., 2-2-2-3 for a four beat NI-meter). For convenience, the eighth-note duration will be used as the base IOI for the N-cycle, and thus in most instances the beat-cycle will involve quarter and dotted quarter notes.

In figure 8.1, let us presume that the underlying subdivisions of each duration are present, so that we clearly have a 12-cycle (the importance of having the N-cycle explicitly articulated will become apparent over the course of our discussion). Let us also presume, for now, that each onset in the figure articulates a beat. Under these conditions this pattern must be related to an NI-meter; the problem is where to place the interpolated beat within the span of the half note duration. Note the difference between this problem and the interpolation discussed with figure 7.3. There the question was whether or not one should interpolate a beat at all. Here the question is not whether but where to interpolate a beat. The answer is straight forward. In order to avoid an ambiguity between

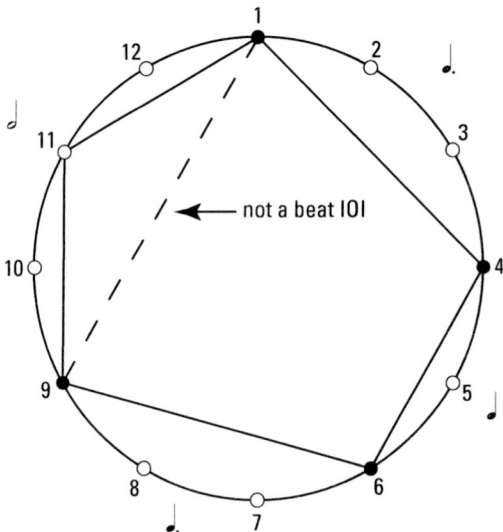

Figure 8.1. "Gapped" ♩ ♩♩ ♩ durational pattern relative to 5-beat NI meter (3-2-3-2-2 beat cycle).

beat IOIs, this pattern must be heard in the context of a 3-2-3-2-2 NI-meter (the interpolated beat is marked with an open dot on the N-cycle in fig. 8.1). Here WFC 5 also comes into play, as any other partitioning of the half note would give rise to a 3-1 or 1-3 beat relationship that WFC 5 prohibits.

The opposite problem occurs when we have "too many notes," such that we are not sure of the location of a beat-level articulation relative to overabundant subdivision. Rahn's "chromatic collections" (pitch-class collections with more than seven notes) are analogous to these metrically overdetermined rhythmic surfaces. Rahn gives the following example (1991, p. 50):

C D E F F♯ G A B

If one tries to treat this as an eight note scale, there are numerous ambiguities and contradictions, given the successive half-steps E–F–F♯–G. However, if instead one fits these pitch-classes into the context of a seven-note diatonic scale, then either F or F♯—but not both—can be regarded as a proper scale degree. The result is a scale form with far fewer ambiguities and contradictions, either C Major or G Major. Thus, this eight-tone set relates to one of two diatonic collections, in each instance with one extra chromatic tone. As Rahn notes, "In general, if eight-tone collections consisting of the diatonic collection and what might be termed an extra note are analyzed in terms of seven rather than eight scale degrees, then simpler, more elegant interpretations arise in every case, save the symmetrical 8-26 collection" (1991, p. 49).[1] Rahn's main point here is to show the special status of the seven-tone diatonic scale in the context of the 12-note chromatic set, and why this scale or similar scales tend to crop up in various musical cultures (see also Carey 1996, 2000; Clough & Douthett 1991; Clough, Cuciurean, & Douthett 1997; Cohn 1997). For our purposes, we can see how the process by which Rahn determines chromatic notes is analogous to the problems of determining the organization of a NI-beat cycle in complex rhythmic surfaces.

There are a number of possible NI-meter construals of a ♩♩♪♩♩♪ pattern. The eighth notes cannot be beats, given WFC 5 as well as (we shall presume) their relatively short duration. But it is not clear whether the eighths should be regarded as always off the beat, always on the beat, or a combination of both. Figure 8.2 shows the ways in which the pattern can be related to various NI beat-cycles (different paths are indicated by solid versus dashed lines on the beat-cycle). First, note that beat articulations at N-cycle locations 5 and 6 and 10 and 11 are mutually exclusive: if five is a beat onset, then six cannot also be a beat onset, and vice versa. Note also that in all cycles, N-cycle location 8 articulates a beat and thus is a good location for the half-measure.

Table 8.2 lists the four possible paths that create well-formed beat-cycles in accordance with WFCs 2 and 3. Paths 1, 3, and 4 involve various rotations of the 2-2-3-2-3 NI beat-cycle. In path 1, both eighths occur on the beat. In path 4, both eighths are off the beat. In path 3, the first eighth occurs off the beat, while the second occurs on the beat. Path 2 involves an alignment with a different beat-cycle, one with both long beats adjacent (2-2-3-3-2). As will be discussed later, this beat pattern involves a hierarchic manifestation of maximal evenness. Moreover, the presence of a perfectly symmetrical half-measure may well affect the

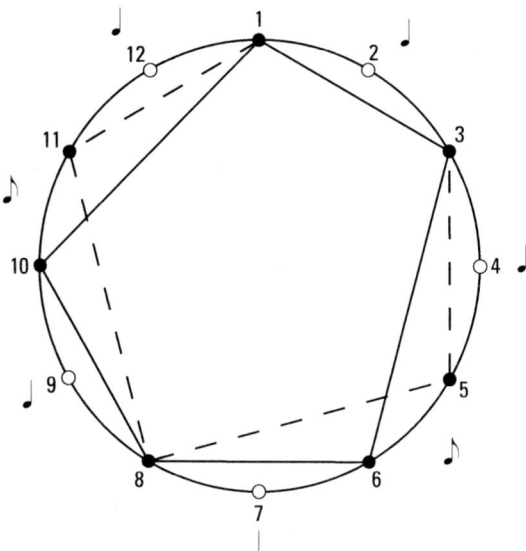

Figure 8.2.   Possible NI-meter construals of ♩♩♪♩♩♪♩ durational pattern.

Table 8.2. Four Paths Creating Well-Formed Beat Cycles

Path	Time-points on the N-cycle	Metric IOI pattern
1.	1-3-5-8-10	2-2-3-2-3
2.	1-3-5-8-11	2-2-3-3-2
3.	1-3-6-8-10	2-3-2-2-3
4.	1-3-6-8-11	2-3-2-3-2

listener's sense of the downbeat, so that rather than the 2-2-3-3-2 rotation, one will more likely hear the pattern relative to 2-2-2-3-3 or 3-3-2-2-2 rotations.

Figure 8.3 diagrams the ♩♩♩♪♩♩♪ rotation of the pattern from figure 8.2; note that this is analogous to shifting the barline one quarter note backward as if what had been an anacrustic note is now regarded as downbeat. As is indicated in figure 8.3, this rotation of the pattern fits very well into a six-beat I-meter. The first four notes align perfectly with the beats and with the half-measure. Interestingly, *none* of the remaining notes align with any beat articulations; instead, we have a syncopated figure. This syncopation is not enough to displace the established sense of beat or bar, and, indeed, in hearing the pattern as syncopated both the isochronous beat-cycle and the symmetrical half-measures emerge.

If, in the case of figures such as ♩♩♪♩♩♪♩, not every note onset articulates a beat, perhaps this is also true for patterns such as ♩♩♩♩. What if we throw out the initial assumption that each articulation in a metrically gapped rhythmic figure must occur on a beat? To return to the tonal analog, it would be akin to entertaining the possibility that a gapped collection may contain some chromaticism.

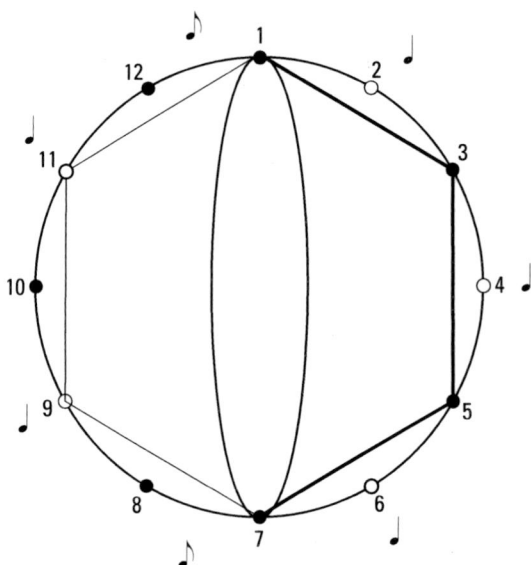

Figure 8.3. ♩♩♪♩♩♪ rotation of the pattern from figure 8.2, relative to I-meter ($\frac{6}{4}$).

For example, the five note collection C _ E F# G _ B contains two gaps. The most natural scalar context for this five note collection is G major, given the presence of F# and the absence of any other accidentals, notably C# or B♭. But if we regard the F# as a chromatic note, we can then construe the collection to have an additional gap: C _ E _ F# G _ B, that is, in terms of a C major scale. In this way, we relate the five-tone collection to another well-formed scale, construing one tone as outside of the C major pitch class set. And indeed, this is what we do in many instances.[2]

Returning to the ♩.♩♩♩ pattern, figure 8.4 gives this pattern relative to a four beat I-meter, that is, $\frac{12}{8}$ time. Here the first dotted quarter matches the first beat IOI, but then surface rhythm steadfastly fails to align in any consistent way with the rest of the measure. This is not to say that one cannot hear this figure in the context of $\frac{12}{8}$, but it would need to be well established (and possibly supported in other parts of the musical texture) in order for the listener to do so. It would be difficult, if not impossible for the listener to either initially construe this pattern relative to $\frac{12}{8}$ in this fashion, or maintain it absent other metrical cues. Figure 8.5a relates this pattern to $\frac{6}{4}$. Interestingly, it may be easier for the listener to hear the figure this way, even though the second and third notes of the pattern are articulated off the beat. In part this may be because of the simpler relation between beats and offbeats in the context of binary versus triplet subdivision, but it may also be because of the way the half note at the end of the rhythm meshes with two of the component subcycles of the meter. A musical instantiation of this pattern is given in example 8.1. As with figure 8.4, to hear this pattern in the context of $\frac{6}{4}$ requires cues for the beat-cycle in other parts of the musical texture, but to initially construe or maintain $\frac{6}{4}$ would seem to take less attentional

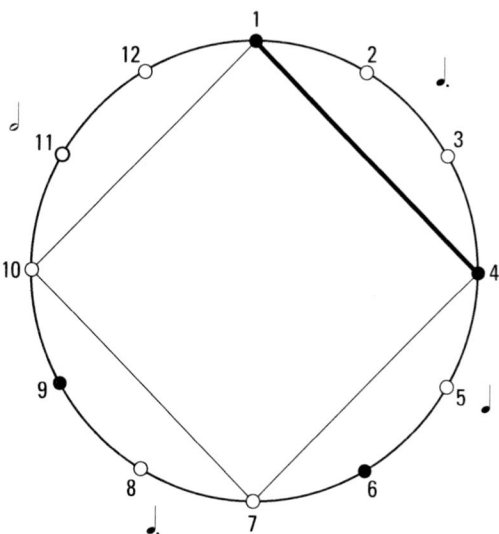

Figure 8.4.   Gapped ♩.♩♩♩ pattern relative to 12/8.

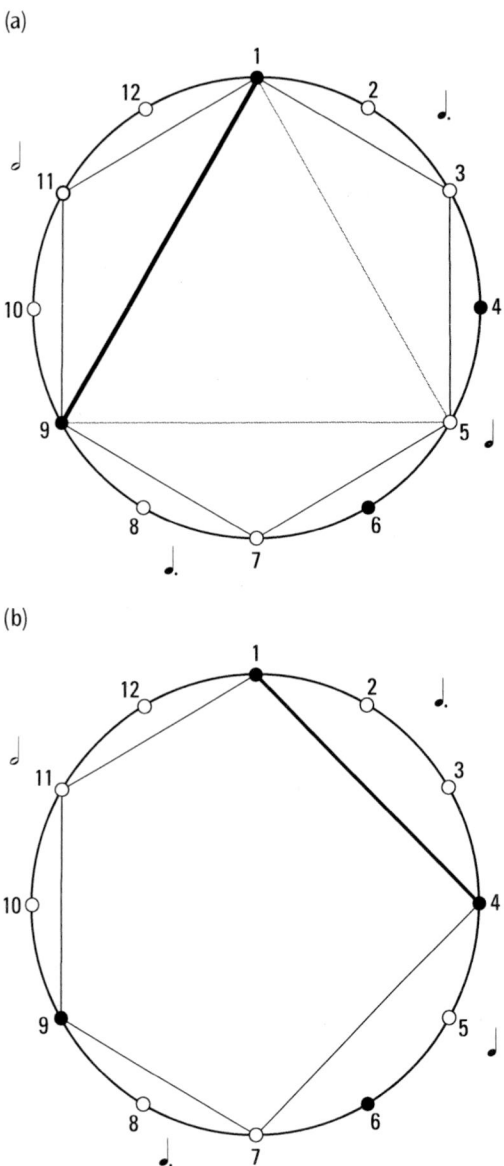

Figure 8.5. Two more metric contexts for the gapped ♩♩♩♩ pattern. (a) Relative to ⁶₄; (b) relative to 5-beat NI meter (3-3-2-2-2 beat cycle).

effort than ¹²₈. Finally, figure 8.5b shows a possible alignment of the rhythmic pattern with a 3-3-2-2-2 NI-meter. In this case, the third note of the pattern would fall off the beat at time-point 7, and then the pattern would realign with articulation of the half note at time-point 9. Yet this is highly doubtful, for in NI-meters durational patterns, especially if they are repeated, strongly tend to articulate beat onsets. Even if the 3-3-2-2-2 meter had been well established, it

Example 8.1. Musical illustration of ♩♩♩♩ pattern in the context of ⁶₄ (composed by the author).

is quite likely that repetitions of the ♩♩♩♩ figure would give rise to a metric shift, that is, to the 3-2-3-2-2 beat-cycle.

The 8-cycle

Eight has one prime factor, 2 ($8 = 2^3$), and so the only I-meters it may contain will be duple; given their familiarity, I need not discuss them here. A three beat meter in the context of the eight-cycle will be non-isochronous and will involve rotations of a 3-3-2 pattern. This beat-cycle occurs in many musical styles, from Indian music (it is one of the 35 sūlādi tālas of Karnatak music theory) to Latin jazz, where it is sometimes called a habanera or danza pattern. The danza figure is typically played on cowbell, claves, or another high-pitched percussion instrument. It is also found in bassline ostinatos, as in example 8.2a . The habanera proper, including the well-known example in Bizet's *Carmen*, is an Afro-Cuban dance form, and its characteristic rhythm and bassline is given in example 8.2b. Note that the 3-3-2 grouping is latent in the habanera figure.

The 3-3-2 pattern often occurs in the context of an I-meter, as dotted quarter, dotted quarter, quarter note in ⁴₄, for example. Placing patterns such as example 8.2a in the context of ⁴₄ implies that (a) performers should count and listeners should entrain under an I-meter, and (b) one will hear the second note as syncopated. And indeed, this is often how this rhythm may be heard, especially

(a)

(b)

Example 8.2. Latin Jazz bassline/rhythm patterns. (a) "Habanera" or "Danza" pattern; (b) typical Afro-Cuban version of the "Habanera" pattern.

by performers who are reading it in $\frac{4}{4}$. However, it is also possible to hear the three-beat pattern without syncopation; as at times performers may use one metric framework while listeners use another. Rahn's list (1987) of NI rhythmic patterns found in sub-Saharan music includes all three rotations of the basic 3-3-2 pattern, although he found that the L–L–S version is more common than L–S–L or S–L–L.

Finally, there is the possibility of an NI two beat meter in the context of an 8-cycle, a 3-5 pattern, as illustrated in figure 8.6. Of course, this pattern may occur as a surface rhythm in the context of a three-beat, 3-3-2 meter (as per the dotted lines in the example), but that is not my concern here. Can this 3-5 pattern function as a two-beat NI meter? It is not maximally even, but as two Ss are > one L, this meter does not contain any ambiguities or contradictions. Rahn (1987), Nketia (1963, 1974), and Arom (1991) give no instances of this rhythm in the context of an 8-cycle. Arom does remark that in central African musical practice one often finds a half measure that is not maximally even, which he terms the principle of *rhythmic oddity*. Keeping in mind that the metric cycles and rhythmic patterns Arom discusses are all based on even N-cycles, he says that these [rhythmic] figures "are nevertheless so arranged that the segmentation *closest to the middle* will invariably yield two parts, each composed of an *odd* number of minimal values. . . . They follow a rule which may be expressed as 'half−1/half+1" (1991, p. 246). For an 8-cycle, this means that the half-measures will be 4 − 1 and 4 + 1, or 3 and 5. Yet tellingly, Arom's example for the eight-cycle is a 3-3-2 figure (1991, p. 246).

Nonetheless, the lack of specific examples of a 3-5 beat-cycle, as opposed to 3-5 half-measures, does not make this meter impossible; in listening to this pat-

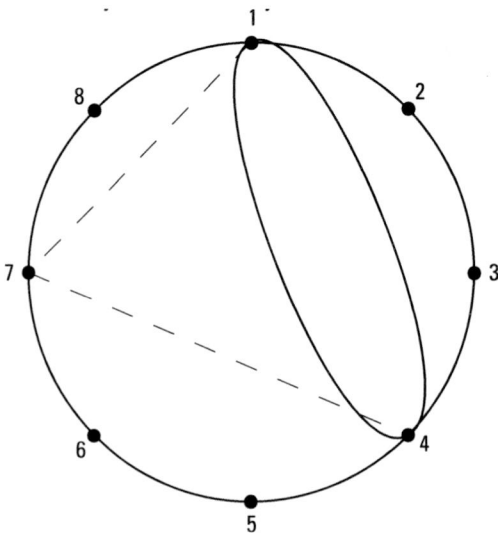

Figure 8.6.   8-cycle with 3+5 beat cycle.

tern at a variety of tempos, with and without a layer of subdivision explicitly present, hearing 3-5 as a beat-cycle did seem possible to me, at least in some contexts.[3] When I played the 3-5 pattern without any accompanying subdivision and over a wide range of tempos, I found it sounded like an expressively performed rhythm in a triple meter, for example, a quarter note pickup followed by a half note in the context of $\frac{3}{4}$. This was the case over a wide range of tempos. However, if the N-cycle articulations were explicitly present, there seemed to be a narrow range of tempos in which I could hear this as a two beat, S-L or L-S measure. If the IOIs on the N-cycle were much longer than 150 ms, the 5 decomposed to 3-2; this was manifest as a virtual articulation that separated the last two articulations of the N-cycle into a separate group, giving rise to a sense of the missing beat. Likewise, at very fast tempos, in which the N-cycle IOIs were shorter than 115 ms, the 3-5 sounded like a triplet subdivision figure as the underpinning articulations became a blur or trill. But within the 115–150 ms range, it seems possible (perhaps with special attentional effort) to hear a 3-5 two-beat pattern if the N-cycle articulations were explicitly present.

Thus, in a very particular musical context, in a critical tempo range, where the texture is metrically saturated, and in which the surface patterning is strongly implicative of the NI beats, it may be possible for a 3-5 two-beat meter to be heard. This means that in some contexts the well-formedness constraint based on maximal evenness may be relaxed. It is likely that the simplicity of this pattern—a mere two beats within in a N-cycle of relatively low cardinality—helps engender this meter, even though it is not maximally even. And while this meter may be possible, it clearly seems to be far less common, as its absence in the discussions and surveys of Rahn, Nketia, and Arom suggest.

The 12-cycle

Unlike the 8-cycle, the 12-cycle may be isochronously organized into duple or triple measures, as 12 has the prime factors $2^2 \times 3$. There are seven possible beat patterns in the 12-cycle; these are given in table 8.3.[4] The three-, four-, and six-beat I-meters do not require comment. The two-beat meters both involve beats

Table 8.3.   Possible Beat Patterns in the 12-Cycle

Beats	I vs. NI	Time Signature or NI pattern
2	I	$\frac{6}{8}$ w/fast sextuplets
2	NI	5+7 at very fast tempos
3	I	$\frac{3}{4}$, quadruplet subdivision
4	I	$\frac{12}{8}$, triplet subdivision
5	NI	2+2+3+2+3
5	NI	2+2+2+3+3
6	I	$\frac{6}{4}$, duplet subdivision

Example 8.3. African "Bell pattern" (based on 12-cycle), notated with and without rests.

that contain six or seven subdivisions and so they bump up against a tempo constraint. At all but the fastest tempos these beats will be exceedingly long, and as they get longer an intermediate level that would carry the tactus is almost certain to emerge. Moreover, the 5-7 pattern faces the same challenges as the 3-5 pattern discussed earlier. The 5-7 is another example of Arom's principle of rhythmic oddity and hence is not maximally even, but, in contrast to the 3-5, the 5-7 relationship more closely approximates the 1:1 beat ratio of a maximally even two-beat meter, which may make it more palatable. Given the constraints on subdivision and beat length, as well as the tendency for the 5s and 7s to decompose into shorter units, a 5-7 two-beat meter in the context of a 12-cycle is perhaps impossible.

The 2-2-3-2-3 formation is the bell pattern that occurs in many African musics. Example 8.3 shows how the bell pattern IOIs align with the series of notes and rests Nketia uses in many of his transcriptions; Example 8.4a and 8.4b show the bell pattern relative to two melodies (see Nketia 1963b, p. 88). As is common in these songs, a rest (literally, stopping the sound of the bell) is used to truncate the first part of the pattern, making the 7-5 half-measures quite plain. At Nketia's indicated tempo the N-cycle IOIs are ≈ 200 ms.

Example 8.5 is an Akan maiden song that uses a 2-2-2-3-3 pattern; at Nketia's indicated tempo the N-cycle IOIs are 170 ms (from Nketia 1963b, p. 132).

(a)

(b)

Example 8.4. Examples which use the Bell pattern, after Nketia (1963b), p. 88. (a) Akatape dance; (b) Akan dance.

| O | dwaa | B'ro | ni | baA | kwa | si | Den | te'ee | E | Bu | oo, | O |

Example 8.5. "Kawsi Dente" (Akan mainden song), after Nketia (1963b), p. 132.

Example 8.6, which uses the same metrical type but in the 3-3-2-2-2 rotation, may be more familiar to most readers; it is the opening measures of Bernstein's "America" again. I have included it to make the point that these sorts of NI-meters do occur in western music. Although Rahn does not list any instances of the 3-3-2-2-2 or 2-2-2-3-3 pattern, Nketia does give examples of both rotations in songs and in drumming and dance music. Tellingly, however, there are *no* examples of any other rotations of this metrical type. Likewise, only some rotations of the 2-2-3-2-3 beat-cycle seem to be used in African music. Table 8.4 lists the occurrences of those rotations in a number of sources. In the case of Arom, it is not always clear what rotation he is presenting; the entries in table 8.4 are my best inferences from Arom's text and examples. In some cases from Nketia, the musical examples involve ambiguous surface rhythms such as 2-2-1-2-3-2, and it is not clear if the 1 in these timelines goes with the previous or the following 2, giving rise to the "?" entries in the table. Of the five possible rotations of the 2-2-3-2-3 metrical type, the 2-2-3-2-3 rotation is by far the most common in these sources; 2-3-2-2-3 is also well represented. These two forms are explicitly noted by Nketia when he speaks of 5-7 and 7-5 partitions of the 12-cycle; his diagram is reproduced in example 8.7 (Nketia 1974, p. 129).[5] The relative absence of other rotations of the 2-2-3-2-3 metrical type may simply be a contingent fact of African musical style and practice, although it may relate to certain features of the those rotations. Here it will be helpful to note the location of the half-measure in each rotation with a vertical line. In the 2-2-3 | 2-3 and 2-3 | 2-2-3 rotations, each half-measure ends with a long beat; these long beats mark a cumulative duration that naturally gives rise to closure (see Narmour 1990, p. 11, pp. 105–12).[6] However, as the 3-2-2 | 3-2 rotation does occur, it would seem that event-to-event proximity becomes less salient when metric patterns are regarded as cyclical gestalts. About all that can be said regarding the preference for certain rotations is that the lack of any clear cases of the 2-3-2-3-2 pattern suggests that in any rotation, the Ls need to be distributed consistently at the beginning (3-2 | 3-2-2 or 3-2-2 | 3-2) or end (2-3 | 2-2-3 or 2-2-3 | 2-3) of each half-measure. In the case of the 2-3-2-3-2 pattern, the placement of L is in-

Example 8.6. Opening measures of Bernstein's "America."

Table 8.4. Rotations of the 2-2-3-2-3 Beat Cycle in Examples from Rahn (1987), Nketia (1963a, 1963b, 1974), and Arom (1985)

Source	22323	23232	32322	23223	32232
Rahn 1987	√ (lots)			√	√
Nketia 1963a	√	?	?		
Nketia 1963b	√				
Nketia 1974	√			√	
Arom 1985			√		√

herently inconsistent (either 2-3 | 2-3-2 or 2-3-2 | 3-2), which may make it less preferable as an entrainment pattern.

Both the 2-2-3 | 2-3 and 2-2-2 | 3-3 beat-cycles raise a number of interesting issues and problems for maximal evenness; cyclical diagrams of each metrical type are given in figure 8.7. In terms of their beat-cycles, the 2-2-3-2-3 pattern is maximally even while the 2-2-2 | 3-3 is not—in the latter, the long beats "clump" together. On the level of the half-measure, however, the situation is reversed (in the example, half-measures or potential half-measures are indicated with dashed lines). In figure 8.7a, it is clear that a half-measure within the 2-2-3-2-3 pattern cannot be maximally even. By contrast, in 8.7b we see how the 2-2-2 | 3-3 pattern does have maximally even half-measures. Both patterns are used in a wide variety of musics, and this means that WFC 6 must be modified in light of these observations. Originally I said that, by definition, both the N-cycle itself and regular meters are maximally even which led to the following constraint for NI meters:

WFC 6 (version 1): All subcycles must be maximally even.

Example 8.7. 7+5 and 5+7 partitions of the 12-cycle, after Nketia (1974), p. 129.

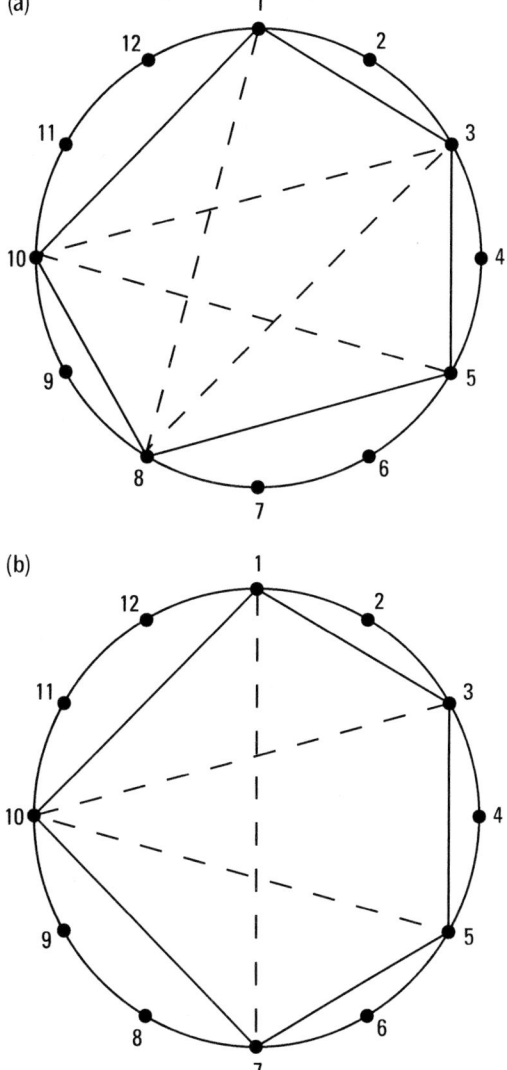

Figure 8.7. 5-beat subcycles in the 12-cycle; potential half-measures marked with dotted lines. (a) 2-2-3-2-3 cycle ("Bell Pattern"); (b) 2-2-2-3-3 cycle ("America").

Now we must take a broader view, and consider maximal evenness as it is hierarchically manifest, that is, not just maximal evenness on each individual subcycle but also for the meter as a whole. WFC 6 must be recast:

> WFC 6 (version 2): The meter as a whole must be as maximally even as possible. Individual subcycles need not be perfectly maximally even; they may deviate from maximal evenness provided this deviation does not produce ambiguities or contradictions on the non-maximally even subcycle.

In its initial formulation, WFC 6 required strict maximal evenness as a way of insuring that a meter would involve no ambiguities or contradictions. As the complexity of a meter increases, measured both in terms of increased cardinality of its N-cycle as well as number of subcycles, maximal evenness cannot always be maintained on every subcycle, nor can ambiguities be wholly eliminated. Indeed, as seen in the case of the 2-2-3-2-3 cycle, maximal evenness on the beat-cycle precludes maximal evenness on the half-measure level and vice versa. Although we still require a more or less even distribution of attentional energy throughout the metric cycle, it becomes clear that we do not (and indeed cannot) require perfect maximal evenness.

We also see that more complex meters do admit some ambiguity. In the 2-2-2 | 3-3 beat-cycle, while the half-measures have the same specific time interval (6 N-cycle IOIs), each contains a different number of beats given the different specific beat sizes, that is, three S versus two L. This is the metric analog to the tritone in the diatonic scale, as the tritone can be regarded as an augmented fourth or a diminished fifth, depending on one's orientation in the scale.[7] It is perhaps because of this mild ambiguity that the 2-2-2-3-3 pattern is at times characterized as a mixed or modulating meter, that is, as a measure of $\frac{3}{4}$, which is then followed by $\frac{6}{8}$, then $\frac{3}{4}$, then $\frac{6}{8}$, and so on. In part this may be due to the conventions of Western music notation (additive time signatures being a fairly recent invention), but it may also be due to the instability created by its ambiguity. Moreover, the clumping of the Ss and Ls in the 2-2-2-3-3 pattern can aid and abet a sense of metric shifting by giving rise to a fluctuating sense of tempo, or perhaps a quirky kind of rubato. Nonetheless, as the 12-cycle emerges over time it stabilizes and makes the five-beat subcycle clear.

The 16-cycle

Like the 8-cycle, the 16-cycle has only 2 as its prime factor ($16 = 2^4$), and so once again here we will find only duple I-meters. As the cardinality of the N-cycle increases, so does the number of possible beat cycles it may contain. Table 8.5 lists all of the possible beat cycles for the 16-cycle. The two-beat cycle consisting of two "octuplets" is included here, again more as a theoretical possibility than as a meter that actually occurs in musical practice. For not only must the IOIs on the N-cycle be very rapid (≤150 ms) lest the beats get too long. In addition, the internal organization of each octuplet must not decompose into any intermediate levels of structure that could shift the listener's perception of the tactus to a four- or eight-beat cycle.

The three-beat cycles are both non-isochronous, but rather different in structure and affect. The 4-6-6 pattern is analogous to the 2-3-3 pattern in the 8-cycle, and indeed is akin to the 2-3-3 pattern that has an additional layer of subdivisions, as in example 8.8. The 5-5-6 pattern is very close to a perfect

Table 8.5. Possible Beat Cycles for the 16-cycle

Beats	I vs. NI	Typical meter/subdivision
(2)	I	$\frac{2}{2}$ w/"Octuplets"
3	NI	4-6-6 (akin to 233 pattern in 8-cycle)
3	NI	5-5-6 (almost perfect $\frac{1}{3}$ measures)
4	I	$\frac{4}{4}$ w/running 16ths
4	NI	4-3-4-5
4	NI	4-4-3-5 (?)
5	NI	3-3-3-3-4
6	NI	3-3-2 | 3-3-2 (ME; only 3 rotations)
6	NI	3-2-3 | 2-3-3 (not ME)
7	NI	3222 | 322 (ME)
7	NI	323 | 2222 (not ME, but perfect $\frac{1}{2}$ meas)
8	I	$\frac{8}{4}$ or $\frac{8}{8}$

"third-measure." Note that the 5-5-6 is maximally even relative to the 16-cycle, while the 4-6-6 is maximally even relative to an eight element subcycle; this is another reason that an eight element subcycle may be perceptually salient in the latter case. In both the 4-6-6 and the 5-5-6 patterns tempo is critical; if the N-cycle IOIs are longer than 150 ms these beats are apt to decompose into twos and threes, with a corresponding shift of tactus. I have not found any cases of 5-5-6 cycle; this may be because of the problems of the 5:6 ratio between the two beat classes discussed earlier.

Non-isochronous four-beat cycles in the 16-cycle would have to involve three specific beat intervals with the relationships 3:4:5. As noted earlier, there are various difficulties and constraints for a meter with three specific beat intervals. Not withstand those problems, with this set of beat intervals two metrical types are theoretically possible, 4-3-4-5 and 4-4-3-5. In the former, a symmetrical half-measure is not possible, although its beat cycle is closer to being maximally even than the 4-4-3-5. Conversely, the 4-4-3-5 pattern does permit a perfect half-measure. These two metrical types raise the same issues regarding the hierarchical manifestation of maximal evenness as did the 2-2-2-3-3 versus 2-3-2-2-3

(a)

(b)

Example 8.8. Musical illustration of related three beat patterns in 8- and 16-cycles. (a) 2-3-3 pattern; (b) 4-6-6 pattern (ornamented version of 2-3-3).

types in the context of the 12-cycle. Table 8.5 contains one five-beat pattern. The 3-3-3-3-4 cycle is maximally even and it is also possible to partition it into half-measures following Arom's principle of rhythmic oddity: 3-3-3 | 3-4 (i.e., $(8 + 1) | (8 - 1) = 9 | 7$). This is the most maximally even half-measure possible in a five-beat cycle.

Although these three-, four-, and five-beat NI meters meet all of our well-formedness criteria, I have unfortunately found no clear examples of their use in musical practice, although the 3-3-3-3-4 pattern is related to the 3-3-3-3-2-2 pattern discussed later. However, other five element patterns are found in various musical contexts. As noted earlier, Locke (1998) gives a ♩♩♩♩♩ pattern as the basic bell (gankogui) timeline in Gahu, and Rahn (1983) includes ♩♩♩♩♩ and ♩♩♩♩♩. These are not beat cycles, however, but only surface rhythms, as these patterns face numerous and ultimately insurmountable problems of metric well-formedness. As they involve three beat classes in a 2:3:4 relationship, problems of ambiguity are present from the start. Moreover, these patterns are decidedly not maximally even. Rahn (1983) notes that the ♩♩♩♩♩ pattern is typically present along with a ♩♩♩♩♩♩♩ pattern in another part of the rhythmic texture. Thus, to avoid ambiguity and to enhance maximal evenness, in most cases the surface fours will decompose into a pair of twos, so that these five element patterns may be heard in the context of a non-isochronous seven beat meter.[8]

Alternatively, some of these five-element patterns also may be heard in the context of an eight-beat I meter. In the ♩♩♩♩♩ and ♩♩♩♩♩ patterns, the clustering of the two dotted quarters means that the other intervals will strongly reinforce the I-meter as shown in figure 8.8. In both figures 8.8a and 8.8b, there is only one time-point, time-point 4, in which the note onsets in each pattern do not align with a beat, and that articulation may readily be regarded as a syncope in each.

To fit six beats into a 16-cycle under our well-formedness constraints requires four long and two short beats—four 3s and two 2s. There is one maximally even six-beat cycle in the 16-cycle, given in figure 8.9a , and it is nicely symmetrical. Its three rotations (3-3-2 | 3-3-2, 3-2-3 | 3-2-3, and 2-3-3 | 2-3-3) all form perfect half-measures; notice that because of its symmetry there are only three distinct rotations of this beat cycle, rather than six. This beat pattern is not explicitly mentioned in discussions of 16-cycles in the sources cited earlier, as it can be accounted for in terms of an 8-cycle that is repeated; this is something akin to non-Western hypermeter, although few if any sources on non-Western music would use that term. Figures 8.9b and 8.9c give the two other possible arrangements of four threes and two twos in the 16-cycle; neither are maximally even. Figure 8.9b has six distinct rotations, some of which have perfect half-measures (3-2-3 | 2-3-3), while others do not (2-3-2 | 3-3-3). Once again we find a hierarchic manifestation of maximal evenness, or a lack of it.

Here we also may see how rotation may affect the emergence of a metrical type, as those rotations that involve perfect half-measures, compensating for the lack of maximal evenness on the beat level, may be preferable metric frame-

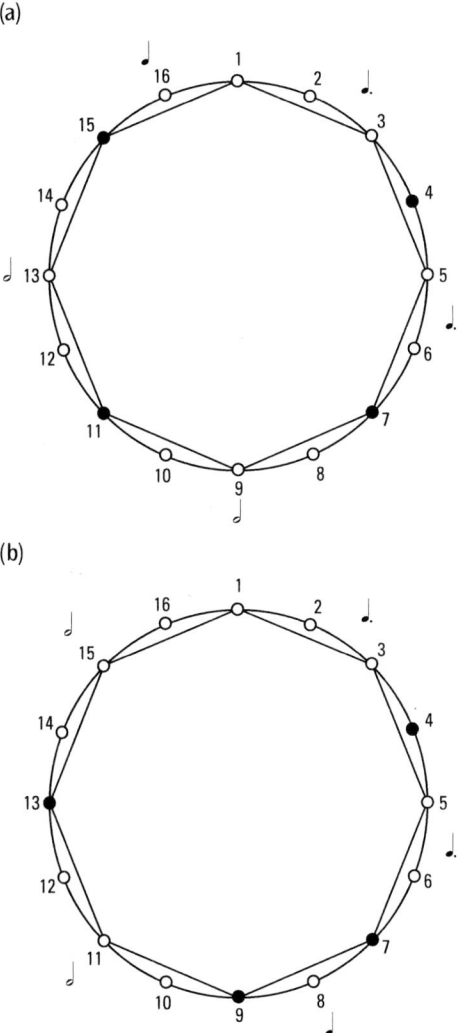

(a)

(b)

Figure 8.8. 5-element durational patterns relative to a 16-cycle. (a) ♩♩♩♩♩ relative to an 8-beat I-meter; (b) ♩.♩♩♩♩ relative to an 8-beat I-meter.

works. By contrast, the 3-3-3-3-2-2 pattern given in figure 8.9c, while not maximally even, occurs as surface rhythm in numerous musical contexts, from Irish reels to Brazilian bossa novas. There are two possible metric contexts into which this pattern may be placed. The first is an I-meter with both eight and four element subcycles. If the I-meter has been established before the 3-3-3-3-2-2 pattern appears, it is relatively easy to hear the nonisochronous IOIs as a series of syncopations or hemiolas against the I-meter, a figure that metrically "rights itself" at the end of each measure. The second context, noted earlier, involves a 3-3-3-3-4 metric framework. In this latter case we have a five-beat NI-metric

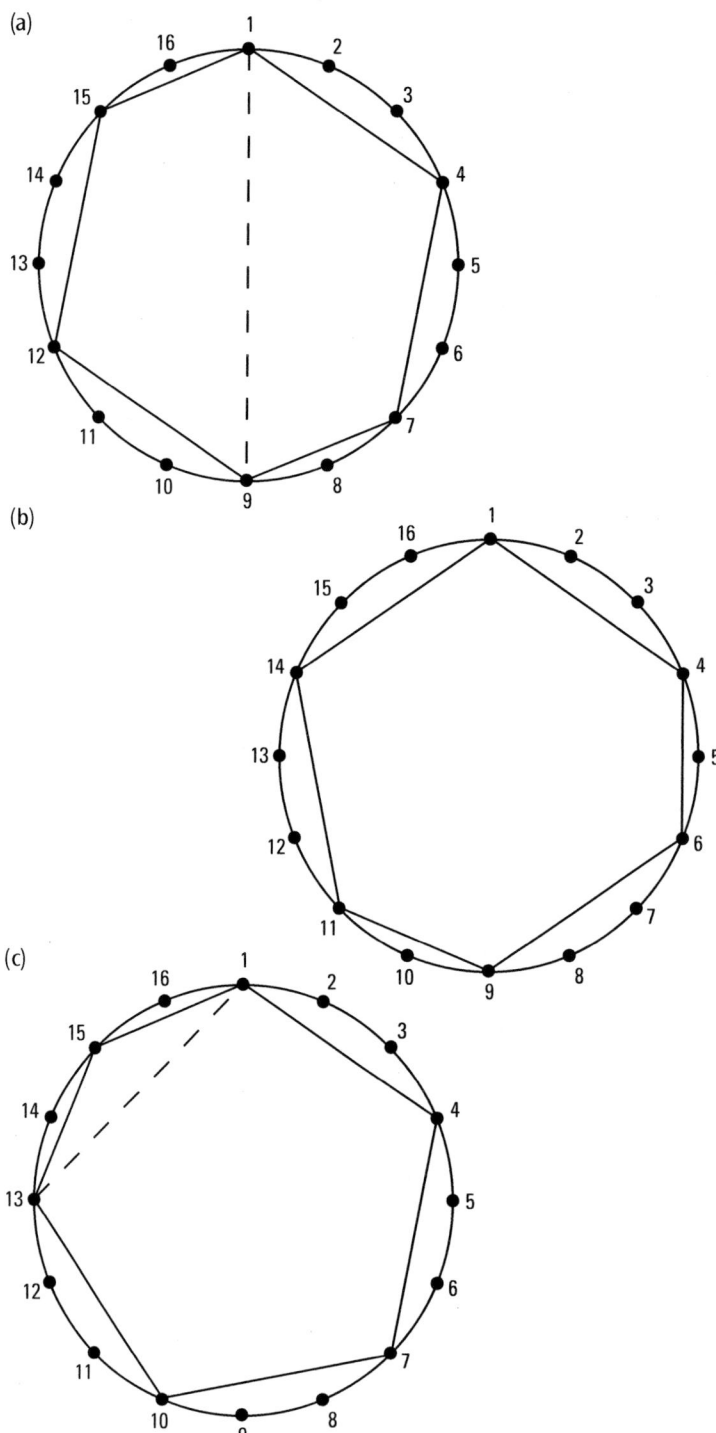

Figure 8.9.   6-beat patterns in the 16-cycle. (a) 3-3-2-3-3-2 beat cycle ("double Habanera" meter); (b) 3-2-3-2-3-3 beat cycle; (c) 3-3-3-3-2-2 (3-3-3-3-4) beat cycle.

framework, and the two 2s that occur at the end of the 3-3-3-3-2-2 pattern are subdivisions of the 4. And indeed, the last "2" in this pattern often sounds less like a beat and more like a subdivision-level anacrusis to the following downbeat. This may be related to the absolute value of the IOIs on the N-cycle and beat-cycle levels. If the N-cycle IOIs are in the $100-150$ ms range, then twos are $200-300$ ms, while 3s and 4s are $300-450$ ms and $400-600$ ms, respectively. · Note how this tends to put the 2s on one side of the 250 ms threshold and the 3s and 4s on the other.

Finally, there are the seven-beat cycles, 3-2-2 | 3-2-2-2 and 3-2-3 | 2-2-2-2. Once again the hierarchical manifestation of maximal evenness comes into play, as the former cycle is maximally even on the beat cycle but not on the half-measure cycle, whereas the latter is not maximally even on the beat cycle but does involve a perfect half-measure. Notice also that in the 3-2-3 | 2-2-2-2 cycle some rotations will involve the maximally even half-measure and others cannot.

NI-meters in N-cycles of Other Cardinalities

In India there are two distinct musical practices, the northern Hindustani and the southern Karnatak (also spelled Carnatic). Both have rich theoretical traditions as well, and they provide many examples and discussions of NI-meters. In India, players and listeners are taught the practice of "counting tāla," that is, establishing and then maintaining a cyclical pattern of time against which the unfolding musical performance may be understood. One counts tāla by claps, waves of the hand (for "silent" beats), and on one's fingers, and so every articulation of a particular N-cycle is given a bodily action or gesture. Yet one must be cautious in moving from tāla practice to ascriptions of meter. As Powers and Widdess note:

> It is a fundamental principle of tāla that while the pattern of irregularly spaced audible claps marks the rotation [i.e., not rotation as a kind of permutation as defined earlier] of the cycle, it does not necessarily indicate the rhythmic organization of musical events within the timespan so measured. Not only is there an almost infinite variety of possible rhythmic configurations within any tāla cycle, but a tāla may even be characterized by an internal rhythm [i.e., meter] different from that implied by the clap-pattern. Thus the Karnatak Jhampā tāla, in its most common misrā variety, is structured by claps as 7-1-2, but the characteristic rhythm of melodies in this tāla is (2-3)-(2-3). . . . Similar internal rhythms operate to a greater or lesser extent in many of the other tālas of both the Karnatak and Hindustani systems. (2001, p. 198)

Tāla patterns thus do not necessarily give a direct representation of the metric entrainment that circumscribes and guides them. Indeed, in Jhampā tāla the characteristic surface rhythm of the melodies may be a better indication of the metric underpinnings of the music than the tāla itself.

In Hindustani music, tālas are often associated with particular drum patterns, knows as thekās, such that tālas "tend now to be defined and identified in terms of their thekā, rather than by the Karnatak practice emphasizing clap patterns" (Powers & Widdess 2001, p. 200). In both Karnatak and Hindustani music there are many tala patterns that clearly relate to I-meters, such as the 4-4-4-4 Tintāl pattern in Hindustani music (the most common Hindustani tala) and Ādi tala 4-2-2 in Karnatak music. In these cases the beat cycle in relation to the N-cycle is fairly clear; in Tintāl each 4 may constitute a beat, while in Ādi tāla the 2 serves as the beat unit, for example.

In Hindustani practice there are a few prime N-cycles: 7-cycles (Rūpak tāla, Tīvra tāla) and an 11-cycle (Savārī tāla). As one would expect, the former involve 3-2-2 beat patterns. The latter is more interesting. According to our WFCs, only a limited number of beat-cycles are possible in the 11-cycle; these are given in figure 8.10. A four-beat cycle will involve a 3-3-3-2 pattern (or one of its other rotations), while a five-beat cycle will involve a 2-2-2-2-3 pattern. Yet Savārī tāla involves the following clap pattern 2-(2)-2-(2)-1½-1½ (here the parentheses indicate a wave rather than a clap). Although it is clear that this means that one should place a clap between two articulations on the 11-cycle, the metric implications of this are murkier. On the one hand, it could mean that in Savārī tāla the true cardinality of the N-cycle is 22, and the counting pattern represents the following beat pattern 4-4-4-4-3-3. On the other hand, it could mean that this is really a five-beat pattern of the 2-2-2-2-3 variety, and that the last clap is in some sense a submetrical event, although one would want to determine the actual timings of these claps (and of the music which is playing while the claps occur). One does well to keep Powers and Widdess's comments on the Jhampā tāla in mind here, and note that the clapping behavior is not necessarily directly indicative of the listener's metric entrainment.

Most Hindustani tālas, however, involve nonprime N-cycles, especially even N-cycles, as there is a strong tendency for symmetrical half-measures. Thus, for example, there is Jhaptāl, based on a 10-cycle arranged (2-3)-(2-3), and Dīpcandī, based on a 14-cycle arranged (3-4)-(3-4).

In Karnatak theory there are a number of prime N-cycles, although in practice most are nonprime. In the Sūlādi system of tālas, variants of the Dhruva tāla involve a number of prime N-cycles. The Dhruva tāla is of the form X-2-X-X, where X is the laghu, an element whose length can involve 3, 4, 5, 7, or 9 units, although 4 is the most common value. This gives rise to N-cycles of cardinality 11, 14, 17, 23, and 29. Where the laghu = 3, the result is an unproblematic beat-cycle of the form 3-2-3-3. For the other tālas there are serious violations of maximal evenness. Moreover, when the laghu is 5, 7, or 9, the short "beat" is considerably less than one half the duration of the long, and thus serious con-

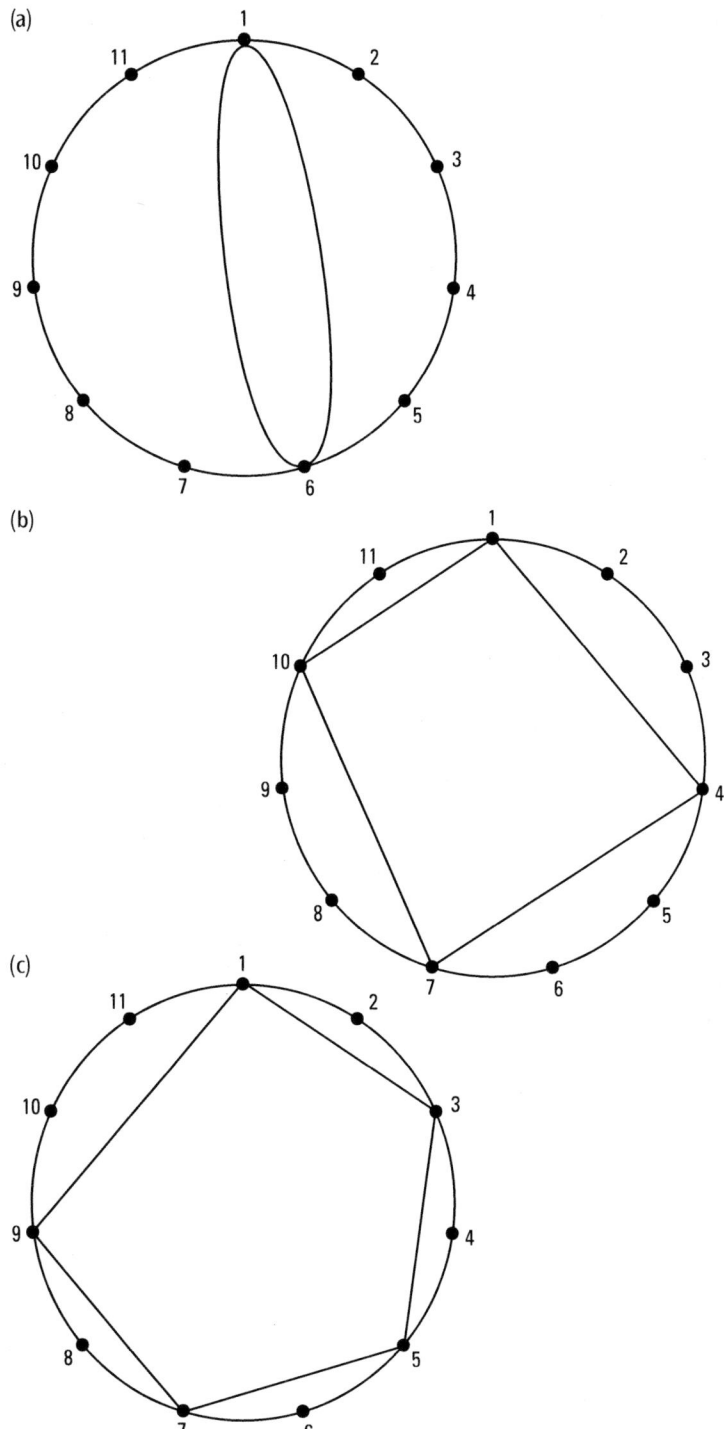

Figure 8.10. Beat cycles within the 11-cycle. (a) 5-6 beat cycle; (b) 3-3-3-2 beat cycle; (c) 2-2-2-2-3 beat cycle.

tradictions result. It is thus doubtful that these tālas represent metric patterns. Rather, they are again akin to the case of Jhampā tāla noted earlier.

Summary and Discussion

Increases in N-cycle cardinality lead to greater variety and complexity of beat cycle patterns. Table 8.6 lists all of the possible beat cycles in N-cycles of cardinality 4 to 16. It also tracks the number of rotational variants in each NI beat-cycle (for NI beat cycles only 2:3, 3:4, or 3:5 beat-class relationships were considered). Here we can see a steady, albeit nonlinear, increase in the range of metric possibilities as N-cycle cardinality increases. By the same token, this does not give rise to an unmanageable number of metrical types, especially as one considers that a listener's knowledge of them is often not exhaustive. As we have seen, most of the prime N-cycle cardinalities are rarely used even in musical cultures and styles in which they can occur and that many of the rotations of various NI-meters tend not to be used as well. The fact that there is a large, although manageable number of metrical types has important implications for the following chapter.

We also see that the 12-cycle is metrically rich relative to its cardinality, with seven possible beat cycles and nine distinct NI phase rotations. This, of course, stems from the fact that its prime factors ($2^2 * 3$) allow for various symmetries and additive patterns. If we wish to avoid higher primes as factors in order to avoid the beat-class ratio problems they will entail, the next smallest N-cycles that will permit similar patterns are the 24-cycle and the 36-cycle (that is 12×2 or 12×3). Given the perceptual limits on the overall duration of a metrical

Table 8.6. Possible Beat Cycles in N-Cycles 4–16

N-cycle Cardinality	Number of beat cycles	Number of NI rotations
4	1	0
5	1	2
6	2	0
7	1	3
8	4	5
9	2	4
10	4	5
11	3	15
12	7	9
13	4	18
14	6	18
15	6	19
16	11 (12)	39
TOTALS	52 (53)	137

cycle, and the 100 ms minimum for IOIs on the N-cycle itself, these larger cycles would only be possible at very rapid tempos. Thus, the 12-cycle is combinatorially privileged within the range of perceptually viable metric cycles.

In exploring the 12-cycle, it became apparent that maximal evenness must be considered hierarchically, rather than simply level by level. This led to a revision of WFC 6, which allows for some cycles in a meter to have less than perfect maximal evenness, provided that the meter as a whole achieves an optimal distribution of attentional peaks over the course of the cycle. This relaxation of maximal evenness is also contingent on avoiding contradictions and minimizing ambiguities. For we also saw that higher-order ambiguities will arise in NI meters in which there are perfect half-measures as in the 3-3 | 2-2-2 beat cycle. While ambiguities on the beat cycle itself are forbidden by WFC 5, in some cases the desire for maximal evenness will create half-measures that contain different numbers of beats.

Once again scale theory provided useful models for understanding how we can metrically interpret a rhythmic surface. Indeed, we often face metrically over- or underdetermined rhythms, and yet we still must entrain appropriately to them. To be sure, having a large repertoire of highly practiced metric behaviors is a great help, for matching a rhythmic figure to a known meter assists the entrainment process just as our knowledge of scale patterns helps us grasp a sense of scale and key. There is also the special case of the "chromatic" interpretation of an otherwise underdetermined rhythmic figure via template matching. In those instances, we make use of our overlearned metric behaviors and knowledge of style-specific rhythmic figures (and their normative metric placement) to instantiate an appropriate meter.

Finally, rotation of a beat-cycle can influence its metric plausibility. Some rotations of a non-isochronous pattern are more likely to be construed as surface rhythms of an I-meter rather than as the IOIs of the beat cycle of a NI-meter, whereas others more naturally lead to NI-meter construals. The presence or absence of a half-measure seems to be an important factor in this regard. While in theory a NI-beat cycle of cardinality N will have N distinct rotations, in practice only some are used.

9

The Many Meters Hypothesis

Ecological Validity in Conceptions of Meter

As we saw in chapter 4, metrical types involve an N-cycle of a given cardinality and a particular configuration of subcycles; collectively these correspond to a hierarchically coordinated set of metric periodicities. Each metrical type may be further individuated by taking the absolute timing values of the average IOIs on each of its component cycles into account, giving rise to several tempo dependent varieties of each metrical type.

But neither metrical types nor tempo-metrical types are representations of a listener's entrainment relative to a specific listening experience. A metrical type is merely an architecture of periodic relationships, while a tempo-metrical type is a subcategorization of metrical types based on the average IOIs on each level. However, if entrainment consists in matching one's attention to a pattern of periodicities present in the music, then such matching optimally involves not an averaged pattern of expectations but a specific set of timing relationships. It is well known that in real-world musical performance IOIs on any metrical level are almost never isochronous. Moreover, as studies of performance and listener expectation have shown, these values can and do systematically vary from isochrony in complex ways. What may appear as a local form of variance among successive IOIs—what are known as expressive deviations or expressive variations—can emerge as part of a larger pattern of temporal regularity. Studies have also shown that listeners can internalize patterns of expressive variation and base their temporal expectancies and judgments upon them. These kinds of expectancies would not occur if metric entrainment merely consisted of an averaged set of periodic expectations.

Therefore, an ecologically valid conception of meter does not simply involve a set of abstract metrical types, or even tempo-metrical types, although these are both very useful ways of approaching metrical structure and behavior. Rather, metric entrainment involves a complex matching of listener expectations to hierarchically structured patterns of temporal invariance that are characteristically present in the music. Patterns of expressive variation are often specific to particular styles, genres, and even performers, and most listeners are highly familiar with at least a few specific musical styles and performers. It is in the context of this kind of concrete knowledge and experience that one's metric skills are formed and honed.

Listening to Music as a Skilled Behavior

In studies of rhythmic perception and performance, a distinction is often made between skilled subjects, that is to say trained musicians (usually instrumentalists) and unskilled or naive subjects under the fuzzy category of nonmusicians (e.g., Drake, 1998, 2000; Duke 1994; Duke, Geringer et al. 1991; Franek, Mates et al. 1991; Shaffer 1982; Shaffer & Clarke1985). This would seem to be an obvious distinction to make in one's subject pool, as musicians spend hours honing their rhythmic behaviors, learning to categorize durational patterns in terms of richly organized metric schemas. Thus one would expect musicians to be far better at most experimental tasks that involve temporal judgement, synchronization, and so forth. Yet the differences between musician and nonmusician subjects in various experiments are not as great as one might expect, and indeed, in some cases (see, e.g., Handel & Oshinsky 1981; Peper, Beek et al. 2000), little or no difference is apparent between them. To be sure, there are large within-category differences among subjects, and as Bruno Repp (1999a) has observed, musicians rarely do badly (though some do much better than others), while nonmusicians run the gamut and the poorest performers are almost always nonmusicians. Likewise, in some contexts, musical training clearly does enhance subject performance (e.g., Yee, Holleran et al. 1994, in which the task involved subdivision of a target interval).

Nonetheless, the differences in rhythmic perception and performance between musicians versus nonmusicians are not as great as one might initially expect. There are two possible explanations as to why this is so. The first is that the experimental tasks, such as tapping to a metronome or judging the duration of an empty interval to a remembered standard, are so unlike real-world musical contexts that a musician's training simply does not apply. That is, the complex behaviors that regulate musical performance and perception are context-specific and do not carry over to nonmusical or quasi-musical tasks.

The second explanation is that the perceptual and behavioral differences between musicians and nonmusicians may not be nearly so great as has been presumed (Smith 1997). While musicians develop special skills in order to be able to sing and play, it does not follow that they will have a significantly greater exposure to music than non-musicians. Music is a more or less ubiquitous presence in the soundscape of our lives, and so most people will have listened to thousands of hours of music by the time they are young adults. Therefore most of us, and hence most experimental subjects, are highly experienced listeners. Indeed, some of us may have a special interest in one or more particular musical styles, and thus have a sensitivity to the rhythmic nuances of that style, whether it is the cadences of different hip-hop poets, the differing senses of swing among jazz drummers, or the phrasing habits of particular classical pianists. Such nuances are almost always produced and judged in a metrical context.

Our musical aptitude and competence is actually a bundle of related skills, as it involves recognizing timbres (which allows us to identify vocalists and musicians by the characteristic sounds of their voices and instruments), judging intonation, tracking melodies and melodic contours, applying a knowledge of standard musical forms and lyrical building-blocks, and, last but not least, metrically entraining in the most efficacious manner to grasp and anticipate the unfolding rhythms. Our metric skill in musical contexts is related to other skilled rhythmic behaviors, such as speech production and comprehension, our auditory and visual tracking of moving objects, and, most important, kinematic or motor control behaviors from walking and running to dancing and participating in sports. All of these activities require rhythmic control of our own bodies as well as temporal coordination with others. We have many opportunities to practice these behaviors, starting in early childhood. Musical performance requires additional skills, but the skills involved in musical performance rest on a substrate of basic rhythmic skills. The more familiar we are with a particular kind of rhythm, the more skilled our attentional behaviors tend to become. Thus, while a neophyte may recognize a jazz drumming pattern, a more experienced listener will be able to discern particular styles (swing vs. bop vs. cool) and even individual performers (Tony Williams vs. Jack DeJohnette vs. Art Blakey).

In order to have such metric expertise we must do two things. First, we must retain the fine-grained details of prior metric experiences and behaviors. This retention enables us to build a repertoire of context-specific strategies for attending to particular kinds of music. Second, we must be able to quickly and correctly bring the metric habit(s) from this repertoire to bear on the given musical context.

Meter and Expressive Variation

In a recent article, Luke Windsor and Eric Clarke remark in passing, "Since the work of Seashore (1938), the discovery that pianists intentionally and systematically (although not necessarily consciously) deviate from notated durations has been refined to suggest that such deviations from the score are systematically related to the structure of the music being played" (1997, p. 129). Although Seashore is often credited with the first studies and observations of expressive variation, the awareness of intentional and systematic deviations from notated durations by musicians in performance goes back quite a bit farther. Here is Wolfgang Caspar Printz, writing in 1676:

> Further, the position in the measure has a peculiar power and virtue which causes notes that are equal to one another, according to the time signature, to seem longer or shorter. . . . The apparent difference in length of notes that are equal according to their time or value, is called *Quantitas Temporalis Intrinseca*, or the inner duration. (p. 18; cited in Houle 1987, pp. 80–81)

Definitions of *Quantitas Intrinseca* appear in many sources, beginning in the late 17th through the 18th centuries. Johannes Walther gives the following definition in his *Musikalisches Lexikon* of 1732:

> *Quantitas notarum extrinseca & intrinseca* [lat.]—the apparent [or outward] and the inner value of the notes. According to the former, every note is performed equal to other notes of the same value, but according to the latter the notes are of unequal length: since, to be specific, the uneven-numbered parts of the beat are long and the even numbered ones short. (1732, p. 507, cited in Houle 1987, p. 82)

It is not always clear whether these music theorists believed quantitas intrinseca to be a phenomenal, objective aspect of performed durations or if it was a subjective aspect of the listener's perception of musical rhythm. On the one hand, many discussions of performance practice take quantitas intrinseca explicitly into account, as they acknowledge that the "inner value of the notes" stems from minute variations in timing and dynamics that result from certain fingerings, bowings, and so on (see Houle 1987, pp. 85–123). To be sure, there is a difference between ergonomic factors which give rise to unavoidable temporal nuances and expressive variations that are under the control of one's conscious musical volition (see Penel & Drake 2000). But one should note that the choice of a particular fingering or bowing is not just made to optimize ergonomic factors, but in many instances is a deliberate choice, made to produce a certain effect of timing, articulation, and dynamics. On the other hand, as Houle points out, "Printz does not advocate lengthening or shortening the duration of notes . . . he implies that it is only the listener's perception of their 'peculiar power and virtue' that distinguishes long from short" (1987, p. 81). Similarly, John Holden, writing in 1770, claims:

> There is no occasion to make the beginning or emphatic part of the measure always stronger or louder than the rest, though it is sometimes best to do so;

for it is not so much the superior loudness of the sound, as the superior regard which a hearer is led to bestow upon it that distinguishes one part of the measure from another. (cited in Houle 1987, p. 79)

Whereas Holden specifically notes the presence (or absence) of dynamic stress in marking metrical structure, as has been noted expressive lengthening of an IOI can be heard as an increase in intensity, and vice versa (Handel 1989; Povel & Okkerman 1981). Holden's "superior regard" thus seems remarkably prescient of Repp's work cited later (1995a, 1998b). It is clear from these sources that it has long been understood that proper metrical performance does not entail mechanical regularity or slavish patterns of dynamic accent.

More recently, expressive variation in timing has been studied under a number of terms, including overholding and underholding (Seashore 1967/1938), systematic variation (Gabrielsson 1982), timing microstructure, composer's "pulses" (Clynes 1986), expressive transformation (Clarke 1985, 1989), and expressive timing (Repp 1998b). Using a variety of measurement techniques, from pianos with optical sensors on each key to various MIDI instruments and controllers, as well as digital signal analysis, researchers are now able to examine the timing patterns in musical performances with great precision and detail. Example 9.1

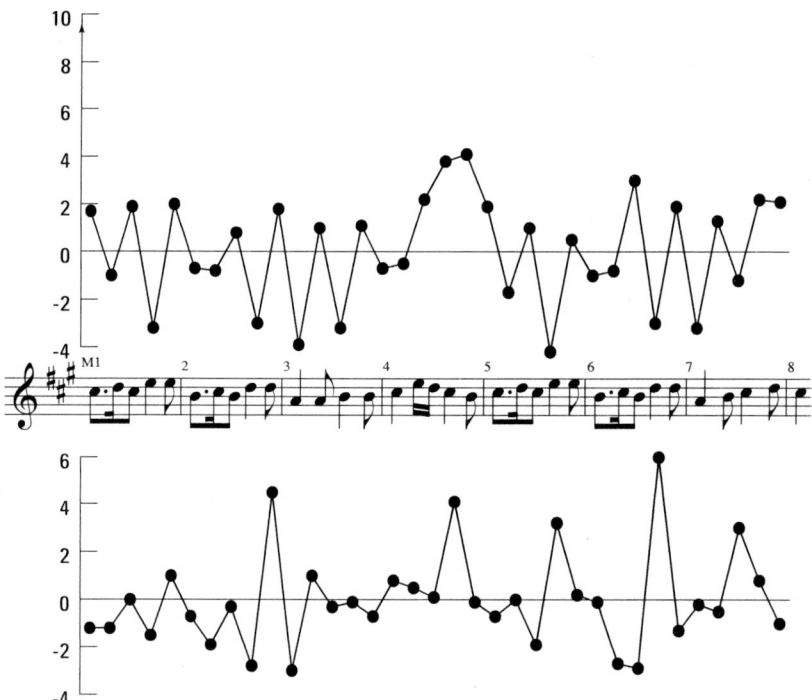

Example 9.1.   Two expressive performance analyses of Mozart's Piano Sonata K. 331, first movement, after Bengtsson and Gabrielsson (1983), fig. 4, p. 36.

from Bengtsson and Gabrielsson (1983) shows how various notes in two performances of the melody of Mozart's Piano Sonata K. 331, first movement, have been changed relative to a perfectly mechanical or deadpan performance. Notes above the line are stretched and those below are compressed relative to the average tempo/IOI value. In both performances there is a tendency to lengthen the penultimate IOIs in each measure, and this extends the duration of the quarter note that falls on the second beat of each measure (remember, this is a slow compound triple meter). Downbeats are not lengthened; indeed, in the first performance they are consistently compressed. In the first performance higher-level timing patterns also come into play, as there is a tendency to lengthen phrase endings which affects their component metric timings.

Example 9.2 is the average timing profile from several performances of the opening measures of Chopin's *Etude in E Major*, Op. 10, No. 3, from Repp (1998c). In contrast to example 9.1, its composite rhythm is a constant stream of sixteenth notes, thus giving precise timing information for every interval of subdivision. As a result, Repp was able to gather a more detailed timing profile than did Bengtsson and Gabrielsson (but one should keep in mind that differences in pitch and rhythmic organization will of course affect the timing profiles of any examples). Repp does not give a baseline for the average tempo/IOI value for this passage but simply charts the absolute value of each IOI in milliseconds. Chopin's *Etude* is performed at a very slow tempo, such that the notated $\frac{2}{4}$ is not the meter that is heard. Note the IOIs for most of the sixteenth notes are in the 400–500 ms range (with some considerably longer), and so the eighth-note is likely to be heard as the tactus and the notated half-bar as the actual measure. If

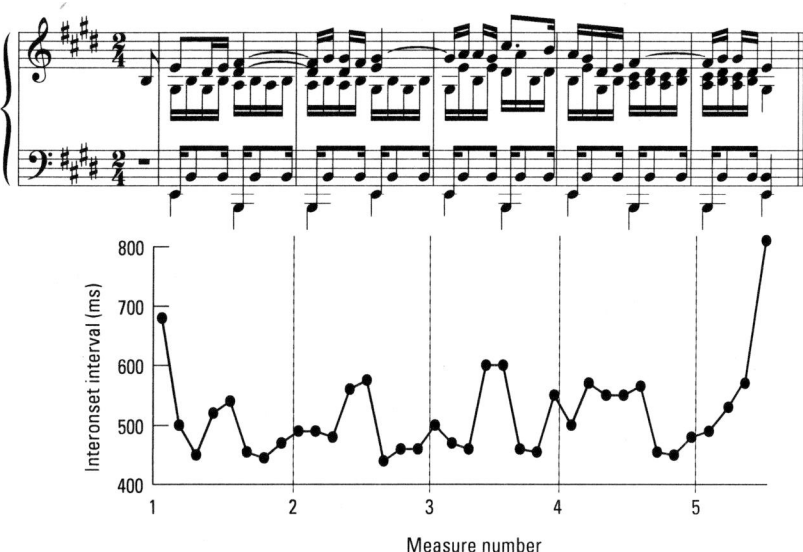

Example 9.2. Typical timing profile from performances of the opening measures of Chopin's Etude, Op. 10, no. 3, after Repp (1998c), fig. 3, p. 797.

the expressed meter is $\frac{2}{8}$, we see that lengthened IOIs tend to coincide with down-beats. Moreover, the downbeats of every other $\frac{2}{8}$ measure are relatively longer, marking the ends of two-bar groups (that is, the second half of each notated measure).

As Sloboda has pointed out, expressive variation may be grasped as the quality of musical motion or expression: "we can hear rhythmic imprecision and rubato with appropriate training, but fine differences in timing are more often experienced as differences in the quality (the 'life' or 'swing') of a performance" (1985, p. 30). Here a distinction is drawn between *structure* and *expression*. That is, between a "canonical" sense of musical rhythms based on a literal reading of scores and involving precise and perfect timings and ratios, versus the interpretive additions which occur under performance, what we might call the added value given by the performer who makes the music expressive, rather than deadpan.[1] Clarke put this very clearly: "The features of a performance are co-determined by structural properties of the music and the organizing processes of the performer" and also "Musical structures may be thought of possessing a double aspect: a relatively fixed canonical representation equivalent to the notations in a score and a more flexible and indeterminate representation that is evident in expressive performance" (1985, p. 211). This double aspect is implicit in the very terms expressive variation or expressive deviation, which imply variance or deviation of timing and dynamics from some rhythmic norm.

Clarke gives the following examples to illustrate the difference between canonical and expressive realizations of a rhythmic sequence. Example 9.3a shows a durational sequence in which a quarter note = 1000 ms. In this hypothetical case—perhaps a computer performance of a MIDI file—the performer has a perfect internal clock, and that clock controls various procedures such as "produce two even durations" or "produce a long-short" relative to it. Example 9.3b is meant to show how expressive variations are actually produced. Clarke notes that, as systematic patterns of expressive variation have been regularly observed, and that these deviations are related to structural characteristics of the music, "this suggests that the clocklike mechanism that times these beat intervals is modifiable, or programmable, so as to vary its momentary rate" (1985, p. 230). Thus, in example 9.3b, the control processes are the same as in example 9.3a, but the clock rate itself has been systematically and continuously modified.

The same distinction between structure and expression underlies analysis-by-synthesis approaches to musical expression in which various systematic deviations are introduced to an otherwise deadpan performance, and judged either quantitatively or subjectively against human performance (Bengtsson & Gabrielsson 1983; Clynes 1986; Desain 1992; Friberg, Sundberg, et al. 1987; Schulze 1989a). Moreover, there is an entire area of computer-music research the goal of which is a system that would take musical sound as input and produce a notated score as output (see Large 2000a, for a summary of this research). These research projects presume that scores are good representations of musical struc-

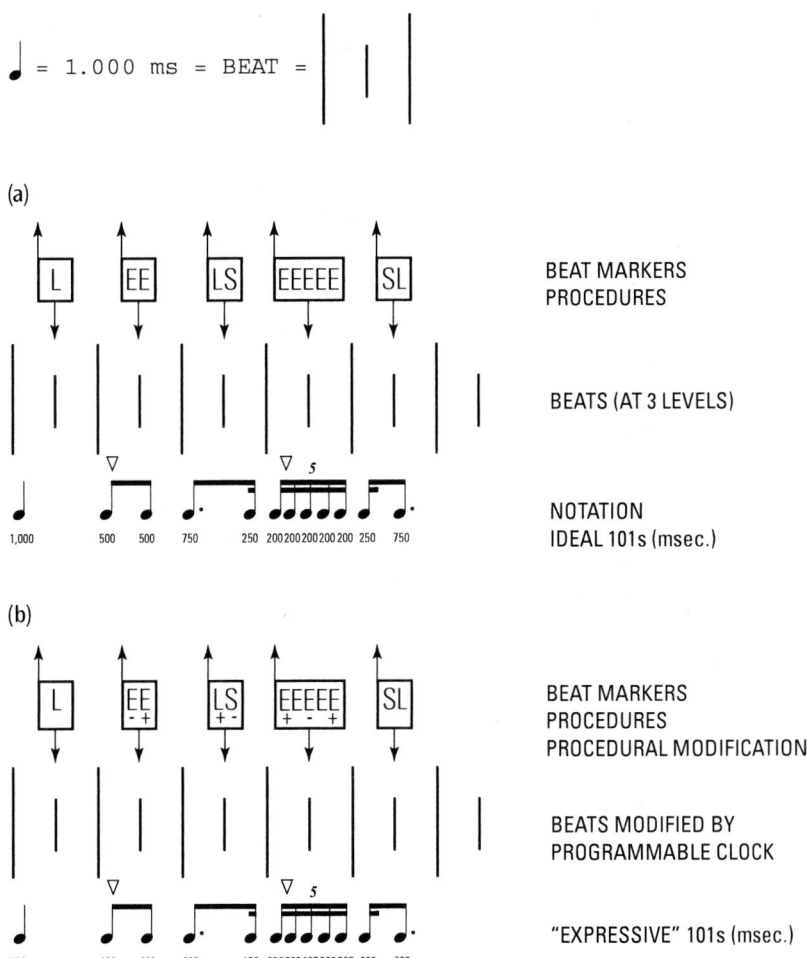

Example 9.3. Diagrams of canonical vs. expressive timing, after Clarke (1985). (a) Deadpan performance of rhythm (fig. 7, p. 226); (b) expressive performance of rhythm (fig. 8, p. 231).

ture, hence, recovering the score from the acoustical signal is equivalent to recovering the structure (or a "structural description") of the music.

However, the structure versus expression dichotomy, as well as models of musical rhythm and meter based on this distinction, may be questioned on a number of grounds. First, there is the presumption that that a musical score is a more or less veridical representation of musical structure. Musical notation has always been a kind of shorthand, a rough set of directions which guide a competent performer. Whereas some aspects of the structural relationships captured in musical notation are doubtless incorporated in our mental representations of music, it does not follow that these representations need to obey the same topological and orthographic constraints as western notation. Musical structure (whatever that may ultimately be) is not literally represented in a musical score.

Nor do scores represent what we expect to hear. Repp's work has shown that we expect an expressive profile that is related to the unfolding musical structure (and this structure includes meter, melody, articulation, and so forth). In his studies Repp found that:

> Despite ubiquitous individual differences, expressive timing is governed by certain principles and constraints, and listeners evidently possess implicit knowledge of these principles, which leads them to expect lengthening of IOIs where performers typically linger and shortening of IOIs where performers typically rush. When music is played without any expressive timing, as in the present experiments, IOIs that are expected to be [relatively] long sound too short (a positive bias, as bias is defined here), whereas IOIs that are expected to be short sound too long (a negative bias). These biases seem to be elicited automatically by the same structural properties that cause performers to modulate their timing. (1998a, p. 135)[2]

Repp's research shows that these lengthenings and shortenings are not deviations from the norm—they *are* the norm. The structural properties that cause performers to modulate their timing involve the relative duration of a series of events, their metric position, and their grouping.[3]

The distinction at issue here is this: Do expressive variations depend on patterns of relative duration and grouping—manifested most strongly and consistently by lengthening the final element of a group—or are these expressive timings embodied in the meter apart from any particular rhythm, or both? Repp (1998b, 1998c, 1998d) has argued that in the case of the Chopin Etude he studied, expressive variation is primarily dependent on rhythm, not meter. However, this argument and those of other researchers is based on selective study of particular rhythmic patterns in particular metrical contexts—hence we know a lot about the rhythmic particulars in Mozart's A major Sonata and Chopin's E major Etude. Indeed, one of the primary aims of these studies was to examine the performance of real musical examples in ecologically valid contexts, and this is of course laudable. But given their design, these studies have not involved the systematic study of every possible metric variant of a rhythmic pattern.

A consideration of a set of such variants is revealing; one such family of variants is given in example 9.4. The basic rhythmic pattern is a Long–Short–Short, with the durational proportions 2:1:1. Different groupings give rise to three rotations: L–S–S (in poetic scansion, the dactyl), S–L–S (the amphibrach), and S–S–L (the anapest). Articulation and dynamics, as well as expressive timing, would be used by the performer to distinguish among these three groupings/ rotations. However, each of the three rotations can be placed in a different alignment with a four-beat meter.[4] When placed into a particular metric context the

Example 9.4. Metrical and rhythmic (grouping) permutations of ♩♩♩ figure.
(a) Dactyl group, long note on downbeat; (b) Amphibrach group, long note on
downbeat (first note as anacrusis); (c) Anapest group, long note on downbeat
(first two notes as anacrusis); (d) Anapest group, first note on downbeat; (e) Amphibrach group, last note on downbeat (rare—tends to shift downbeat to long
note); (f) Dactyl group, long note off dowbeat (rare—tends to shift downbeat to
long note); (g) Amphigrach group, first note on downbeat; creates syncope relative
to half-measure; (h) Dactyl group, last note on downbeat (*very* rare, if not impossible);
(i) Anapest group, middle note on downbeat (*very* rare, if not impossible).

performer's task now becomes more difficult, for he or she must convey both the grouping *and* its metric position (e.g., dactyl on the downbeat versus dactyl on beat three). Of course, these are rhythmic tasks that musicians carry out all the time, but while some of these tasks are fairly easy, others are practically impossible.

In examples 9.4a, 9.4b, and 9.4c, the long note always occurs on the downbeat of the measure; these may be thought of as the "default" metric placements for each of the three groupings. Of the three, I presume that the amphibrach (ex. 9.4b) would involve a distinctly different pattern of timing and articulation, as the quarter note on beat 3, which is the end of the group, might be stretched relative to the following quarter on beat 4. Note, however, that one can alter the relative length of beats 2 and 3 without affecting the larger relation of beats 1 and 4 to beats 2 and 3. The next two sets are even more interesting. Example 9.4d is found commonly enough (for example, in the finale of Haydn's "London" Symphony). Likewise, the syncopated pattern in example 9.4g is also not uncommon. However, the remaining variants are almost impossible to perform. For example, if one projects the grouping pattern of example 9.4e with appropriate timings to mark group boundaries, the result is also the projection of a syncopated figure—that is, example 9.4g. In a similar fashion, the patterns in examples 9.4f and 9.4h lead to the dactyl pattern and metric alignment of example 9.4a, with the long note concurrent with the downbeat.

What example 9.4 demonstrates is that the expressive variations that indicate the group boundaries of a rhythmic figure and its metrical orientation are co-constrained and mutually reinforcing. This makes it difficult to draw a hard distinction between metrical and rhythmic timing. While one can systematically change both the metrical position and grouping boundaries for a rhythmic figure, not all orientations are metrically viable.

We may examine the separability of metrical and rhythmic timing from another angle. Consider the familiar tune "Happy Birthday." There is its normative, slightly off-key performance (at a moderate tempo) by a group of enthusiastic nonmusicians at most birthdays (at least in the United States). Now consider how "Happy Birthday" may be performed in other musical styles: as a marching band piece, as a cha-cha, or as a big-band jazz tune. Let us presume that each of these versions keep the melody at the same tempo so that we are dealing with the same tempo-metrical type. Likewise, as the structural tones of the melody and their rhythmic grouping do not change, their rhythmic timing factors also should be invariant. But the timing profiles *will* change from arrangement to arrangement and from style to style. Although some cues for these different styles lie in instrumentation, accompaniment, and so forth, others are manifest in the performance of the melody itself. Those differences lie in the nuances of metrical timing that are part and parcel of the marching band, cha-cha, and big-band musical styles.

The Many Meters Hypothesis

The consideration of example 9.4 leads to another question: Is it possible to have expressive variants of a particular permutation? If the answer is yes, at least in some cases, this means that tempo-metrical types may be further individuated. Based on the preceding discussion, I will presume the following before attempting to individuate metrical types further:

> If a temporally regular pattern of events within certain perceptual ranges is consistently present in the environment and we have enough opportunities to engage with it, we will adapt our attention to match it.
>
> We are able to retain those patterns of attention and use them again when we encounter similar temporal contexts.
>
> We use these retained timing patterns not only to direct our behavior in performance, but also to make musical observations and judgements when we listen in order to differentiate among performers and musical styles, to note exaggerations from normal timing patterns such as rubato, and so forth.

From these presumptions, I derive the *Many Meters Hypothesis* (MMH):

> A listener's metric competence resides in her or his knowledge of a very large number of context-specific metrical timing patterns. The number and degree of individuation among these patterns increases with age, training, and degree of musical enculturation.

While acknowledging that there are common structural aspects among many meters, my claim is that there can be expressive varieties of particular tempo-metrical types. And while, on the one hand, this means collapsing the double aspect of fixed versus indeterminate metrical representation, as noted by Clarke earlier, on the other, it leads us to acknowledge a far greater number of individuated metric behaviors. Our knowledge of musical meter consists of a large number of style-, genre-, performer-, and tempo-specific attentional patterns. Moreover, our sense of what makes one meter distinct from another may be encoded in terms of the motional character and expressive properties of different metrical timing patterns, as well as the rhythmic figures which characteristically occur within them. Thus, we are aware of differences in the "life or swing" of a performance, as Sloboda has noted, precisely because we have internalized their characteristic timing patterns and other parametric differences. The fact that these differences exceed the limit of resolution of musical notation does not render them less structural. As I have argued, what makes something a march and not a galop, for example, is in large part the characteristic metrical timing patterns of each genre—timing patterns that remain relatively fixed even though specific rhythmic figures vary from piece to piece within a given genre. And if we listen to marches and galops with any frequency, those characteristic timings will become part of our habitual entrainments to them.

Our metrical experience and knowledge proceeds from the concrete to the more abstract. Figure 9.1 illustrates a hypothetical scenario as to how we might build up an internalized knowledge of a number of expressive varieties of a particular tempo-metrical type. Imagine a competent listener—a college student, say—who likes popular music, is familiar with film scores, knows various forms of commercial music, and so on, but who is ignorant of jazz. In particular, this student knows nothing of (having never heard) the characteristic swing patterns of classic and big-band-era jazz. The student decides to take an introductory course in jazz history, and is presented with Count Basie's "One O'Clock Jump." This piece is in a fast $\frac{4}{4}$ time, with "swung" 8-notes that involve expressively timed triplet subdivisions of the beat; complete triplets are often present in the drums and other instruments. Figure 9.1a is a loose representation of the particular timing pattern involved in that piece—a 12-cycle that indicates the characteristic timing of the compound subdivision of a four-beat measure (drawn as a circular beat cycle with "petals" for the subdivisons/12-cycle for reasons that will become clear in a moment).[5] Our student listens to this piece many times, and so we may presume that the timings in figure 9.1a are well learned. As it is the only swing pattern the student knows, it forms the basis for all future encounters with other pieces in this style and at this tempo. Then the student goes and listens to Benny Goodman's "Down South Camp Meeting," another classic big-band standard with a very similar swing pattern. She now comes to know two varieties of swung eighths for big-band jazz at a fast tempo. Figure 9.1b shows how this metric knowledge might be related, in the form of two expressive varieties of this tempo-metrical type. Note that only one of which will be active at any one time, as is indicated by the use of dotted versus solid lines for the IOIs on the 12-cycle.

The semester is finished, and our student becomes a real big-band jazz aficionado, buying many CDs, going to concerts, and taking swing dance lessons. The student has wonderful conversations with grandparents on the relative merits of various big-bands. The student is now a highly enculturated, quasi-expert listener in this style of music. Example 9.5c is a partial representation of her newly formed knowledge of the expressive varieties of this tempo-metrical type—Basie versus Goodman versus Miller versus Calloway, and so forth. That is, knowledge of the "big-band swung eighth fast tempo metrical type" consists, at least in part, of something akin to the set of particular timing patterns illustrated in figure 9.1c. This set of timing patterns may be related to other varieties of the 12-cycle/1-4-7-10 subcycle fast tempo-metrical type, and those varieties in turn will relate to other varieties of this metrical type at different tempos.[6] Thus, a particular listener's knowledge of a given metrical type may incorporate

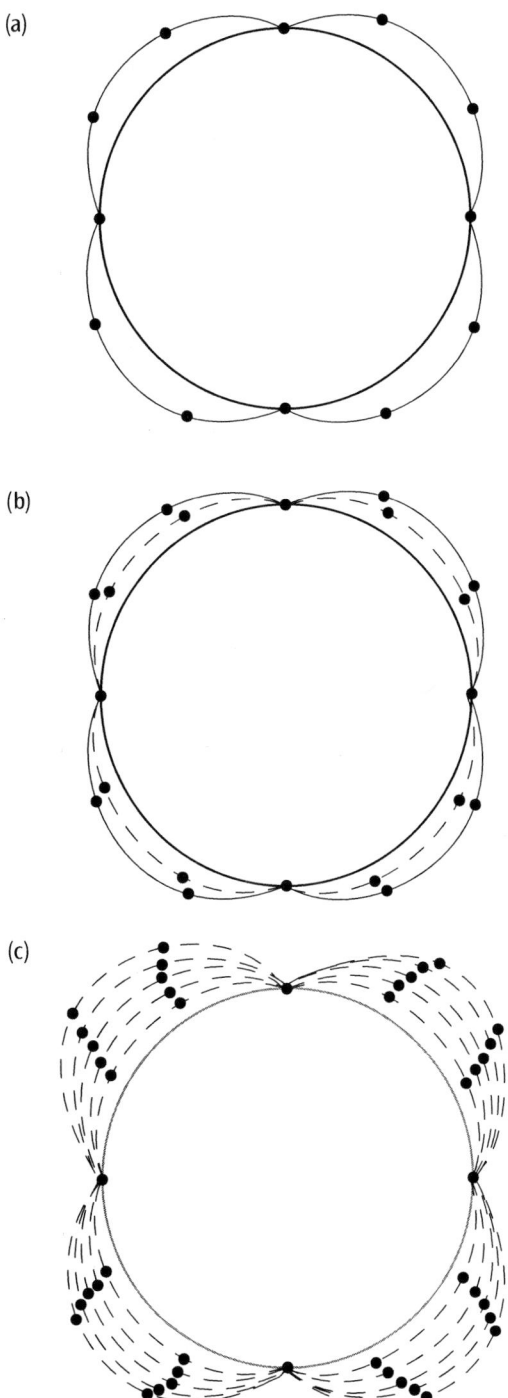

Figure 9.1. Expressive timings of a tempo-metrical type. (a) Single tempo-metrical type with particular timing values; (b) same tempo-metrical type with "old" (inactive, in dashed lines) and "new" (active in black) timing values; (c) a set of expressively individuated timings for a tempo-metrical type.

tens, and in some cases, hundreds, of interrelated, context-specific patterns of timing behavior.

Support for and Challenges to the MMH

Competent listeners can grasp a beat and meter very quickly, as well as adapt readily to metrical alterations. We are all familiar with the "radio dial" phenomenon of jumping from station to station and from song to song. Yet we are usually able to latch on to the meter and tempo almost instantly when we do this. Having a sizable repertoire of ready-made meters would facilitate such rapid metric recognition, and explain the ease and skill with which we are able to entrain not only to a sense of beat, but often to several metrical layers even before we have heard a complete measure.

Some observations on musical practice and performance also provide support for the MMH. To be able to play a passage at a variety of tempos is not a simple mater of scaling the durational proportions of its rhythm(s). For if the IOI of one or more elements in a pattern crosses a boundary or reaches a limit, there is a change in the subjective sense of the pattern. This perhaps explains why musicians typically must practice a passage at incrementally increasing or decreasing metronome settings in order to have command of the music across a range of tempos. At very fast tempos the 100 ms limit on the performance of short notes in a pattern comes into play—the shortest notes in a pattern can only get so short—and this interferes with scaling (e.g., Friberg & Sundström 2002).

In a nonmusical context, Gentner (1987) examined the data on a variety of timing behaviors such as arm movement, typing, running, and walking, and found that a generalized motor program in which the durations were simply scaled according to some multiplier (i.e., simply do everything twice as slowly, or half again as fast) did not fit the data. Gentner also noted, however, that "it seems implausible and grossly inefficient that a separate motor program would be stored for every variation of the action that can be performed. Furthermore, with a separate motor program for each variation, there would also be no direct way to perform novel variations of an action." (1987, p. 255). This makes sense in some contexts, such as typing, in which one rarely types the same pattern of words over and over. Gentner's objections have less weight for musical performance, precisely because in music there is little room for novelty; one doesn't add extra notes in the middle of a Beethoven sonata, for example. Even improvised musical styles, such as jazz and various folk musics, involve well-practiced motor sequences in performance and typically not the creation of new, unpracticed motor sequences on the spot. To be sure, however, within-tempo variations of a particular expressive tempo-metrical type would involve variations of an action, and these accord with the MMH. In the event that one is called on to perform novel variations of an action or attend to an unfamiliar musical style, the performer or listener is then thrown back to a more basic temporal strategy akin to a generic tempo-metrical type.

Musicians who are highly skilled within a particular style often have the ability to mimic other performers, and to a high degree this mimicry involves reproducing their characteristic timing patterns. To do so, the musical mimic must have individual representations of the characteristic metric behaviors of each of their imitative subjects, and make use of them in performing their musical impersonations.[7] It also has been observed that musicians do not readily cross musical styles—a great classical pianist may be unconvincing when performing a jazz ballad, for example. One reason for such crossover difficulties may be that the timing behaviors musicians have learned so well for the performance of one style are not appropriate for another. And because these timing behaviors are so well learned—the product of decades of practice and reinforcement—it is difficult to suppress overlearned performance habits when trying to sing or play in a new style. This also may explain why listeners have different degrees of discernment: someone who is a keen judge of jazz performers may not be a good judge of classical pianists, and vice versa.

The difficulties musicians have in crossing stylistic boundaries or incrementally scaling the tempo of a passage suggest that skilled musical performance is highly task-specific. While this may in part relate to biomechanical preferences and constraints, as certain tempos may optimize finger and arm dynamics, for example, it also may relate to our central timekeepers and the need to establish distinct timing representations for a motor program at different tempos. As Gentner has observed, it certainly does not seem very efficient to have to build a bevy of metrical representations or motor control programs in order to deal with each and every metrical context. However, what we know of neural architecture and the size of available neural populations suggests that efficiency need not be a paramount concern. Robert Gjerdingen reminds us that:

> The fact that meter is something we can mentally create inside ourselves has tended to lead scholarly discussions of it toward notions of sophisticated cognitive processing. And perhaps in some esoteric repertoires a measure of sophistication is indeed required to discern a meter. Yet in the vast majority of music heard by ordinary people, meter is quite a down-to-earth affair. Could it be that the perception of, and internal synchronization with the simple periodicities of basic musical features actually depends on low-level processes? The neural metronomes discussed above are simple "avalanche" circuits of the type found in many primitive organisms. . . . Could the low-level processing of meter thus help to explain its subjectively visceral feel? (1989, pp. 90–91)

To Gjerdingen's visceral feel I would add its motional quality. Although I do not want to venture too far into a neurobiological account of meter, if to encode any one meter requires a fairly small and simple neural network, and if the human brain contains a very large number of neurons, then it becomes plausible to propose that we have many such networks, each able to be tuned to a particular metrical resonance. In other words, there would seem to be no neurobiological argument against the MMH.

Pressing, in his discussion of the music of the African-American or "black Atlantic" diaspora, which includes jazz, blues, gospel, reggae, rock, and hip-hop, goes into some detail on the notion of "groove" or "feel." These are terms that are commonly used by practitioners of these musics to refer to, in Pressing's words, "a cognitive temporal phenomenon emerging from one or more carefully aligned rhythmic patterns" (2002, p. 288). It is clear that the ordinary language use of the term "groove" describes not just a tempo-metrical type but also an expressive timing component, as grooves have a particular gestural and kinetic quality. While grooves are related to the rhythmic patterns that tend to occur within them, they are nonetheless independent of those patterns.

Gentner's call for a parsimonious model for motor behavior, however, points to some significant challenges the MMH must overcome. The MMH makes most sense when dealing with a musical "expert" in a familiar context: the expert automatically makes use of the most appropriate attending framework or set of performance timings. But we aren't or weren't always experts, and even experts are faced with situations in which their expertise is of limited value. How does the MMH fit into a developmental account of music perception and cognition? Does one develop, along with a sense of an expressively particular tempo-metrical type a more generic sense of that tempo-metrical type? Similarly, when an expert listener is faced with an unfamiliar musical style, does the expert employ a previously acquired meter, pressing it into service and hoping for the best, as it were? Or does expertise involve (in part) facility at creating new varieties of a tempo-metrical type, perhaps starting from a generic tempo-metrical type that has less-focused expectation and lower attentional peaks? There are also questions of stability and retention relative to each instance of a particular tempo-metrical type. If I encounter a context where a prior meter seems apt, but is then is further modified by that experience, how do I retain the old meter?

Another challenge to the MMH involves our perception of continuous tempo change. If our metric habits involve a large number of tempo-specific metrical types, then when faced with an accelerando or ritard, then why don't we hear a series of jumps in the temporal continuity of such passages? If one grants that the neural architecture that underlies our metrical behaviors in listening and performing is highly interconnected, contains a great deal of redundancy, and is massively parallel, then the MMH has the potential to explain not only our sense of continuity in such passages but also our sense of tempo change. A metric pattern—that is, the listener's sense of the meter at any given point in his or her musical experience—involves the coordination of several levels of attentional periodicity. The metric diagrams given in this chapter and in previous chapters might be thought of as a set of active temporal periodicities that are embedded in an extended thicket of possible periodic relationships; in this sense figure 9.1 is a massive oversimplification of the way newly acquired metric knowledge is related to existing metric knowledge. When we encounter a continuous tempo change, the mismatch between expectations and the actual onsets of musical events will initially be manifest only at lower levels; whereas a lower-level periodicity might need to change, higher levels might not immediately need to be recast. In this way, temporal continuity is maintained, as not every level of a metric cycle changes at once. At the same time, as the set of active periodicities shifts (and especially if one or more of the periodicities crosses one of the temporal thresholds discussed in chapter 2), this may then give rise to our awareness that the tempo is in fact changing, as opposed to a more local flexing of tempo that is characteristic of expressive variation or rubato.

Summary and Discussion

Our experience of music is always an experience of a particular piece or performance. We do not encounter "generic $\frac{4}{4}$" or even "$\frac{4}{4}$ at a tempo of quarter-note = 120" but a pattern of timing and dynamics that is particular to the piece, the performer, and the musical style. Therefore, to give an ecologically valid account of meter, we must move beyond a theory of tempo-metrical types to a metrical representation that involves particular timing relationships and their absolute values in a hierarchically related set of metric cycles. While these patterns of timing and dynamics may be highly particularized, they are not unique; they are replicable (i.e., when a performer plays the same piece on different occasions these same patterns tend to recur) and also transferable (i.e., when a performer plays a different piece in the same style and with some of the same structural aspects, they may be redeployed).

The temporal skill of performers has been documented through the growing body of research on timing and dynamics in musical performance, research that has shown how musicians are able to control their timing to a high degree and with remarkable consistency. Here I have argued that most listeners have similar skills, skills that manifest themselves in their ability to recognize the characteristic timing behaviors of particular performers and make critical judgments regarding performances and performance practice. We develop these skills through our deep immersion in a musical culture.

Patterns of timing and dynamics have long been explained in both music theory and psychology in terms of rhythmic or metric structure versus expression— a purposeful pattern of variations or deviations from the values that are specified in the musical score. Yet the structure versus expression dichotomy is based on the mistaken premise that scores are veridical representations musical structure.

The MMH is an alternative to the structure versus expression dichotomy. A pattern of expression that is characteristic of a performer or style may be regarded as a distinct meter under this hypothesis, an expressive variety of a tempo-metrical type. Skilled performers and listeners thus have large repertoires of these context-specific meters at their disposal. The former may use particular meters when called on to play the same passage at different tempos, or with different expressive qualities (either their own sense of timing, or consciously imitating the timing and phrasing of others). Likewise, listeners will use particular expressive varieties both in attending to and their judgment of performances and performers.

Conclusion

Recapitulation

Hearing in Time began with the observation that meter is a musically specific instance of our more general capacity of entrainment, the sympathetic resonance of our attention and motor behavior to temporal regularities in the environment. Composers and performers often play on our metric abilities, either through their careful choice of tempos that tickle one or more metric thresholds, or in their use of patterns that invite but then thwart our ability to form coherent metric cycles (Stravinsky is perhaps the unchallenged master at this latter ploy). At other times, music does not challenge our ability to entrain so much as demand it, as it calls us to get up and dance, whether it is a jaunty polka or an Afro-Cuba tango. But perhaps the quintessential example of entrained behavior is when we tap our foot along to a tune, as our synchronized motor responses require a grasp of the rhythmic regularities of both the music and of our own bodies.

As meter is a kind of entrainment, it is subject to the same temporal limits that have been observed with respect to a wide variety of perceptual and motor behaviors. These limits, from 100 ms to about 5 to 6 seconds, define a temporal window for meter. Indeed, one of the reasons for "attending metrically" is that a hierarchical arrangement of our temporal attention allows us to expand the upper bound of the temporal window from 1.5 to 2 seconds for individual inter-event intervals to a longer, composite span of time. There are also a number of important thresholds within this temporal window, and they define important ranges within it: from 100–250 ms, from 250–1500 ms, and 1500 ms to 5–6 seconds, with a strong "attractor" around 600 ms. Studies have shown that our perception and cognition of periodicities within these ranges differs—and hence our subjective experience of rhythms of different temporal magnitudes will also differ. One thing that meter does is to integrate these different kinds of time into a coherent perceptual framework. In this way, we are able to grasp both the *temps longs* and the *temps courts* that Fraisse distinguished, as well as relate them to each other.

The thesis that meter is a kind of entrainment, and a consideration of what psychological research can tell us about it, provides the background for the two main music-theoretic inquiries of the book: (1) how can we best represent meter and then use those representations to talk about its various formal and perceptual properties, and (2) what constitutes a well-formed meter in light of this research? The latter question also invites the corollary: What constitutes a well-formed meter in light of the wide-ranging rhythmic practices of both Western and non-Western musics?

The circular representations for meter developed here aim to capture the stable, cyclical aspects of metric entrainment. They are independent of any particular rhythmic surface, although they relate to those surfaces in very specific ways. The circular diagrams show how various levels interrelate, and they also can be used to show how various levels may come and go over the course of a piece, as one attentional pattern may morph into another. Given the conjecture that perceiving a beat involves at least a latent sense of its subdivision, these diagrams readily show the relationship between the N-cycle and beat cycle of a metric hierarchy. They also allow one to grasp well-formedness via the coordination of subcycles within the N-cycle and through the apparent symmetry or near-symmetry in their arrangement. Last, but certainly not least, these diagrams treat meters as hierarchic gestalts, and make clear the distinctions between meters of different hierarchic depths.

The well-formedness conditions for meter developed here differ from previous work in the following ways. They specifically include temporal limits for various metrical levels and yoke them to certain absolute values. The WFCs given here admit both I-meters and NI-meters, and so can accommodate a broader variety of the world's musical practices. The WFCs work collectively, such that meters that satisfy them will be regular enough to permit a stable pattern of entrainment, but allow for that stability to be manifest in various ways. The WFCs eliminate the need for distinctions between additive versus multiplicative meters, as well as meter versus hypermeter.

The inclusion of temporal limits in the WFCs recognizes the perceptual and cognitive aspects of metric well-formedness. Maximal evenness further emphasizes this, for as has been shown, maximal evenness makes both formal and attentional sense, providing for an optimal arrangement of attentional energy within a certain amount of time, and coordinating peaks of attention to a baseline of short attentional intervals, that is, the N-cycle. Maximal evenness is also yoked to the timing of motor behaviors, as the symmetry or near-symmetry of maximally even meters prevents the mixture of short/rapid intervals with longer, slower ones. This avoids meters that would have correlates with herky-jerky movement patterns. To put it another way, well-formed meters serve to guide smooth, well-formed motor behaviors, given the ways that metric well-formedness leads to harmony among the component periodicities of the metric hierarchy. The WFCs also draw on analogous work in the theory of musical scales, although they differ from scalar well-formedness most importantly by the metric prohibition against including N-cycle units on higher levels, such that a subdivision can never function as a beat. By contrast, in the case of tonal/scalar relationships, a half-step that functions as the integer unit of the tonal space can have both a chromatic and a diatonic identity. Even so, maximal evenness, as well as avoiding ambiguity and contradiction, in the senses developed by Rahn, is important to both scalar and metrical contexts.

Finally, I have proposed the Many Meters Hypothesis as a way of mediating between the abstract, theoretical category of a tempo-metrical type and the timing behaviors we actually encounter as listeners and performers. In real-world musical contexts, meters never occur apart from the rhythms that initiate and sustain them, and in human performances these rhythms involve some degree of expressive variation. The elimination of these expressive variations is indicative of a deadpan or computer-generated performance, just as their exaggeration marks the presence of rubato. If our metrical patterns of attending stem from our encounters with expressively varied rhythms, then it seems parsimonious to simply include those expressive timings into the metric framework itself. While one can approach expressive variation and our knowledge of it in terms of tempo-metrical types with flexible timing, to the extent that these timing differences mark the distinctive characteristics of musical styles and in some cases individual performers, they serve to categorically differentiate the meters produced or heard in such contexts.

For this reason, I hold to the kind of metric nominalism that the Many Meters Hypothesis entails: metric competence is cashed out in our having a large number of context-specific behavioral responses to rhythmic stimuli. Greater competence involves being able to reproduce or discern a greater number of tempo-metrical types as well as a greater number of expressive differences within each tempo-metrical type. As these differences mark different, albeit closely related, temporal behaviors, they involve different meters.

The Many Meters Hypothesis also acknowledges that most listeners are highly enculturated metric experts, barring some physical, auditory, or neurological disability. Most of us have listened to music for countless hours in our lives. Similarly, as we often walk, run, take turns in conversation, march, dance, and engage in many other rhythmic behaviors, we are highly practiced in the production of various rhythms, both alone and in synchrony with others. Thus, it should not surprise that we are so adept at dealing with the complex rhythmic surfaces that music presents to us.

Coda: Metric Complexity and Rhythmic Complexity

This book was originally conceived as an exploration of metric complexity; my initial aim was to come up with a taxonomy of metric complexity along with the principles that distinguish more versus less complex meters. A number of presumptions seemed obvious—meters with many hierarchic levels are more complex with those with fewer; meters with non-isochronous levels are more complex than those that are wholly isochronous, and so forth. However, as I continued my research these presumptions became less and less secure. The late Jeff Pressing gives an overview of the problems in measuring and musical complexity beginning with this observation:

> Patterns are fundamental to all cognition. Whether inferred from sensory input or constructed to guide motor actions, they betray order. Some are simple, others are more complex. . . . Are there psychological forces pushing us along this dimension? Seemingly so. The drive to simplify and regularize is seen in familiar *Gestalt* ideas of pattern goodness and Prägnanz, which hold in many situations. The drive towards complexity can be seen in the accretional processes of individual development, or in the incremental sophistication of many cultural behaviors such as systems of musical design. (1999, online source)

Pressing gives various perspectives on complexity, including hierarchical complexity, which involves multileveled structures, dynamic or adaptive complexity, which is a mark of systems that can show a rich range of behaviors, as well as information-based complexity, which gauges the complexity of an object or behavior relative to the shortest description required to describe or generate it. Pressing does not focus on melody or rhythm alone, but rather on the overall complexity of various musical patterns. He gives the following example, a set of all of the "metrical permutations" of a two-note descending figure (see conclusion example.1). He describes the situation it presents as follows:

> Given perfectly literal and metronomic performance, as from a computer notation package realization, or an idealized literal performer, and apart from an identified starting point, the aural results from cases a, c, d, & f, are identical (forming category 1), as are cases b & e (category 2). . . . If, in contrast, the [performance] of the patterns were made by musicians, then we should have differential evidence of distinct mental models (metrical frameworks) at work. The evidence will be of two kinds: dynamics and timing. Not only should mean and variance of dynamics and interonset intervals betray the distinct mental model [of each figure], but so should the patterns of correlation between these variables. (1999, online source)

Pressing then goes on to model the various difficulties each permutation presents to the performer, primarily in terms of beat alignment: from perfect align-

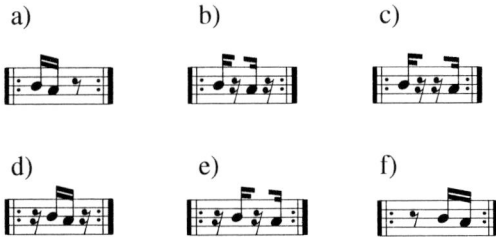

Example 1.   Variations on a two note descending figure, after Pressing (1999), fig. 2 (online source) (measures labeled a) through f)).

ment for pattern b (both notes align with the beat) to what he considers the most difficult, pattern e (both notes off the beat).[1]

Pressing, of course, is right: these six different cases will be performed and heard differently, and he is also right in noting that some are easy to play and others much harder. My question is, on the account of meter I have proposed, would these involve distinct metrical frameworks? I would claim that they do not—in all six cases, we have here a 4-cycle (presuming, as per Pressing's discussion, that the sixteenths carry the beat). If we also note that the metric framework will involve a differentiation of timing (and dynamics) relative to metric position, we can see how shifting the figure will produce different IOIs for each figure. One short example should suffice: If we presume that the four beats within each measure involve an initial and a final stretch due to expressive variation, such that they display a L−S−S−L pattern, then case (a) will be expressively timed L−s, while case (d) will be s−s. I will also presume that differences in the lengths of notes and rests will keep the overall pattern duration constant. Now, of course, these permutations may be cashed out in some other form of metrical timing, but I trust the point here is clear: it isn't a distinct metrical framework that is involved with each permutation, but a distinct relationship between the metrical framework and each rhythmic figure.

If these six figures involve the same meter, then it cannot be *metric* complexity that makes some easy to play and others more difficult. And this gets to the heart of the problem of metric complexity: just as meters do not exist apart from rhythmic surfaces that initiate and sustain them, so too with metric complexity. Whereas we can speak in some ways of the complexity of various tempo-metrical types, the more relevant complexity is that which emerges from the interaction between a metric framework and a rhythmic surface. Moreover, while some metric behaviors are more complex than others, other metric behaviors are more difficult than others. These are not the same thing. A simple pattern composed of but a few layers of activity, at either an extremely fast or extremely slow tempo, will probably prove harder to establish and maintain than a richer and more variegated metrical hierarchy at a moderate tempo. Likewise, maintaining a rich metric hierarchy, even one involving a non-isochronous meter, may be unproblematic if the musical texture articulates each metric level and its organization. By contrast, maintaining a simple isochronous meter, where one needs to constantly interpolate missing beats, discount various kinds of rhythmic noise such as trills or grace notes, may prove far more challenging.

For these reasons, I largely abandoned my sense that non-isochronous meters are inherently more complex than isochronous meters. Meter is, I have been arguing, a form of behavior. Playing the gankogui, with nuances of dynamics and articulation, is an amazingly complex rhythmic activity. So is playing Chopin with a significant amount of rubato. Listening to either is also a complex task, and yet we do this with ease, for our individual delectation and for our collective enjoyment.

Three Parting Thoughts

Thought number 1: NI-meters and I-meters are more alike than different; this observation also has been made recently by David Temperley (2001, p. 289). *Hearing in Time* argues that both obey the same set of well-formedness conditions; that both are highly practiced rhythmic behaviors; that both kinds of meters must be regarded as hierarchic gestalts and not as an affiliation or summation of independent levels of structure. This last point is important and worth dwelling on for a moment. If we view meters as gestalts, then the distinction between additive and multiplicative meters is specious. As noted earlier, this is a distinction between notational systems, and not the meters themselves. More important, when we consider how both I-meters and NI-meters are actually performed it becomes clear that neither can be produced by multiplicative operations (such as those proposed by Jones and Boltz 1989), given the expressive variations that are involved. One cannot simply feed-forward a beat IOI in order to predict the next event onset, as the timing patterns are more complicated than that. Recall the diagram of the gankogui pattern from the Gahu rhythm discussed in chapter 7:

> . . . M M L L S M M L L S M M L L S M M L L S M M L L S . . .

There I remarked that it is clear that there is a five-element sequence, even if one is not certain which element stands as the downbeat. Now consider an oversimplified example of expressive variation in an I-meter (here B is a slightly stretched beat and b is slightly compressed beat):

> . . . B b b B B b b B B b b B B b b B B b b B B b b B . . .

Notice that this creates the same effect, as the regularities of the expressive timing indicate that here we have a four-beat pattern, even if we aren't sure which beat is the downbeat. Thus expressive variation in an I-meter functions much like the variegated beat pattern of a NI-meter: they both make the higher-level periodicities clear. The difference is that in NI-meters the distinction(s) among the beats is "engineered" into the formal structure of the meter, while in I-meters these distinctions may be added (and, I would conjecture, usually are added) via conventions of expressive variation. In both cases a process of template matching will help indicate which beat is the downbeat, given the listener's familiarity with characteristic patterns of expressive variation. I hasten to add that in holding to the MMH, these expressive variations are not really additions at all, but information that is integrated into the timing values of stylistically differentiated tempo-metrical types.

Thought number 2: subdivision is important. In other studies of meter subdivision has received little (if any) attention, but here I have tried to give the littlest notes their due. This is made clear in *Hearing in Time*'s WFCs and the pride of place they give to the N-cycle, as it is the foundation for the other levels of structure. The cardinality and the prime factors of the N-cycle determine what kinds of beat cycles (and other subcycles) will be possible within it. The N-cycle is the one level that must be isochronous, since it defines the isochrony or non-isochrony of all other levels. The importance of subdivision goes beyond these formal requirements, however. Subdivisions are the baseline for the level of rhythmic activity and energy in the music; as such Nketia's characterization of them as the "density referent," is most apt. Beats that are composed of rapid quadruples or sextuplets have a very different character from those involving simple duplets, even if the beat-level IOIs are the same. Even when not phenomenally present, we need to have a sense of the beat's subdivision, as it plays such an important role in defining the gestural qualities of melodic and rhythmic figures. This notion is supported by the relationships among the thresholds for beat versus subdivision perception, and so it would seem that hearing latent subdivisions in undivided beats involves very basic or low-level aspects of our auditory perception.

Thought number 3: the results of psychological research in rhythmic perception and cognition are old news to musicians. This isn't because musicians and music theorists are well versed in the early work of James, Wundt, and Woodrow (let alone more recent research). Rather, it is just that the various capacities and thresholds that have been studied and quantified in the psychological laboratory are commonsense aspects of everyday musical practice. They are intuitively known to composers when they write their music and to performers in their choices of tempo. At the same time, most musicians including performers, composers, and theorists are unaware of the psychological significance of what they do every day.

By now I hope it is obvious how much research in music perception and cognition can add to music theory and musical analysis, and vice versa. There also are critical implications for this research that could lead to a cognitive theory of musical gesture, motion, and affect. Like painterly manipulation of perspective and color, the way in which a melody or rhythmic pattern strikes our senses in many ways depends on our perceptual abilities. A shimmering melody, an almost inert rhythm—such characterizations depend on our perceptual and cognitive limits and the ways those limits are incorporated into a metrical framework.

These innate limits and abilities are, I presume, universal. Although they may be manifest in different cultures in different ways, I believe they help explain why we tend to respond to the rhythms of the world's musics in the same, visceral way. In hearing metrically we engage one of our most basic perceptual and behavioral capacities. So when we gather to listen to music, we synchronize our attention to its melodies and rhythms, and we tap our toes and dance and sway, whether it is Bach, bossa nova, be-bop, or Balkan dances. In so doing, we are hearing in time, together.

Notes

Introduction

1. For a more extended discussion of the distinction between rhythm and meter, see London (2001), part I, section 1.

2. One could turn this around and say the motor behavior is what drives the attentional behavior—this is the argument pursued by Todd (1995, 1996a, 1996b; Todd, O'Boyle, et al. 1999; as well as Iyer 2002). Although this is a question of some import for neurophysiology and neuropsychology, i.e., whether or not it is the toe-tapping the drives my attention or the attention that drives my toe, the musical upshot is the same: meter resides in the interaction between the listener and the temporal events in the music he or she is listening to.

1. Meter as a Kind of Attentional Behavior

1. This "negative asynchrony" depends on both the tempo of the pacing signal and the response mode (i.e., hand or finger versus foot tapping). At slower tempos there is greater variability in the synchronization, but as tempo increases the negative asynchrony diminishes; it disappears entirely around 500–600 ms IOI. However, when subjects are asked to synchronize with longer tones (300 ms in duration) rather than simple ticks of the metronome, performance improves (see Wohlschläger and Koch 2000, p. 116).

2. It should be noted that Boltz's study, like many others in music perception and cogntion, suffers because of problems in the design of its stimulus materials. The temporal variants introduced in the second half of each stimulus necessarily affected their rhythmic and tonal syntax. Unfortunately, as Boltz is neither a composer nor music theorist, these stimuli displayed various degrees of musical grammaticality. As a result, in some cases it may not be temporal accent structure that gave rise

to her results, but simply that unstylistic or ungrammatical melodies may have been judged to be less closed than grammatical ones.

3. It should be noted that Gallun and Reisberg (1995) were unable to replicate Dowling et al.'s results, as they changed the pretest, experimental task, and stimulus set in their experiments. Also, the particular configuration of their randomly generated distractor tones may have influenced their results. Rather than random distractors, better results would have been obtained with carefully composed interleavings (with the aid of composer or theorist conversant with tonal melodic syntax) that would control for the accidental creation of alternate melodic and harmonic patterns.

4. Subjective rhythmization has its analogs in visual perception, and these have long been known (Boring 1942; Schumann 1900).

5. Povel (1984) equates metric malleability with rhythmic ambiguity; for him, such ambiguity obtains precisely when there are two or more equally plausible metric grids for a given rhythmic pattern (p. 325). As we will see in chapter 5, malleability and ambiguity, while related, are not quite synonymous.

6. Examples of listeners projecting a particular meter on more or less a metrically neutral surface have been offered as evidence for the *categorical perception* of duration or meter (e.g., Clarke 1987a, 1990, 1993; Cutting 1976; Gabrielsson 1983; Schulze 1989a; Windsor, 1993). Categorical perception in the case of duration means whether, for example, two successive durations are heard as the same/even or different/uneven, even if the durations are unequal (in the former instance) or nearly equal (in the latter). Such categorical perceptions of duration may be yoked to our sense of meter. For example, even durations may be part and parcel of successive IOIs in a duple meter, whereas uneven durations may be heard relative to a triple meter (where the longer duration comprises two beats or subdivisions, while the shorter involves but one). Recently, Clarke (2000) has questioned whether these are bona-fide cases of categorical perception. Although it is true that some aspects of musical structure and meaning are not categorical, it also would seem that in the particular case of meter, our perception of rhythmic patterns is indeed categorical in that we attend to the musical surface in terms of one attentional frame and not another.

7. It will be assumed that meter in the musical foreground, cued by durational patterns, phenomenal accents, melodic contours, expressive variations, and so forth, works largely independent of tonal criteria, such as harmonic change or scale step. While there are some significant interactions between pitch and rhythm (Van Noorden 1975, 1982), there is considerable evidence that rhythm and meter is perceptually and conceptually *prior* to tonal criteria (Boltz 1995; Deutsch 1980; Jones 1976; Jones, Boltz, & Kidd 1982; London 1990; Schmuckler & Boltz 1994).

8. Narmour (1990) and Taggart (1996) have both commented on how style structure can work in a top-down fashion to influence our interpretation of rhythmic events.

9. For summaries of research on the mental representation of temporal intervals and timekeepers, see Sloboda (1983, 1985), Pressing (1995), Vorberg and Wing (1996), and Large and Jones (1999).

10. I thank Michael Spitzer (private communication) for pointing out some of these terminological relationships to me; a discussion of Koch and Sulzer is also given in Hasty (1997, pp. 27–28).

11. Figure 1.2 shows the relative strength and salience of each oscillator at any given point in the cycle, and this allows one to determine whether an event that occurs in the trough between two peaks is heard as late relative to the previous peak, or early relative to the following peak. So, for example, a between-peak event is marked as early (relative to the strong beat) since at the time of its occurrence, the measure-level oscillator shown by the dashed line is generating a greater sense of expectancy than beat-level oscillator shown by the dotted line. As a result, the between-peak event is "captured" by the following downbeat.

12. This presumes that rhythmic and metric clarity is desired, and this is normally the case. But in some contexts metric ambiguity may be desired, and therefore one cannot simply require all correct performances to clearly project a metrical structure.

13. The performer may have levels of attending (i.e., have metrically broad anticipations) that the listener does not because the performer has greater familiarity with the music—and after all knows what is coming in a way the listener may not. By contrast, a performer who is focused on local problems of execution may not be attending to broader metric levels as could the listener at that very moment, as the listener is not burdened by the problems of fingering, breath support, and so on.

2. Research on Temporal Perception and its Relevance for
Theories of Musical Meter

1. Bilmes (1993) proposes the term "Tatum" to refer to the shortest possible unit of subdivision in honor of the great jazz piano virtuoso Art Tatum.

2. Apparent motion in vision occurs only at very short temporal intervals (20–60 ms), whereas auditory stimuli give rise to sense of continuity and movement over much longer intervals (i.e., the range in which one can hear a sense of beat of pulse). Thus, the analogy here is between the fact that apparent motion arises in both perceptual modalities, and not between the specific temporal ranges in which it occurs in each modality.

3. Royal (1995) provides an excellent summary of this research (pp. 45–49).

4. I have specifically avoided saying that the triplet defines the long-short of uneven subdivision in terms of an exact 2:1 durational ratio, as this durational value is usually not present in actual performance (see, for example, Collier and Collier 1996 for a review of studies of performance timing of swing rhythm in jazz performance). That is, the triplet itself is subject to expressive timing variations, and these in turn relate to the observed durational ratios.

5. Schulze (1989), Clarke and Windsor (1992), Windsor (1993), and Large (2000) have studied categorical perception of an entire measure, that is, on how one hears a shift from $\frac{3}{4}$ to $\frac{6}{8}$ (and vice versa) as the ratio of an L–S interval is systematically manipulated. Large especially found evidence of a "hysteresis effect," whereby the same

ratio is heard as either a $\frac{3}{4}$ or $\frac{6}{8}$ measure depending on the prior context: if possible, we tend to maintain a metric context rather than shift it. Similar studies have not, to my knowledge, been undertaken on the smaller time scales related to metric subdivision, but one would expect that similar behaviors indicative of categorical perception of beat subdivision would also occur.

6. My conjecture that hearing a beat requires hearing at least a *potential* for subdivision may be related to human movement, which is always cyclic. For example, if the hand makes a beating motion (up and down), it must move away from and then return to its initial position to make each beat. The return motion is more or less in antiphase with the beat. If the beat rate is so fast that the return movement cannot be completed, then it is physically impossible to beat. And if beat perception is parasitic on the motor system, then in a Gibsonian sense, perceiving a beat is perceiving the affordance of (physically) beating time. I am grateful to Bruno Repp for pointing this out to me.

7. Musically it is clear that the $\frac{8}{4}$ level is more apt to emerge than $\frac{12}{4}$, because an eight-beat unit is marked by a shift in the bass, increased dissonance, and as the piece continues beyond the given excerpt, by explicit two-bar patterning.

8. Barnes and Jones (2000) provide some evidence that periodicities in this range may have a weak influence on attending behaviors; see pages 290–1 for a cautionary discussion.

3. Meter-Rhythm Interactions I: Ground Rules

1. Vazan and Schober's results run parallel those of Chambers and Reisberg (1985), who studied the reconstrual of ambiguous visual figures.

2. Pressing (private communication) has pointed out that even when using a composite pattern to produce a polyrhythm, performers will still favor one stream, such that it serves as the metric ground for the other. Expert performers may become adept at using either stream as the metric ground at moderate tempos, but at tempo extremes they, too, are only able to use one stream as the metric ground.

3. Desain and Honing (1994) have included a beat interpolation component as part of their more general "beat extraction" model, but their model does not interpolate a metrical layer that is continuously absent from the rhythmic surface.

4. Metric Representations and Metric Well-Formedness

1. It is worth noting that tonality is similarly "invisible"—given that most scores contain a key signature and that certain pitches are present, both successively and in combination, hearing a chord progression "in E♭," is, like hearing a rhythmic pattern "in simple triple time" a perceptually emergent property of the music.

2. Lerdahl and Jackendoff's notation is drawn from Komar (1971), and it also has much in common with Liberman's (1975) metric diagrams for speech prosody.

3. As we will see in subsequent chapters, one can speak of half-measures even in

cases where one has an odd number of beats, or when the beats themselves are non-isochronous. Thus, half measures need not be exactly (or even nearly, as would be the case with expressive variation) ½ of the N-cycle.

4. Povel notes that in a metrical system "one interval can be used to organize the others" (1984, p. 319), and here this is true with respect to the N-cycle, but *only* with respect to the N-cycle. As we will see, it does not hold with respect to IOIs on other levels.

5. Whereas "time lines" such as 2-1-2-1-2 and others (e.g., 2-2-1-2-2-2-1) may be familiar to students of various non-Western musics, it is argued later and in the following chapters that such timelines do not represent meters per se but, rather, the organization of surface rhythms.

6. This is a variant of the nomenclature for metric cycles developed by Cohn (1992).

5. Meter-Rhythm Interactions II: Problems

1. Rothstein's analysis is actually a bit more subtle and complicated than this, as he notes that the primary meter is not $\frac{2}{4}$ but $\frac{4}{4}$ (that is, every odd-numbered bar functions as a downbeat). However, this $\frac{4}{4}$ level of activity also entails $\frac{2}{4}$ half-measures, and if I were to take up Rothstein's point of view, I would argue that the presence of the shadow meter undermines the $\frac{4}{4}$ level such that the primary meter collapses from $\frac{4}{4}$ to $\frac{2}{4}$—the primary meter requires a constant reiteration of its accentual pattern to refute the "shadow downbeats." Either way, figure 5.1 is a reasonably fair description of at least some of the metric conflict Rothstein claims to be present in this passage.

2. Krebs (private communication) has clarified that when he speaks of "metrical" and "anti-metrical" strata, he is speaking of only a single meter against which another pattern is dissonant. I remain uneasy, however, in using terminology and concepts derived from tonal phenomena to describe rhythm and meter (see London 2002b).

3. This pattern, and variations upon it, could be very useful in studies of beat interpolation (i.e., a tapping test, in which listeners are instructed to interpolate either one or two beats, whichever seems to be rhythmically "natural"/"correct"/etc.). One could use the "literal figure" (a deadpan timing of 1800 ms – 300 ms – 300 ms) as a standard, against which one could vary the IOI of the long note as well as the IOI(s) of the shorter notes for a priming stimulus. Alternatively, performance timings of this figure gathered from musicians playing the figure in different notational contexts also may be of interest, as they may use various strategies of expressive variation to convey the sense of triple versus quadruple meter (and indeed, whether or not listeners could reliably tell would be most interesting).

4. This example also involves an elision between the end of the consequent phrase in measure 8 and the beginning of the following phrase, also in measure 8. For the eighth measure not only starts with a rest but also involves a new motivic pattern, and once we realize this (when the motive is sequenced in measure 9), we hear measure 8 as both the end of one phrase and the beginning of the next—making the accented rest all the more salient.

6. Metric Flux in Beethoven's Fifth

1. Of course, the conductor will need to give some cue for the entrance of the 2nd violins in measure 6. One can have a quiet release, and then cue the upbeat for the 2nd violins in the left hand, thus effacing the downbeat in measure 6. It is also possible to cue the release of the fermata with a downbeat gesture, and the resultant "bump" (slight sforzando) on the release may mark a downbeat. Or one can have quiet release, and then conduct a downbeat to cue the 2nd violin entrance—but this effectively adds a downbeat and hence an extra measure to the music. I am grateful to my Carleton colleague Hector Valdivia for his helpful discussions on how to conduct this and other passages in this movement.

7. Nonisochronous Meters

1. As we shall see, it is problematic to claim that non-isochronous meters are more complex than isochronous meters *tout court*. Thus, I am rejecting the use of the term "complex meters" that I had previously employed (London 1995).

2. A 4-5 subcycle is also possible, although given the timing constraints on both the N-cycle and on the beats themselves, it is more likely that a 4-5 pattern would emerge as a half-measure cycle concurrent with a 2-2-2-3 beat-cycle. See discussion of analogous cases in 12- and 16-cycles in the next chapter.

3. In the case of four beats in a 9-cycle, WFC 5 also comes into play, as it precludes having a 1-2-3-3 pattern. Note that the 1-2-3-3 pattern is not maximally even.

4. In the case of triple meters one might analogously speak of "third-measures," that is, of the most symmetrical spacing for three beats within the N-cycle. If N has 3 as a prime factor (e.g., and for all practical purposes, if N = 6, 9, 12, 15, 18, 21, or 24), then one may have "perfect third measures." For other values of N, maximal evenness may be calculated as follows: $N \div 3$ yields an integer value, V, plus a remainder, R. If R = 1, then the best possible third measure involves a pattern of V, V, and V + 1 elements. If R = 2, then the best possible third measure involves a pattern of V, V + 1, and V + 1 elements. So, for example, if N = 10, the best possible "triple measure" involves a 3-3-4 pattern.

5. Relationships such as 2:5, 2:9, 3:7, and so forth are sometimes presented as if they described the relationship between specific beat classes, in the case of various Tālas in Indian music, but here it is argued that these represent rhythmic rather than metric patterns.

6. Nketia acknowledges this limitation on beat length in African NI meters, as he discusses both maximum and minimum beat length relative to an underlying cycle of rapid pulses (i.e., the N-cycle), as well as the maximum and minimum lengths for phrases containing such beats (1963b, p. 91.)

8. NI Meters in Theory and Practice

1. "8-26" refers to a system of indexing pitch-class collections according to their interval content developed by Allen Forte (1973). The 8-26 collection corresponds,

for example, to the pitch-classes C D E F G G# A B. If one maps these pitch-classes in a circular fashion (much as we have mapped a metric 12-cycle), their symmetry becomes apparent, as well as the fact that if one wishes to have two successive whole steps (the intervals C–D and D–E in this instance), then in this set the distribution of the remaining pitch-classes is the best one possible in terms of maximal evenness. The most maximally even distribution of eight pitch classes in a chromatic series is a regular alternation of half- and whole-steps, the "octatonic" scale.

2. Two examples of our construal of a diatonic set/key from a "gapped chromatic" collection can be found in popular culture, that is, cartoon theme music. North American readers of a certain age may be familiar with the Hanna-Barbera cartoon series *The Jetsons*. Its theme, relative to C major, starts with the notes C–E–F#–G. North American readers of a somewhat younger age may be familiar with the current cartoon *The Simpsons*, whose theme, also relative to C major, begins C–E–F#–A–G. It becomes clear as the melodies continue that both are clearly in C major, and in both cases the F# is a "wrong" (that is to say, chromatic) note.

3. The following report is clearly no substitute for a properly done laboratory study of listener responses to this pattern at various tempos. Nonetheless, I include it for thoroughness of discussion and also as a preliminary to further empirical research. The listening material involved presentations of a 3-5 figure registrally distinct from a stream of underlying pulses (on those "trials" when the N-cycle pulses were present). A score written under the *Encore* music notation package served as the performance controller, and Macintosh Quicktime MIDI instrument sounds were used; listening was via headphones. All performances were "deadpan," without expressive timing variations.

4. In table 8.3, one might consider a NI four-beat pattern, where the beats are 3-2-3-4. This can be discounted for the same reasons we discounted the 4-3-2 pattern in the context of the 9-cycle in chapter 7. Rahn (1983) does find some examples of the 3-2-3-4 pattern in African drumming, but he notes that, as our WFCs would predict, where one drum articulates this pattern another usually plays a 3-2-3-2-2 figure; in such cases the 4 is decomposed into two 2s to avoid ambiguity.

5. In example 8.7 the timeline is given as 2-2-1-2 | 2-2-1 or 2-1-2 | 2-2-1-2, but as Nketia makes clear in his other examples, these relate to a 2-2-3 | 2-3 or 2-3 | 2-2-3 beat cycle.

6. Povel and Essens (1985) found that the middle tones of a group of three or more tones tend to be perceived as unaccented, while the boundary tones are likely to be heard as accented—although their use of the term accent is generic, and does not distinguish between rhythmic and metric accent. To the extent that rhythmic and metric accent tend to be congruent (and even more so in the case of NI-meters) patterns that do not involve this accentual congruence will tend to be avoided.

7. Note that the 2-2-3-2-3 beat cycle involves two specific beat classes (2 or 3) and two specific half-measure classes (5 or 7). Because each half-measure class (5 or 7) is composed of the same quantity and kind of beat classes (5 = one 2 and one 3; 7 = two 2s and one 3), no such ambiguity is involved.

8. Nketia (1963b, pp. 81–85) notes how elements in a time line may be omitted, so that a sequence which "normally" contains five, six, or seven claps or gong-strikes may be reduced by omitting some of these articulations, resulting in longer IOIs be-

tween some adjacent elements; Nketia specifically notes this practice with respect to five-versus seven-element clap patterns.

9. The Many Meters Hypothesis

1. As has been shown (Penel & Drake 1998; Repp 1999a), even when performers are instructed to give a "deadpan" performance, they nonetheless produce timing patterns similar to "expressive" performances of the same music.

2. Repp, like many other researchers, at times refers to expressive timing variations as a kind of tempo variation. This does not seem quite right. If these variations exhibit a higher order pattern of acceleration or deceleration (over a moderate or longer term, i.e., a half-phrase or more), then it would seem appropriate to characterize them in terms of tempo variation. If, however, there is only a moderate amount of variation, and it does not affect higher-order periodicities, then this would not seem to be a tempo-related phenomenon, but part of the normative and systematic fluctuation of IOIs that is characteristic of what is perceived as a stable tempo.

3. Penel and Drake (1998) have argued that some expressive timings are the result of low-level constraints in the auditory system, and thus expressive variations are a means of compensating for these constraints. As a result, in order for a series of notes to sound even, they must be played unevenly—these are "obligatory" timing variations. There can be additional timing variations, over and above this psycho-acoustic compensation, and these "voluntary" timing deviations can and do serve expressive/interpretive purposes. Repp (1998c) gives a fairly robust counterargument.

4. This discussion of rhythmic archetypes relative to a metric context is modeled after and greatly indebted to Cooper and Meyer (1960).

5. I have not tried to capture the exact timings here for each time-point on the 12-cycle, as my aim here is illustrative rather than analytical.

6. Or maybe not—an interesting question arises as to whether tempo or metrical type is the stronger form of relation. That is, metric similarly and overlap (in terms of the underlying timing mechanisms which give rise to particular metrical behaviors) may be more related to tempo than metrical type. Thus, for example, a 16-cycle and a 6-cycle may be more closely related (provided their beat cycle IOIs fall within the same range) than two 16-cycles at markedly different tempos. This is clearly a subject for more empirical research.

7. Geoff Collier (private communication), in carrying out his study of timings used by jazz drummers, found that his expert subjects were quite ready and able to imitate other well-known drummers, and indeed could produce on demand their characteristic "grooves" (i.e., timing patterns for typical jazz rhythms such as a ride cymbal pattern).

Conclusion

1. Pressing makes one error in his description of his patterns, or perhaps it is a typographical mistake: pattern c is not like any of the other patterns, in that as it loops, it will form an ascending figure, and not a descent.

Bibliography

Agawu, Kofi. 1995. *African Rhythm: A Northern Ewe Perspective*. Cambridge: Cambridge University Press.

Allan, Lorraine. G. 1979. The Perception of Time. *Perception and Psychophysics* 26(5): 340–54.

Allan, Lorraine. G., and Alfred. B. Kristofferson. 1974. Successiveness Discrimination: Two Models. *Perception and Psychophysics* 15(1): 37–46.

Arlin, Mary. 2000. Metric Mutation and Modulation: The Nineteenth-Century Speculations of F.-J. Fétis. *Journal of Music Theory* 44(2): 261–322.

Arom, Simha. 1991. *African Polyphony and Polyrhythm*. Martin Thom, Barbara Tuckett, and Raymond Boyd, trans. Cambridge: Cambridge University Press.

Babbitt, Milton. 1962/1972. Twelve Tone Rhythmic Structure and the Electronic Medium. In *Perspectives on Contemporary Music Theory*, ed. Benjamin Boretz and Edward T. Cone. New York: Norton: 148–79.

Baddeley, Alan D. 1976. *The Psychology of Memory*. New York: Basic Books.

Balzano, Gerald J. 1987. Measuring Music. In *Action and Perception in Rhythm and Music*, ed. Alf Gabrielsson. Stockholm, Royal Swedish Academy of Music, vol. 55: 177–99.

Barnes, Ralph, and Mari Riess Jones. 2000. Expectancy, Attention, and Time. *Cognitive Psychology* 41: 254–311.

Beek, Peter J., C. E. Peper, et al. 2000. Timekeepers versus Nonlinear Oscillators: How the Approaches Differ. In *Rhythm Perception and Production*, ed. Peter Desain and W. Luke Windsor. Lisse: Swets and Zeitlinger: 9–33.

Bengtsson, Ingmar, and Alf Gabrielsson. 1983. Analysis and Synthesis of Musical Rhythm. in *Studies of Music Performance*, ed. J. Sundberg. Stockholm, Royal Swedish Academy of Music. 39: 27–60.

Berry, Wallace. 1976. *Structural Functions in Music*. Englewood Cliffs, N.J.: Prentice Hall.

——— 1985. Metric and Rhythmic Articulation in Music. *Music Theory Spectrum* 7: 7–33.

——— 1989. *Musical Structure and Performance*. New Haven, Conn.: Yale University Press.

Bharucha, Jamshed J., and John H. Pryor. 1986. Disrupting the Isochrony Underlying Rhythm: An Asymmetry in Discrimination. *Perception and Psychophysics* 40(3): 137–41.

Bilmes, Jeffrey A. 1993. Timing is of the Essence: Perceptual and Computational Techniques for Representing, Learning, and Reproducing Expressive Timing in Percussive Rhythm. MA Thesis, MIT.

Bolton, T. L. 1894. Rhythm. *American Journal of Psychology* 6: 145–238.

Boltz, Marilyn G. 1989. Rhythm and Good Endings: Effects of Temporal Structure on Tonality Judgements. *Perception and Psychophysics* 46(1): 9–17.

———— 1991. Some Structural Determinants of Melody Recall. *Memory and Cognition* 19(3): 239–51.

———— 1993. Time Estimation and Expectancies. *Memory and Cognition* 21(6): 853–63.

———— 1995. The Generation of Temporal and Melodic Expectancies During Musical Listening. *Perception and Psychophysics* 53(6): 585–600.

———— 1998. Tempo Discrimination of Musical Patterns: Effects Due to Pitch and Rhythmic Structure. *Perception and Psychophysics* 60(8): 1357–73.

Boring, Edwin G. 1942. *Sensation and Perception in the History of Experimental Psychology*. New York: Appleton-Century.

Bregman, Albert S. 1990. *Auditory Scene Analysis: The Perceptual Organization of Sound.* Cambridge, Mass.: MIT Press.

Brower, Candace. 1993. Memory and the Perception of Rhythm. *Music Theory Spectrum* 15(1): 19–35.

Brown, Howard M. 1980. Tactus. In *The New Grove Dictionary of Music and Musicians,* ed. Stanley Sadie. London, Macmillan, 18: 518.

Caplin, William. 1981. Theories of Harmonic-Metric Relationships from Rameau to Riemann. PhD Diss., University of Chicago.

Carey, Norman. 2000. Coherence and Failure: A General Theory of Ambiguity and Contradiction. Paper read at the Annual Meeting of the *Society for Music Theory,* Toronto, November 5th.

Chambers, Deborah, and Daniel Reisberg. 1985. Can Mental Images Be Ambiguous? *Journal of Experimental Psychology: Human Perception and Performance* 11(3): 317–28.

Christensen, Thomas, and Nancy K. Baker, Eds. 1995. *Aesthetics and the Art of Musical Composition in the German Enlightenment.* Cambridge Studies in Music Theory and Analysis. Cambridge: Cambridge University Press.

Clarke, Eric F. 1985. Structure and Expression in Rhythmic Performance. In *Music Structure and Cognition,* ed. P. Howell, I. Cross and R. West. London, Academic Press: 209–36.

———— 1987. Categorical Rhythmic Perception: An Ecological Perspective. In *Action and Perception in Rhythm and Music,* ed. Alf Gabrielsson. Stockholm, Royal Swedish Academy of Music, No. 55: 19–33.

———— 1989. The Perception of Expressive Timing in Music. *Psychological Research* 51: 2–9.

———— 1990. Expression and Communication in Musical Performance. In *Proceedings of the International Symposium on Music, Language, Speech, and Brain,* Stockholm, ed. J. Sundberg, L. Nord, and R. Carlson. New York: Macmillan: 184–93.

———— 1993. Imitating and Evaluating Real and Transformed Musical Performances. *Music Perception* 10(3): 317–41.

———— 1999. Rhythm and Timing in Music. In *The Psychology of Music,* ed. Diana Deutsch. New York: Academic Press: 473–500.

———— 2000. *Categorical Rhythm Perception and Event Perception.* Sixth International Conference on Music Perception and Cognition, Keele University, U.K.

Clarke, Eric F., and W. Luke Windsor. 1992. Dynamic Information for Metre. *Fourth Workshop on Rhythm Perception and Production,* Bourges, France.

———— 1993. Using Probe Events to Investigate the Perception of Meter. *Biannual Meeting of the Society for Music Perception and Cognition,* Philadelphia, Pa. June 17.

———— 2000. Real and Simulated Expression: A Listening Study. *Music Perception* 17(3): 277–313.

Clough, John, and Jack Douthett. 1991. Maximally Even Sets. *Journal of Music Theory* 35(1 and 2): 93–173.

Clynes, Manfred. 1986. When Time is Music. In *Rhythm in Psychological, Linguistic, and Musical Processes,* ed. James R. Evans and Manfred Clynes. Springfield, Ill.: Thomas: 169–224.

Clynes, Manfred, and Janice Walker. 1982. Neurobiologic Functions of Rhythm, Time, and Pulse in Music. In *Music, Mind, and Brain,* ed. Manfred Clynes. New York: Plenum Press: 171–216.

Cohn, Richard. 1992. Metric and Hypermetric Dissonance in the Menuetto of Mozart's Symphony in G-minor, K. 550. *Integral* 6: 1–33.

Collier, Geoffrey L., and James L. Collier. 1994. An Exploration of the Use of Tempo in Jazz. *Music Perception* 11(3): 219–42.

———— 1996. Microrhythms in Jazz: A Review of Papers. *Annual Review of Jazz Studies* 8: 117–39.

Collier, Geoffrey L., and Charles E. Wright. 1995. Temporal Rescaling of Simple and Complex Ratios in Rhythmic Tapping. *Journal of Experimental Psychology: Human Perception and Performance* 21(3): 602–27.

Collyer, Charles E., and Russell M. Church. 1998. Interresponse Intervals in Continuation Tapping. In *Timing of Behavior: Neural, Psychological, and Computational Perspectives,* ed. David A. Rosenbaum and Charles E. Collyer. Cambridge, Mass.: MIT Press: 63–87.

Collyer, Charles E., Hilary A. Broadbent, et al. 1992. Categorical Time Production: Evidence for Discrete Timing in Motor Control. *Perception and Psychophysics* 51(2): 134–44.

Collyer, Charles E., Hilary A. Broadbent, et al. 1994. Preferred Rates of Repetitive Tapping and Categorical Time Production. *Perception and Psychophysics* 55(4): 443–53.

Cone, Edward T. 1968. *Musical Form and Musical Performance.* New York: Norton.

Cooper, Grosvenor, and Leonard B. Meyer. 1960. *The Rhythmic Structure of Music.* Chicago: University of Chicago Press.

Cutting, James E., Burton S. Rosner, et al. 1976. Perceptual Categories for Music-like Sounds: Implications for Theories of Speech Perception. *Quarterly Journal of Experimental Psychology* 28: 361–78.

Desain, Peter. 1992. A (De)Composable Theory of Rhythm Perception. *Music Perception* 9(4): 439–54.

Desain, Peter, and Henkjan Honing. 1992. Time Functions Function Best as Functions of Multiple Times. In *Music, Mind, and Machine,* ed. Peter Desain and Henkjan Honing. Amsterdam: Thesis Publishers: 149–66.

———— 1994. Does Expressive Timing in Music Performance Scale Proportionally with Tempo? *Psychological Research* 56: 285–92.

———— 1994. Advanced Issues in Beat Induction Modeling: Syncopation, Tempo, and Timing. Proceedings of the *1994 International Computer Music Conference.* San Francisco: International Computer Music Association: 92–94.

———— 1999. Computational Models of Beat Induction: The Rule-Based Approach. *Journal of New Music Research* 28(1): 29–42.

Deutsch, Diana. 1980. The Processing of Structured and Unstructured Tonal Sequences. *Perception and Psychophysics* 28: 381–89.

Deutsch, Diana, and John Feroe. 1981. The Internal Representation of Pitch Sequences in Tonal Music. *Psychological Review* 88(6): 503–522.

Dowling, W. Jay. 1973. The Perception of Interleaved Melodies. *Cognitive Psychology* 5: 322–37.

Dowling, W. Jay, and Dane L. Harwood. 1986. *Music Cognition.* Orlando: Academic Press.

Dowling, W. Jay, Kitty Mei-Tak Lung, et al. 1987. Aiming Attention in Pitch and Time in the Perception of Interleaved Melodies. *Perception and Psychophysics* 41(6): 642–56.

Drake, Carolyn. 1998. Psychological Processes Involved in the Temporal Organization of Complex Auditory Sequences: Universal and Acquired Processes. *Music Perception* 16(1): 11–26.

Drake, Carolyn, and Marie-Claire Botte. 1993. Tempo Sensitivity in Auditory Sequences: Evidence for a Multiple-Look Model. *Perception and Psychophysics,* 54, 277–86.

Drake, Carolyn, Mari Riess Jones, et al. 2000. The Development of Rhythmic Attending in Auditory Sequences: Attunement, Referent Period, Focal Attending. *Cognition* 77(3): 251–88.

Drake, Carolyn, and Caroline Palmer. 1993. Accent Structures in Music Performance. *Music Perception* 10(3): 343–78.

Drake, Carolyn, Amadine Penel, et al. 2000a. Tapping in Time with Mechanically and Expressively Performed Music. *Music Perception* 18(1): 1–23.

Drake, Carolyn, Amadine Penel, et al. 2000b. Why Musicians Tap Slower Than Non-Musicians. In *Rhythm Perception and Production,* ed. Peter Desain and W. Luke Windsor. Lisse: Swets and Zeitlinger: 245–48.

Duke, Robert A. 1989. Musicians' Perception of Beat in Monotonic Stimuli. *Journal of Research in Music Education* 37(1): 61–71.

———— 1994. When Tempo Changes Rhythm: The Effect of Tempo on Nonmusicians Perception of Rhythm. *Journal of Research in Music Education* 42(1): 27–35.

Duke, Robert A., John M. Geringer, et al. (1991). Performance of Perceived Beat in Relation to Age and Music Training. *Journal of Research in Music Education* 39(1): 35–45.

Dunlap, Knight. 1910. Reaction to Rhythmic Stimuli with Attempt to Synchronize. *Psychological Review* 17(6): 399–416.

Eck, Douglas, Michael Gasser, et al. 2000. Dynamics and Embodiment in Beat Induction. In *Rhythm Perception and Production,* ed. Peter Desain and W. Luke Windsor. Lisse: Swets and Zeitlinger: 157–70.

Efron, R. 1973. An Invariant Characteristic of Perceptual Systems in the Time Domain. In *Attention and Performance IV,* ed. S. Kornblum. New York: Academic Press: 713–36.

Epstein, David. 1995. *Shaping Time: Music, the Brain, and Performance.* New York: Schirmer.

Essens, Peter J. 1986. Hierarchical Organization of Temporal Patterns. *Perception and Psychophysics* 40(2): 69–73.

Essens, Peter J., and Dirk-Jan Povel. 1985. Metric and Nonmetrical Representations of Temporal Patterns. *Perception and Psychophysics* 37(1): 1–7.

Forte, Allen. 1973. *The Structure of Atonal Music.* New Haven, Conn.: Yale University Press.

Fraisse, Paul. 1963. *Psychology of Time.* New York: Harper.

———— 1982. Rhythm and Tempo. In *The Psychology of Music,* ed. Diana Deutsch. New York: Academic Press: 149–80.

———— 1984. Perception and Estimation of Time. *Annual Review of Psychology* 35: 1–36.

Franek, M., J. Mates, et al. 1991. Finger Tapping in Musicians and Nonmusicians. *International Journal of Psychophysiology* 11(3): 277–9.

Friberg, Anders, and Johan Sundberg. 1995. Time Discrimination in a Monotonic, Isochronous Sequence. *Journal of the Acoustical Society of America* 98(5): 2524–31.

Friberg, Anders, and Andreas Sundström. 2002. Swing Ratios and Ensemble Timing in Jazz Performance: Evidence for a Common Rhythmic Pattern. *Music Perception* 19(3): 333–49.

Gabrielsson, Alf. 1982. Perception and Performance of Musical Rhythm. In *Music, Mind, and Brain,* ed. Manfred Clynes. New York, Plenum Press: 159–69.

———— 1987. Once Again: The Theme from Mozart's Piano Sonata in A Major (K. 331). In *Action and Perception in Rhythm and Music,* ed. Alf Gabrielsson. Stockholm: Royal Swedish Academy of Music. 55: 81–103.

———— 1993. The Complexities of Rhythm. In *Psychology and Music: The Understanding of Melody and Rhythm,* ed. Thomas J. Tighe and W. Jay Dowling. Hillsdale, N.J.: Erlbaum: 93–120.

Gallun, Erick, and Daniel Resiberg. 1995. On the Perception of Interleaved Melodies. *Music Perception* 12(4): 387–98.

Gentner, Donald R. 1987. Timing of Skilled Motor Performance: Tests of the Proportional Duration Model. *Psychological Review* 94(2): 255–76.

Getty, David J. 1975. Discrimination of Short Temporal Intervals: A Comparison of Two Models. *Perception and Psychophysics* 18(1): 1–8.

Gibson, James J. 1966. *The Senses Considered as Perceptual Systems.* Boston: Houghton Mifflin.

———— 1982. *Reasons for Realism : Selected Essays of James J. Gibson.* Hillsdale, N.J.: Erlbaum.

Gjerdingen, Robert O. 1989. Meter as a Mode of Attending: A Network Simulation of Attentional Rhythmicity in Music. *Integral* 3: 67–91.

———— 1993. 'Smooth' Rhythms as Probes of Entrainment. *Music Perception* 10(4): 503–8.

———— 1994. Apparent Motion in Music? *Music Perception* 11(4): 335–70.

Glass, Leon, and Michael C. Mackey. 1988. *From Clocks to Chaos.* Princeton, N.J.: Princeton University Press.

Grave, Floyd. 1995. Metrical Dissonance in Haydn. *The Journal of Musicology* 12(3): 168–202.

Grieshaber, Kate. 1990. Polymetric Performance by Musicians, PhD Diss., University of Washington.

Halpern, Andrea R., and Christopher J. Darwin. 1982. Duration Discrimination in a Series of Rhythmic Events. *Perception and Psychophysics* 32(1): 86–89.

Handel, Stephen. 1984. Using Polyrhythms to Study Rhythm. *Music Perception* 1(4): 465–84.

———— 1989. *Listening: An Introduction to the Perception of Auditory Events.* Cambridge, Mass.: MIT Press.

———— 1992. The Differentiation of Rhythmic Structure. *Perception and Psychophysics* 52(5): 497–507.

———— 1993. The Effect of Tempo and Tone Duration on Rhythm Discrimination. *Perception and Psychophysics* 54(3): 370–82.

Handel, Stephen, and Gregory R. Lawson. 1983. The Contextual Nature of Rhythmic Interpretation. *Perception and Psychophysics* 34(2): 103–20.

Handel, Stephen, and James S. Oshinsky. 1981. The Meter of Syncopated Auditory Patterns. *Perception and Psychophysics* 30(1): 1–9.

Hasty, Christopher. 1997. *Meter as Rhythm*. Oxford: Oxford University Press.

Hauptmann, Mortiz. 1881. *The Nature of Harmony and Meter,* trans. W. E. Heathcote. New York: Novello, Ewer .

Heusler, Andreas. 1925. *Deutsche Versgeschichte*. Vol. I. Berlin: de Gruyter.

Hirsh, Ira J. 1959. Auditory Perception of Temporal Order. *Journal of the Acoustical Society of America* 31(6): 759–67.

Hirsh, Ira J., Caroline B. Monohan, et al. 1990. Studies in Auditory Timing: 1. Simple Patterns. *Perception and Psychophysics* 47(3): 215–26.

Horlacher, Gretchen. 1997. *Rhythmic Counterpoint in Steve Reich's Tehillim*. Paper read at the *West Coast Conference on Music Theory and Analsysis*, University of California at Santa Barbara.

Houle, George. 1987. *Meter in Music, 1600–1800*. Bloomington: Indiana University Press.

Imbrie, Andrew. 1973. Metrical Ambiguity in Beethoven. In *Beethoven Studies I,* ed. Alan Tyson. New York: Norton: 45–66.

Ivry, Richard B., and R. Eliot Hazeltine. 1995. Perception and Production of Temporal Intervals Across a Range of Durations: Evidence for a Common Timing Mechanism. *Journal of Experimental Psychology: Human Perception and Performance* 21(1): 3–18.

Iyer, Vijay. 2002. Embodied Mind, Situated Cognition, and Expressive Meaning. *Music Perception* 19(3): 387–414.

James, William. [1890] 1950. *The Principles of Psychology*. New York: Dover Reprint.

Johnson-Laird, Philip N. 1991. Rhythm and Meter: A Theory at the Computational Level. *Psychomusicology* 10: 88–106.

Jones, Mari Riess. 1976. Time, Our Lost Dimension: Toward a New Theory of Perception, Attention, and Memory. *Psychological Review* 83(5): 323–55.

———— 1981. Only Time Can Tell: On the Topology of Mental Space and Time. *Critical Inquiry* 7: 557–576.

———— 1986. Attentional Rhythmicity in Human Perception. In *Rhythm in Psychological, Linguistic, and Musical Processes*, ed. J. R. Evans and M. Clynes. Springfield, Ill.: Thomas.

———— 1987a. Dynamic Pattern Structure in Music: Recent Theory and Research. *Perception and Psychophysics* 41(6): 621–34.

———— 1987b. Perspectives on Musical Time. In *Action and Perception in Rhythm and Music*, ed. Alf Gabrielsson. Stockholm: Royal Swedish Academy of Music. 55: 153–75.

———— 1990a. Learning and the Development of Expectancies: An Interactionist Approach. *Psychomusicology* 9(2): 193–228.

———— 1990b. Musical Events and Models of Musical Time. In *Cognitive Models of Psychological Time*, ed. R. A. Block. Hillsdale, N.J.: Erlbaum: 207–40.

———— 1992. Attending to Musical Events. In *Cognitive Bases of Musical Communi-*

cation, ed. Mari Riess Jones and Susan Holleran. Washington, D.C.: American Psychological Association: 91–110.

Jones, Mari Riess, and Marilyn Boltz. 1989. Dynamic Attending and Responses to Time. *Psychological Review* 96(3): 459–91.

Jones, Mari Riess, Marilyn Boltz, et al. 1982. Controlled Attending as a Function of Melodic and Temporal Context. *Perception and Psychophysics* 32(3): 211–18.

Jones, Mari Riess, Richard J. Jagacinski, et al. 1995. Test of Attentional Flexibility in Listening to Polyrhythmic Patterns. *Journal of Experimental Psychology: Human Perception and Performance* 21(2): 293–307.

Jones, Mari Riess, Gary Kidd, et al. (1981). Evidence for Rhythmic Attention. *Journal of Experimental Psychology: Human Perception and Performance* 7(5): 1059–73.

Jones, Mari Riess, and Jacqueline T. Ralston. 1991. Some Influences of Accent Structure on Melody Recognition. *Memory and Cognition* 19: 8–20.

Kahneman, Daniel. 1973. *Attention and Effort.* Englewood Cliffs, N.J.: Prentice Hall.

Kelly, Michael H. 1989. Rhythm and Language Change in English. *Journal of Memory and Language* 28(6): 690–710.

Kelly, Michael H., and J. Kathryn Bock. 1988. Stress in Time. *Journal of Experimental Psychology: Human Perception and Performance* 14(3): 389–403.

Kelly, Michael H., and David C. Rubin. 1988. Natural Rhythmic Patterns in English Verse: Evidence from Child Counting-out Rhymes. *Journal of Memory and Language* 27(6): 718–40.

Klapp, Stuart T., Martin D. Hill, et al. 1985. On Marching to Two Different Drummers: Perceptual Aspects of the Difficulties. *Journal of Experimental Psychology: Human Perception and Performance* 11(6): 814–27.

Koch, Heinrich C. 1782, 1787, and 1793. *Versuch einer Anleitung zur Composition,* 3 vols. Leipzig: Adam F. Boehme.

Komar, Arthur J. 1971. *Theory of Suspensions.* Princeton, N.J.: Princeton University Press.

Kramer, Jonathan D. 1988. *The Time of Music.* New York: Schirmer Books.

Krebs, Harald. 1987. Some Extensions of the Concepts of Metrical Consonance and Dissonance. *The Journal of Music Theory* 31(1): 99–120.

——— 1999. *Fantasy Pieces: Metrical Dissonance in the Music of Robert Schumann.* New York: Oxford University Press.

Langer, Susanne. 1953. *Feeling and Form.* New York: Scribners.

Large, Edward W. 2000a. On Synchronizing Movements to Music. *Human Movement Science,* 19: 527–66.

——— 2000b. Rhythm Categorization in Context. Paper read at the *6th International Conference on Music Perception and Cognition,* Keele, UK, August 8.

Large, Edward W., and Mari Riess Jones. 1999. The Dynamics of Attending: How We Track Time-Varying Events. *Psychological Review* 106(1): 119–59.

Large, Edward W., and John F. Kohlen. 1994. Resonance and the Perception of Musical Meter. *Connection Science* 6: 177–208.

Large, Edward W., and Caroline Palmer. 2002. Perceiving Temporal Regularity in Music. *Cognitive Science* 26: 1–37.

Lashley, Karl S. 1951. The Problem of Serial Order in Behavior. In *Cerebral Mechanisms in Behaviour: The Hixon Symposium,* ed. L. A. Jeffress. New York, Wiley: 112–36.

Lee, Christopher S. 1991. The Perception of Metrical Structure: Experimental Evidence and a Model. In *Representing Musical Structure,* ed. P. Howell, R. West and I. Cross. New York, Academic Press: 59–127.

Lehiste, Ilse. 1970. *Suprasegmentals*. Cambridge, Mass.: MIT Press.

Lerdahl, Fred. 2001. *Tonal Pitch Space*. Oxford: Oxford University Press.

Lerdahl, Fred, and Ray Jackendoff. 1983. *A Generative Theory of Tonal Music*. Cambridge, Mass.: MIT Press.

Lester, Joel. 1986. *The Rhythms of Tonal Music*. Carbondale: Southern Illinois University Press.

Liberman, Mark. 1975. The Intonational System of English. PhD Diss, MIT.

London, Justin M. 1990. The Interaction Between Meter and Phrase Beginnings and Endings in the Mature Instrumental Music of Haydn and Mozart. PhD Diss, University of Pennsylvania.

———— 1993. Loud Rests and Other Strange Metric Phenomena, or Meter as Heard. *Music Theory Online* 0(2): http://societymusictheory.org/mto/.

———— 1995. Some Examples of Complex Meters and Their Implications for Models of Metric Perception. *Music Perception* 13(1): 59–78.

———— 1996. The Binary Bias of Metric Subdivision and the Relative Complexity of Various Meters, or, Why is $\frac{9}{8}$ so Rare? Paper read at the *Fourth International Conference on Music Perception and Cognition*, Montreal, Quebec August 14.

———— 1999. Hasty's Dichotomy: A Review-Essay of Christopher Hasty's *Meter as Rhythm*. *Music Theory Spectrum* 21(1): 260–74.

———— 2001. Rhythm. In *The New Grove Dictionary of Music and Musicians*, 2nd edition, ed. John Tyrrell and Stanley Sadie. London: Macmillan, Vol. 21: 277–309.

———— 2002a. Cognitive Constraints on Metric Systems: Some Observations and Hypotheses. *Music Perception* 19(4): 529–50.

———— 2002b. Some Non-Isomorphisms Between Pitch and Time. *Journal of Music Theory* 46 (1&2): 127–151.

Longuet-Higgins, H. Christopher, and Christopher S. Lee. 1982. The Perception of Musical Rhythms. *Perception* 11: 115–28.

Magill, Jonathan M., and Jeffrey L. Pressing. 1997. Asymmetric Cognitive Clock Structures in West African Rhythms. *Music Perception* 15(2): 189–222.

Massaro, Dominic W. 1970. Retroactive Interference in Short-Term Recognition Memory for Pitch. *Journal of Experimental Psychology* 83(1, pt. 1): 32–39.

Mates, J., U. Müller, et al. 1993. Stimulus Anticipation Disappears when Following Slow Tonal Sequences by Finger Tapping. *Homeostatis in Health and Disease* 34(3–4): 185–7.

Meumann. Ernst. 1894. Untersuchungen zur Psychologie und Aesthetik des Rhythmus. *Philosophische Studien* 10: 249–322 and 393–430.

Meyer, Rosalee K., and Caroline Palmer. 2001. Rate and Tactus Effects in Music Performance. Unpublished MS.

Michon, John A. 1964.Studies on Subjective Duration. I. Differential Sensitivity in the Perception of Repeated Temporal Intervals. *Acta Psychologica* 22: 441–50.

———— 1978. The Making of the Present: A Tutorial Review. In *Attention and Performance VII*, ed. J. Raquin. Hillsdale, N.J.: Erlbaum.

Miall, Christopher. 1996. Models of Neural Timing. In *Time, Internal Clocks and Movement*, ed. M. A. Pastor and J. Artieda. Amsterdam: Elsevier, Vol. 115: 69–94.

Monohan, Caroline B. 1993. Parallels Between Pitch and Time and How They Go Together. In *Psychology and Music: The Understanding of Melody and Rhythm*, ed. Thomas J. Tighe and W. Jay Dowling. Hillsdale, N.J.: Erlbaum: 121–54.

Monohan, Caroline B., and Ira J. Hirsh. 1990. Studies in Auditory Timing: 2. Rhythm Patterns. *Perception and Psychophysics* 47(3): 227–42.

Morris, Robert. 2000. Crowns: Rhythmic Cadences in South Indian Music. Paper read at the Annual Meeting of the *Society for Music Theory*, Toronto November 2.

Narmour, Eugene. 1990. *The Analysis and Cognition of Basic Melodic Structures*. Chicago: University of Chicago Press.

Nauert, Paul C. 1997. Timespan Formation in Nonmetric, Posttonal Music. PhD Diss., Columbia University.

Neisser, Ulric. 1976. *Cognition and Reality*. San Francisco: Freeman.

——— 1978. Perceiving, Anticipating, and Imagining. In *Perception and Cognition: Issues in the Foundations of Psychology*, ed/ C. W. Savage. Minneapolis: University of Minnesota Press, vol. IX: 89–105.

Nketia, J. H. Kwabena. 1963a. *African Music in Ghana*. Evanston, Ill.: Northwestern University Press.

——— 1963b. *Drumming in the Akan Communities of Ghana*. London: Thomas Nelson and Sons for the University of Ghana.

——— 1968. *Our Drums and Drummers*. Accra: Ghana Publishing.

——— 1974. *The Music of Africa*. New York: Norton.

Palmer, Caroline. 1996. Anatomy of a Performance: Sources of Musical Expression. *Music Perception* 13(3): 433–53.

Palmer, Caroline, and Michael H. Kelly. 1992. Linguistic Prosody and Musical Meter in Song. *Journal of Memory and Language* 31: 525–42.

Parncutt, Richard. 1994. A Perceptual Model of Pulse Salience and Metrical Accent in Musical Rhythms. *Music Perception* 11(4): 409–64.

Penel, Amadine, and Carolyn Drake. 1998. Sources of Timing Variations in Music Performance: A Psychological Segmentation Model. *Psychological Research* 61(1): 12–32.

——— 2000. Rhythm in Music Performance and Perceived Structure. In *Rhyhtm Perception and Production*, ed. Peter Desain and W. Luke Windsor. Lisse: Swets and Zeitlinger: 225–32.

Peper, C. E., Peter J. Beek, et al. 2000. Considerations Regarding a Comprehensive Model of (Poly)Rhythmic Movement. In *Rhythm Perception and Production*, ed. Peter Desain and W. Luke Windsor. Lisse: Swets and Zeitlinger: 35–49.

Pöppel, Ernst. 1972. Oscillations as Possible Basis for Time Perception. In *The Study of Time*, ed. J. T. Fraser, F.C. Haber, and G. H. Müller. Berlin: Springer-Verlag: 219–241.

Povel, Dirk-Jan. 1981. Internal Representation of Simple Temporal Patterns. *Journal of Experimental Psychology: Human Perception and Performance* 7(1): 3–18.

——— 1984. A Theoretical Framework for Rhythm Percpetion. *Psychological Research* 45: 315–37.

Povel, Dirk-Jan, and Hans Okkerman. 1981. Accents in Equitone Sequences. *Perception and Psychophysics* 6: 565–72.

Povel, Dirk-Jan, and Peter Essens. 1985. Perception of Temporal Patterns. *Music Perception* 2(4): 411–40.

Powers, Harold S., and Richard Widdess. 2001. India, §III, 4(iii)(b): Theory and Practice of Classical Music: Rhythm and Tāla. In *The New Grove Dictionary of Music and Musicians*, 2nd edition, ed. Stanley Sadie and John Tyrrell. London: MacMillan, Vol. 12: 195–202.

Pressing, Jeffrey L. 1995. Testing Dynamical and Cognitive Models of Rhythmic Pattern Production. In *Motor Control and Sensory Motor Integration: Issues and Directions*, ed. D. J. Glencross and J. P. Piek. Amsterdam: Elsevier: 141–70.

——— 1998. Error Correction Processes in Temporal Pattern Production. *Journal of Mathematical Psychology* 42: 63–101.

———— 1999. Cognitive Complexity and the Structure of Musical Patterns. Proceedings of the 4th Conference of the *Australasian Cognitive Science Society,* Newcastle. Online at www.psych.unimelb.edu.au/staff/pressing.html.

———— 2002. Black Atlantic Rhythm: Its Computational and Transcultural Foundations. *Music Perception* 19(3): 285–310.

Pressing, Jeffrey L., Jeff Summers, et al. 1996. Cognitive Multiplicity in Polyrhythmic Pattern Performance. *Journal of Experimental Psychology: Human Perception and Performance* 22(5): 1127–48.

Rahn, Jay. 1983. *A Theory for All Music.* Toronto: University of Toronto Press.

———— 1987. Asymmetrical Ostinatos in Sub-Saharan Music: Time, Pitch, and Cycles Reconsidered. *In Theory Only* 9(7): 23–37.

Repp, Bruno H. 1992. Probing the Cognitive Representation of Musical Time: Structural Constraints on the Perception of Timing Perturbations. *Cognition* 44: 241–81.

———— 1994. Relational Invariance of Expressive Microstructure Across Global Tempo Changes in Music Performance: An Exploratory Study. *Psychological Research,* 56: 269–84.

———— 1995a. Detectability of Duration and Intensity Increments in Melody Tones: A Partial Connection Between Music Perception and Performance. *Perception and Psychophysics* 57(8): 1217–32.

———— 1995b. Quantitative Effects of Global Tempo on Expressive Timing in Music Performance: Some Perceptual Evidence. *Music Perception* 13(1): 39–57.

———— 1998a. Musical Motion in Perception and Performance. In *Timing of behavior: neural, psychological, and computational perspectives,* ed. D. Rosenbaum and C. Collyer. Cambridge, Mass.: MIT Press: 125–144.

———— 1998b. Obligatory Expectations of Expressive Timing Induced by Perception of Musical Structure. *Psychological Research* 61: 33–43.

———— 1998c. Variations on a Theme by Chopin: Relations Between Perception and Production of Deviations from Isochrony in Music. *Journal of Experimental Psychology: Human Perception and Performance* 24: 791–811.

———— 1998d. The Detectability of Local Deviations from a Typical Expressive Timing Pattern. *Music Perception* 15(3): 265–89.

———— 1999a. Detecting Deviations from Metronomic Timing in Music: Effects of Perceptual Structure on the Mental Timekeeper. *Perception and Psychophysics* 61(3): 529–48.

———— 1999b. Relationships Between Performance Timing, Perception of Timing Perturbations, and Perceptual-Motor Synchronization in Two Chopin Preludes. *Australian Journal of Psychology* 51: 188–203.

———— 2000. Subliminal Temporal Discrimination Revealed in Sensorimotor Coordination. In *Rhythm Perception and Production,* ed. Peter Desain and W. Luke Windsor. Lisse: Swets and Zeitlinger: 129–42.

———— (2002). The Embodiment of Musical Structure: Effects of Musical Context on Sensorimotor Synchronization with Complex Timing Patterns. In *Attention and Performance XIX: Common Mechanisms in Perception and Action,* ed. W. Prinz and B. Hommel. Oxford: Oxford University Press: 245–65.

———— (in press). Rate Limits in Sensorimotor Synchronization with Auditory and Visual Sequences: The Synchronization Threshold and the Benefits and Costs of Interval Subdivision. *Journal of Motor Behavior.*

Repp, Bruno H., London, Justin M., et. al. 2004. Production and Synchronization of Uneven Rhythms at Fast Tempi (unpublished MS).

Repp, Bruno H., Windsor, W. Luke, et al. 2002. Effects of Tempo on the Timing of Simple Musical Rhythms. *Music Perception* 19(4): 565–97.

Riemann, Hugo. 1903. *System der musikalischen Rhythmik und Metrik*. Leipzig: Breitkopf und Härtel.

Riepel, Joseph. 1752–86. *Anfangsgründe zur musikalischen Setzkunst*. Regensburg: lm E.F. Baders Buch laden.

Roeder, John. 1998. Review of Christopher F. Hasty's *Meter as Rhythm*. *Music Theory Online*, 4.4. www.societymusictheory.org/mto.

Roederer, Juan G. 1995. *The Physics and Psychophysics of Music: An Introduction*. New York: Springer Verlag.

Rothstein, William N. 1989. *Phrase Rhythm in Tonal Music*. New York: Schirmer Books.

———— 1995. Beethoven with and without *Kunstgepräng*: Metrical Ambiguity Reconsidered. In *Beethoven Forum IV*, ed. C. Reynolds, L. Lockwood and J. Webster. Lincoln: University of Nebraska Press: 165–93.

Royal, Matthew S. 1995. The Perception of Rhythm and Tempo Modulation in Music. PhD Diss., University of Western Ontario.

Sachs, Curt. 1953. *Rhythm and Tempo*. New York: Norton.

Samarotto, Frank. 1999. Strange Dimensions: Regularity and Irregularity in Deep Levels of Rhythmic Reductions. In *Schenker Studies 2*, ed. Carl Schachter and Heidi Siegel. Cambridge: Cambridge University Press: 222–38.

Schachter, Carl. 1976. Rhythm and Linear Analysis: A Preliminary Study. In *The Music Forum IV*, ed. Felix Salzer and Carl Schachter. New York: Columbia University Press: 281–334.

———— 1980. Rhythm and Linear Analysis: Durational Reduction. In *The Music Forum 5*, ed. Felix Salzer and Carl Schachter. New York: Columbia University Press: 197–232.

———— 1987. Rhythm and Linear Analysis: Aspects of Meter. In *The Music Forum 6.1*, ed. Felix Salzer and Carl Schachter. New York: Columbia University Press: 1–59.

Schmuckler, Mark. A., and Marilyn G. Boltz. 1994. Harmonic and Rhythmic Influences on Musical Expectancy. *Perception and Psychophysics* 56(3): 313–25.

Schulze, Hans-Henning. 1978. The Detectability of Local and Global Displacements in Regular Rhythmic Patterns. *Psychological Research* 40: 173–81.

———— 1989a. Categorical Perception of Rhythmic Patterns. *Psychological Research* 51: 10–15.

———— 1989. The Perception of Temporal Deviations in Isochronic Patterns. *Perception and Psychophysics* 45(4): 291–96.

Schumann, F. 1900. Beiträge aur Analyse der Gesichtswahrnehmungen. *Zeitschrift fuer Psychologie* 23: 1–32.

Scruton, Roger. 1997. *The Aesthetics of Music*. Oxford: Oxford University Press.

Seashore, Carl E. [1938] 1967. *Psychology of Music*. New York: Dover Reprint.

Seashore, Robert H. (1926). Studies in Motor Rhythm. *Psychological Monographs* 36(1): 142–89.

Semjen, Andras, Hans-Henning Schulze, et al. 1992. Temporal Control in the Coordination Between Repetitive Tapping and Periodic Stimuli. Proceedings of the *Fourth Workshop on Rhythm Perception and Production*, Bourges, France, ed. A. Auxiette, C. Drake, and C. Gerard: 73–78.

Semjen, Adras, Hans-Henning Schulze, et al. 2000. Timing Precision in Continuation and Syncrhonization Tapping. *Psychological Research* 63: 137–47.

Semjen, Andras, Dirk Vorberg, et al. 1998. Getting Synchronized with the Metronome: Comparisons Between Phase and Period Correction. *Psychological Research* 61: 44–55.

Shaffer, L. H. 1982. Rhythm and Timing in Skill. *Psychological Review* 89(2): 109–22.

——— 1984. Timing in Solo and Duet Piano Performances. *Quarterly Journal of Experimental Psychology* 36A: 577–95.

Shaffer, L. H., Eric F. Clarke, et al. 1985. Metre and Rhythm in Piano Playing. *Cognition* 20: 61–77.

Shove, Patrick, and Bruno Repp. 1995. Musical Motion and Performance: Theoretical and Empirical Perspectives. In *The Practice of Performance*, ed. John Rink. Cambridge: Cambridge University Press: 55–83.

Sloboda, John A. 1983. The Communication of Musical Metre in Piano Performance. *Quarterly Journal of Experimental Psychology* 35A: 377–96.

——— 1985. Expressive Skill in Two Pianists: Metrical Communication in Real and Simulated Performances. *Canadian Journal of Psychology*, 39: 273–93.

Smith, J. David. 1997. The Place of Novices in Music Science. *Music Perception* 14(3): 227–62.

Smith, Karen C., and Lola L. Cuddy. 1989. Effects of Metric and Harmonic Rhythm on the Detection of Pitch Alterations in Melodic Sequences. *Journal of Experimental Psychology: Human Perception and Performance* 15(3): 457–71.

Sorkin, Robert D., and DeMaris A. Montgomery. 1991. Effect of Time Compression and Expansion on the Discrimination of Tonal Patterns. *Journal of the Acoustical Society of America* 90(2, pt. 1): 846–57.

Steudel. U. 1933. Über Empfindungen und Messung der Lautstärke. *Zeitschrift für Hochfrequenz Technik und Electrotechnik* 41: 166 ff.

Stevens, Lewis T. 1886. On the Time Sense. *Mind* 11(43): 393–404.

Sulzer, Johann-Georg. 1792. *Allgemeine Theorie der schönen Künste*. Vol. 2. Leipzig: In der Weidmannschen Buchhandlung.

Taggart, Bruce F. 1996. Rhythmic Perception and Conception: A Study of Bottom-up and Top-down interaction in Rhythm and Meter. PhD Diss., University of Pennsylvania.

Temperley, David. 2001. *The Cognition of Basic Musical Structures*. Cambridge, Mass.: MIT Press.

Todd, Neil P. M. 1995. The Kinematics of Musical Expression. *Journal of the Acoustical Society of America* 97(3): 1940–50.

——— 1996a. An Auditory Cortical Theory of Primitive Auditory Grouping. *Network: Computation in Neural Systems* 7: 349–56.

——— 1996b. Neuronal Representations of Rhythm and Time: Time Without Clocks. *British Association Annual Festival of Science*, Birmingham.

Todd, Neil P. M., Donald J. O'Boyle, et al. 1999. A Sensory-Motor Theory of Rhythm, Time Perception, and Beat Induction. *Journal of New Music Research* 28(1): 5–28.

Treffner, Paul J., and M. T. Turvey. 1993. Resonance Constraints on Rhythmic Movement. *Journal of Experimental Psychology: Human Perception and Performance* 19(6): 1221–37.

van Noorden, Leon. 1975. Temporal Coherence in the Perception of Tone Sequences. Doctoral diss., Technische Hogeschool Eindhoven: The Netherlands.

——— 1982. Two-Channel Pitch Perception. In *Music, Mind, and Brain: The Neuropsychology of Music*, ed. Manfred Clynes. New York: Plenum Press: 251–69.

Vazan, Peter, and M. F. Schober. 2000. The 'Garden Path' Phenomenon in the Perception of Meter. Paper read at the Annual Meeting of the *Society for Music Perception and Cognition*, Toronto, November 3.

Vorberg, Dirk, and R. Hambuch. 1978. On the Temporal Control of Rhythmic Performance. In *Attention and Performance VII*, ed. J. Requin. Hillsdale, N.J.: Erlbaum: 535–55.

Vorberg, Dirk, and Alan M. Wing. 1996. Modeling Variability and Dependence in Timing. In *Handbook of Perception and Action, Volume 2: Motor Skills*, ed. H. Heuer and S. W. Keele. New York: Academic Press: 181–262.

Warren, Richard M. 1993. Perception of Acoustic Sequences: Global Integration versus Temporal Resolution. In *Thinking in Sound*, ed. S. McAdams and E. Bigand. Oxford: Oxford University Press: 37–68.

Wertheimer, Max. 1912/1961. Experimentelle Studien über das Sehen von Bewegung. Reprinted and translated in *Classics in Psychology*, ed. Thorne Shipley. New York: Philosophical Library: 1032–89.

Westergaard, Peter. 1975. *An Introduction to Tonal Theory*. New York: W.W. Norton.

Windsor, W. Luke. 1993. Dynamic Accents and the Categorical Perception of Metre. *Psychology of Music* 21: 127–40.

Windsor, W. Luke, and Eric F. Clarke. 1997. Expressive Timing and Dynamics in Real and Artificial Musical Performances: Using an Algorithm as an Analytical Tool. *Music Perception* 15(2): 127–52.

Wohlschläger, Andreas, and Robert Koch. 2000. Synchronization Error: An Error in Time Perception. In *Rhythm Perception and Production*, ed. Peter Desain and W. Luke Windsor. Lisse: Swets and Zeitlinger: 115–27.

Woodrow, Herbert. 1909. A Quantitative Study of Rhythm. *Archives of Psychology* 14: 1–66.

———— 1932. The Effect of Rate of Sequence Upon the Accuracy of Syncrhonization. *Journal of Experimental Psychology* 15(4): 357–79.

Wundt, Willhelm. 1911. *Grundzüge der physiologischen Psychologie*. Leipzig: Engelmann.

Yee, William, Susan Holleran, et al. 1994. Sensitivity to Event Timing in Regular and Irregular Sequences: Influences of Musical Skill. *Perception and Psychophysics* 56(4): 461–71.

Yeston, Maury. 1976. *The Stratification of Musical Rhythm*. New Haven, Conn.: Yale University Press.

Zuckerkandl, Victor. 1956. *Sound and Symbol: Music and the External World*. New York: Pantheon Books.

———— 1959. *The Sense of Music*. Princeton, N.J.: Princeton University Press.

Index

accent, metrical, 19–23, 26, 53, 61, 65
  defined, 19, 23
  as listener-generated, 19, 25–26
  in NI-meters, 111–114, 115
acousmatic space, 5, 6
additive meters. *See* meters, additive and multiplicative
Africa, music of, 68, 88, 117, 126
  bell pattern in, 128–129, 128 ex. 8.3 & 8.4, 129 ex. 8.5, 131 fig. 8.6a, 166
  West African Gahu drumming in, 85, 111–115, 112 ex. 7.2 & 7.3
analysis, metric, 62–68
  of Beethoven's Fifth Symphony, 89–99
  cyclical representations in, 64–69, 72, 162
  dot notation in, 62, 62 ex. 4.3
  wave analysis in, 63–64, 63 ex. 4.4, 64 ex. 4.5
analysis, rhythmic, 60–61
Arom, Simha, 113, 126–129, 134
attending. *See* attentional behavior
attentional behavior, 11–12, 15–17, 25, 164
  meter as, 6, 9–18, 64
  See also entrainment
attentional framework, 17, 43, 51, 87
  as result of integrative function of meter, 34

See also hierarchy
attentional peaks, 23, 30, 77, 106, 107 fig. 7.4, 141, 162
  in cyclical representations of meter, 64–65, 68–69, 76
attunement. *See* entrainment

Babbitt, Milton
  Composition for Twelve Instruments, 24, 24 ex. 1.5, 85,
Bach, Johann Sebastian
  C Major Prelude from *Well-Tempered Clavier, Book 1,* 40–41, 41 ex. 2.1 & fig. 2.4
  "Goldberg" Variations, 56, 57 ex. 3.6b
beat-classes, 106–110, 115, 140
beat-cycles, 66, 70–71, 76–78
  formation of, 116–140
  maximal evenness and, 105
  in music of Africa, 112–114
beats, 20–23, 27–30, 31–32
  interpolation of missing, 85–86, 118–119
  NI-beats, 106–110
  subdivisions and, 19, 34–38, 46
  See also tactus
Beethoven, Ludwig van
  An die ferne Geliebte, op. 98, no. 6, 81–82, 82 ex. 5.4, 84 fig. 5.2, 88, 95
  Fifth Symphony, 89–99

191

Beethoven, Ludwig van (continued)
　Ninth Symphony, second movement,
　　55–56, 55 ex. 3.5, 58
　"Ode to Joy," 51–52, 52 ex. 3.2, 53
　　ex. 3.3
　Piano Sonata, op. 2, no. 3, 56–57,
　　57 ex. 3.6c
behavior, meter as, 4–6, 25, 166
　learned, 143–144, 153, 157
　studies of, 12–14
　See also entrainment
Bernstein, Leonard
　"America" from West Side Story, 129,
　　129 ex. 8.6 & 8.7
Bolton, T. L., 28–29
Brahms, Johannes
　Symphony no. 4, first movement,
　　53–54, 53 ex. 3.6d
Bregman, Albert, 4,5,30
Brubeck, Dave
　Blue Rondo a la Turk, 100, 101 ex. 7.1
Butler, Charles, 15–16, 16 ex. 1.2

Caplin, William, 55
cardinality, 68
　See also N-cycle
Carnatic. See India, music of
Chopin, Frederic
　Etude in E major, op.10, no.3,
　　147–148, 147 ex. 9.2, 150
　Polonaise in A major, 63, 63 ex. 4.4
Clarke, Eric, 16, 32, 34, 144–145,
　　148, 170 n6
Cohn, Richard, 83, 83 ex. 5.5
contradiction. See maximal evenness
Cooper, Grosvenor & Leonard Meyer,
　　20, 32, 61 ex. 4.2
cycles, 64–69, 66 ex. 4.3, 68 ex. 4.5
　in isochronous and non-isochronous
　　meters, 100–103
　maximal evenness and, 103–106
　well-formedness and, 72–78
　See also N-cycle; subcycle; tactus

entrainment, 4, 6, 12, 14, 17–19,
　　25–26, 92, 97, 161–162
　circular representations of meter
　　and, 64–69
　ecological validity and, 142, 154
　limits to, 27–30, 48, 51, 52

metric dissonance and, 84–88
time discrete vs. time continuous
　models of, 20–21
well-formedness constraints and,
　77–78
envelope, temporal or metric. See limits,
　metric
Epstein, David, 32, 89
expectation. See rhythmic behavior
expressive variation, 28, 52, 72, 75,
　77, 79
　effect on timing ratios, 33–34, 35
　Many Meters Hypothesis and,
　　153–156, 159
　recent research in, 144–153

figure-ground relationship, 48, 50, 58
Fraisse, Paul, 21, 29, 31, 34
"Frere Jacques," 13, 56, 57 ex. 3.6a

Gentner, Donald, 156, 158
Gibson, James J.
　ecological approach to perception,
　　9–10, 14
Gjerdingen, Robert, 4, 30, 157

Habanera, 125, 125 ex. 8.2
half-measure, 68, 68 fig. 4.5, 73, 77,
　　126, 134, 172–173 n.3, 175 n.7
　maximal evenness and, 105–106
"Happy Birthday," 152
Hasty, Christopher, 8, 23, 62–63
Haydn, Josef,
　Symphony in D major no. 104
　　("London"), finale, 151 ex. 9.4d,
　　152
hemiola, 49, 49 ex. 3.1c, 86–87
　See also metric ambiguity; metric
　　dissonance
hierarchy
　circular representations of meter
　　and, 65–69, 162
　maximal evenness and 121, 131,
　　133, 134, 137, 141
　meter as, 17, 25
　metric accent and, 19–20
　metric complexity and, 164–165
　metric depth and, 18–19, 25, 33,
　　37–38
　metric limits and, 27, 46

tactus level and, 32–33
well-formedness and, 72–73, 77–78
See also attentional framework;
    entrainment
Hindustani music. *See* India, music of
Holden, John, 145, 146
hypermeter, 19, 25, 81, 162
    in non-Western music, 134

I-meters. See meters, isochronous
India, music of, 68, 137–140, 174 n.5
interonset intervals (IOI), 4, 27
    subdivision and, 35
    subjective rhythmization and, 33–34
    tactus and, 31–33
indifference interval, 31
invariance, 5, 9–10, 23–24, 25–26,
    84, 143
    in generating or maintaining meter,
    15, 16–17, 50–51
    shift in pattern of, 53, 55
IOI. *See* interonset interval

James, William, 10, 14
Jones, Mari Riess, 11–12, 13, 18, 21,
    33, 50–51, 63
just noticeable difference (JND), 33–34

Kahneman, Daniel, 11
Karnatak music. *See* India, music of
Koch, Heinrich, 15, 21, 31–32, 61
    ex. 4.1
Krebs, Harald, 32, 81, 84, 87, 96, 98

Large, Edward, 20–21, 171–172 n5
Large, Edward & Mari Riess Jones,
    20–21, 22 fig. 1.1, 63
Lerdahl, Fred & Ray Jackendoff, 19–20,
    32, 51, 65
    dot notation, 62, 62 ex. 4.3
    well-formedness rules, 69–72
levels, metric. *See* hierarchy
limits, metric, 27–46, 72, 75
    100ms limit, 27, 28–29, 35–37,
    42–43, 46–47, 72
    1.5–2.0 second limit, 27, 30, 31, 42
    5–6 second limit, 30, 46–47
    See also maximal pulse salience;
    tactus
Locke, David, 111–113, 134

London, Justin, 62, 103, 169 n1, 173
    n2, 174 n1

Many Meters Hypothesis, 153–160
maximal evenness, 7, 103–107,
    114–115, 162–163, 174 n4,
    175 n1
    NI-meters and, 130–132, 133–137,
    141
    See also well-formedness
maximal pulse salience, 31, 38
    See also tactus
measure, measures, 40–46, 51, 53–55
    cyclical representations of meter and,
    64–65
Mendelssohn, Felix
    Midsummer Night's Dream, scherzo,
    63, 64 ex. 4.5
meter, 4–6, 25, 166
meter, accentless, 132
meter, overdetermined, 56–58, 57
    ex. 3.6b
meter, underdetermined, 56–58, 57
    ex. 3.6c
meters, additive and multiplicative,
    no distinction between, 100, 114,
    162, 166–167
meters, isochronous, 72–73, 100–103
    compared to non-isochronous
    meters, 103, 109, 110, 111, 115
    maximal evenness and, 103, 105
meters, non-isochronous, 100, 103,
    125
    accent and, 111, 115
    beat-cycle formation and, 116–117
    maximal evenness and, 103–105,
    114
    NI-rhythm and, 118–125
    tempo and, 110–111, 115
    timing constraints and, 106–110
metric ambiguity, 79–80, 85–86, 88,
    104–105
    in Beethoven's Fifth Symphony, 92,
    93 ex. 6.3, 98–99
    See also metric malleability
metric dissonance, 80–85, 86–88
    as lacking psychological basis, 88
    "polymeter" and, 50
    See also metric ambiguity; metric
    malleability